IN
WORD

IN A WORD

THE ESSENTIAL TOOL FOR FINDING THE PERFECT WORD

MARK BROATCH

NEW
HOLLAND

First published in 2009 by New Holland Publishers (NZ) Ltd
Auckland • Sydney • London • Cape Town

www.newhollandpublishers.co.nz

218 Lake Road, Northcote, Auckland 0627, New Zealand
Unit 1, 66 Gibbes Street, Chatswood, NSW 2067, Australia
86–88 Edgware Road, London W2 2EA, United Kingdom
80 McKenzie Street, Cape Town 8001, South Africa

Publishing manager: Matt Turner
Commissioned by Louise Armstrong
Editor: Nicola Learmonth
Design: Spencer Levine
Layout: Dee Murch

National Library of New Zealand Cataloguing-in-Publication Data

Broatch, Mark.
In a word : The essential tool for finding the perfect word /
written by Mark Broatch.
Includes bibliographical references.
ISBN 978-1-86966-272-1
1. Vocabulary. 2. English language—Glossaries, vocabularies,
etc. I. Title.
428.1—dc 22

10 9 8 7 6 5 4 3 2 1

Printed in China by Everbest Printing Co., on paper sourced from sustainable forests.

CONTENTS

INTRODUCTION

The search for the perfect word can be an exercise in frustration. It can also be – cliché alert – a voyage of discovery.

But what voyage are you on, and who is the captive audience of fellow passengers you hope to inform, persuade and entertain? Are you a professional writer who needs a jog of the memory? An occasional scribbler who's looking for a bit of subtlety and precision? A reviewer or blogger trying out new ways to blast a film, book or album, or praise it to the skies? Or just someone who knows there is the precise word out there for what she wants to say, but just can't find it, or a way to find it?

These days everyone really is a critic. Thanks to the internet, opinions – many vociferous and completely sure of themselves – are everywhere. Blogs and the web in general have given a global voice to everyone who wants one. And because this power can't be taken back – banning the bad, sad and slightly mad typists of the world from their laptops simply to keep the online noise level down – it makes more sense to encourage those who do write to write better. Even if better means encouraging one person to replace 'great' or 'not great' with any of the 5500 mostly adjectival synonyms or associated words that open this book. Rest assured that every effort has been taken to find the best available words: many have been trawled from thousands of articles and reviews from the world's best writers and critics.

For if *In a Word* is aimed at anyone in particular, it's critical writers: those who wish to say something meaningful with insight, precision and, perhaps, humour.

No one who hopes to push their prose beyond mediocrity wants to be like the 'most respected' art critic in Evelyn Waugh's novel *Brideshead Revisited*, who had a painful keenness to be modern and inventive, while saying nothing, badly.

> Mr Ryder rises like a fresh young trout to the hypodermic injection of a new culture and discloses a powerful facet in the vista of his potentialities ... By focusing the frankly traditional batter of his elegance and erudition on the maelstrom of barbarism, Mr Ryder has at last found himself.

If, on the other hand, you're aiming to move the stars rather than bang a cracked drum for dancing bears, as Flaubert almost put it, you need the right tools. Tool No. 1 is the right vocabulary.

Of course, all the words in the world can't give us knowledge or understanding. We may know every line of *Casablanca* but fail to grasp just why Ilsa gets on that plane, or even why the French are running the place. To paraphrase former US Secretary of Defense Donald Rumsfeld, there are things we know we know, and things we know we don't know, but there are also things we don't know we don't know (and thing we don't know we know).

A single book can't fill that chasm – but *In a Word* is intended to point you in the right direction. In this regard, you can think of it as a cheat sheet or aide-mémoire of sorts for the galaxy of words you have in your head but can't quite recall.

In a Word is not a replacement for a dictionary or thesaurus; in fact, you will need a dictionary if you don't know the meaning of some of the undefined words here. But you are probably the sort of person who already owns a dictionary or two, a thesaurus or crossword reference book, and perhaps a half-dozen other language books. Rather than attempting to be comprehensive across the English lexicon, the intention is to be comprehensive in grouping useful words in a useful way.

Choices of subject, style and spelling err on the side of the Commonwealth tradition. Where definitions are given, the one most of use to a critical writer is often given first rather than the one that might appear initially in many dictionaries.

Aside from encouraging precision, expanding the reader's vocabulary and jogging their memory, *In a Word* has one other intention. If you like words, it's a gentle push on that endless, endlessly gratifying voyage of discovering the beauty and variety of English.

How to use

In a Word is grouped into four main sections: Vocabulary, Characterisation, Terminology and Reference.

It takes the form of a series of lists, some defined, as in a dictionary, and some instead grouped in synonyms or semantic associations, as in a thesaurus.

The first section, **Vocabulary**, opens with a Descriptive Thesaurus, gathering categories of praise, denunciation and more neutral description. If you are seeking a word to describe something in a critical way, be it favourably, unfavourably or more neutrally, then the thesaurus should be your first stop. Although you will find nouns here, most of the words are adjectives. Yes, good writers should show rather than tell, and so avoid the weak or inaccurate noun or verb, but there is also nothing quite like the apposite adjective.

For example, if you want to describe someone or something as 'competent', a word that contains a multitude of connotations, you will find 'adroit', 'adequate', 'assured', 'conventional', 'garden-variety', 'kosher', 'middling', 'passable' and 'workmanlike'. If it's 'not new' you are looking for, there's 'antiquated', 'blasé', 'boilerplate', 'conventional', 'fogeyish', 'obsolete', 'schematic' and 'vintage', and 'assemblage', 'caricature', 'homage', 'platitude' and 'typecasting'.

Words within the rest of Vocabulary are divided among four main categories: Useful, Fancy, Plain and Colourful. If you are seeking a word that will give a bit of punch, a Colourful, Plain (short, monosyllabic, often Anglo-Saxon) or Foreign word could be your best bet. Colourful words are those that amuse and delight in their sound and connotation, including the likes of medical terms and tabloidese in Specialist Terms. They add – by means of onomatopoeia, or what wine makers might call mouthfeel – liveliness or a little joy to a sentence. To help with precision, a selection of Useful and Fancy (multisyllabic, probably Latinate and usually ostentatious) words is also given, along with a definition for each. The Useful words listed are those that are used frequently in critical writing but are also often confused and misused. Plain words, by contrast, can help writers keep their prose from straying into the florid and the flabby.

The section then defines some of the many foreign words in English by language of origin, and concludes with a list of common confusions and misspellings.

The second section, **Characterisation**, is devoted to illustrating humans in all their endless actual and fictional variety. If you are attempting to describe a person by appearance or personality, you'll get help here. They may have a limp, a nose like Barry Manilow, teeth like Freddie Mercury, fallen arches, an androgynous air, a Geordie accent, and remind you of a character out of a film or novel. But what state of mind are they in, and what are their interactions with other people? Characterisation will help you define how they look, sound, act and interact, and how they resemble other characters already brought into life by writers and artists over the centuries.

The third section, **Terminology**, is devoted to critical writing. After defining the basics of language and criticism – such as argument and figures of speech – it offers lists of words that might be helpful in writing critically about a subject, or trying to figure out what to pay attention to, particularly if it's art, sport or food. It lists words to aid the description of aspects of life outside human beings, such as weather and geography.

Reference, the fourth section, collects together facts you might be familiar with – US presidents, for example – and others you might not be, such as historical methods of punishment and ways of divining the future. It also lists films, directors, authors and other artists by decade and subject. If you are trying to remember which films featured teachers or trains, for instance, or which are the seminal works of an author, try here.

The **Appendix** contains word associations, including those relating to decades of the late 20th century, and those of other subjects such as religion, death and sex. It also lists websites full of language and useful facts.

Abbreviations used

Adjective = (adj)
Adverb = (adv)
Conjunction = (conj)
Contraction = (contr)
Noun = (n)
Preposition = (prep)
Pronoun = (pron)
Verb = (v)
Verb past participle = (v pp)

SECTION 1
VOCABULARY

'One's vocabulary needs constant
fertilising or it will die.'
— *Evelyn Waugh*

The Descriptive Thesaurus
is intended to help describe
something in a critical way,
whether favourably, unfavourably,
neutrally or ambiguously. If you
are seeking a word that will
give a bit of punch, a Colourful,
Plain or Foreign word could be
your best bet. A selection of
Useful and Fancy words – ones
commonly used and misused in
critical writing – are also defined.
A list of common confusions and
misspellings ends the section.

DESCRIPTIVE THESAURUS

FLATTERING

QUALITIES: NOUNS

ability, affection, alchemy, ambition, authenticity, authority, beauty, belief, challenge, charisma, charm, clarity, complexity, comprehensiveness, confidence, conviction, courage, culture, daring, deliberation, determination, dignity, distinction, dynamism, emotion, empathy, fibre, fireworks, fizz, fun, guts, heart, humour, idiosyncrasy, influence, integrity, intelligence, intensity, invention, mastery, merit, method, nerve, passion, pathos, patience, perfection, persuasion, poignancy, polish, power, principle, promise, restraint, reverence, romance, sass, shrewdness, simplicity, sincerity, skill, sophistication, spirit, subtlety, suspense, sympathy, talent, verve, virtue, wisdom, wit, wonder

COMPETENT

able, acceptable, accomplished, adept, adequate, admirable, admissible, adroit, agreeable, ample, appealing, apt, assured, attractive, average, bourgeois, capable, catchy, charming, clever, commendable, commonplace, conventional, decent, deserving, diverting, effective, efficacious, efficient, endearing, enjoyable, enough, fair, fitting, garden-variety, handsome, impressive, inessential, inoffensive, kosher, legitimate, likeable, middling, minimal, moderate, normal, not bad, okay, ordinary, passable, pleasant, pleasing, praiseworthy, presentable, proficient, professional, proficient, proportionate, prosaic, qualified, realistic, regular, respectable, run of the mill, satisfactory, skilful, skilled, solid, so so, special, sufficient, surprising, sympathetic, talented, tolerable, unacceptable, underrated, unexceptional, unimpressive, unremarkable, unspectacular, useful, usual, valuable, welcome, well-versed, workmanlike, worthwhile, worthy

VERY GOOD

24-carat, ace, amazing, astonishing, astounding, bonzer, breathtaking, brilliant, corking, cracking, dazzling, deluxe, devastating, excellent, exceptional, expert, exquisite, extraordinary, fabulous, fantastic, faultless, fine, first-class, first-rate, flawless, genius, gobsmacking, grand, great, high-quality, impactful, important, incomparable, incredible, indelible, ineffable, insuperable, irresistible, joyful, key, kick-arse, landmark, luxe, magic, magnificent, marvellous, miraculous, must-see, nonpareil, note-perfect, one-of-a-kind, outstanding, overwhelming, perfect, phenomenal, plum, prime-time, prodigious, rare, remarkable, satisfying, seismic, sensational, singular, smashing, special, spiffing, splendid, sterling, stunning, stupendous, sublime, superb, superior, swell, terrific, top-notch, tremendous, unbelievable, uncommon, unequalled, unforgettable, unique, unmatched, unrivalled, unsurpassed, wonderful, wondrous

Very good: nouns

archetype, bee's knees, chef d'oeuvre, classic, cracker, exemplar, ideal, jewel, magnum opus, masterpiece, masterwork, ne plus ultra, nonpareil, objet d'art, paragon, pièce de résistance, prototype, revelation, sleeper, standard, stroke of genius, tour de force, triumph, work of art

ATTRACTIVE OR ENGAGING

absorbing, affable, agreeable, alluring, amiable, amusing, appealing, arresting, attractive, beautiful, beguiling, bewitching, bright, captivating, catchy, charismatic, charming, cheerful, cheery, compelling, congenial, cordial, cute, delightful, dinky, elegant, enchanting, endearing, engrossing, enjoyable, entertaining, enthralling, entrancing, fascinating, favourable, fetching, genial, good-humoured, good-looking, good-natured, graceful, gratifying, gripping, handsome, happy, hypnotic, infectious, interesting, intriguing, inviting, involving, irresistible, kind-hearted, likeable, loveable, lovely, magical, magnetic, mesmerising, nice, optimistic, personable, picturesque, piquant, pleasant, pleasing, pleasurable, prepossessing, pretty, riveting, rosy, satisfying, seductive, spellbinding, striking, suspenseful, sweet, sympathetic, thrilling, warm, warm-blooded, warm-hearted, welcome, winning, winsome

EXCITING

action-packed, beguiling, bewitching, bracing, breathtaking, captivating, careering, cliff-hanging, compelling, dangerous, dazzling, dramatic, electric, enthralling, entrancing, exhilarating, eye-popping, gripping, hair-raising, heart-moving, hectic, impressive, inspiring, intoxicating, intriguing, invigorating, jarring, jaw-dropping, jolting, mind-blowing, mouth-watering, overwhelming, rip-roaring, riveting, soul-stirring, stirring, thrilling

SPIRITED

action-packed, alive, animated, ardent, avid, boisterous, bold, bouncy, brave, bumptious, buoyant, cheeky, courageous, crazy, dynamic, eager, ebullient, energetic, enthusiastic, evangelical, excited, exhilarating, extravagant, exuberant, fast-paced, fearless, feisty, fervent, forward, foxy, fresh, full-throttle, game, gripping, high-spirited, impertinent, impish, impudent, irreverent, keen, knockabout, lively, mettlesome, mischievous, naughty, outrageous, passionate, peppy, pert, playful, plucky, puckish, punchy, racy, rakish, raring, realistic, roguish, rollicking, salty, sassy, saucy, sexy, snappy, sprightly, spunky, unflagging, unrestrained, upbeat, vibrant, vigorous, vivacious, waggish, wholehearted, zany, zealous, zestful, zippy

Spirited: person

bad boy, bounder, bugger, devil, enfant terrible, imp, joker, minx, prankster, rapscallion, rascal, rogue, scallywag, scamp, trickster, wag

SMART

able, academic, adroit, agile, alert, apt, artful, astute, au fait, aware, brainiac, brainy, bright, brilliant, canny, cerebral, clever, clued-up, crafty, cunning, dashing, discriminating, distinguished, educated, elegant, eloquent, enlightened, erudite, expert, eye-opening, genius, gifted, gnomish, high-brow, imaginative, informed, ingenious, insightful, intellectual, intelligent, in the know, judicious, keen, knowing, knowledgeable, learned, lettered, neat, nifty, omniscient, penetrating, perceptive, perspicacious, pointy-headed, prudent, quick, quick-witted, reasonable, sagacious, sane, savvy, scholarly, scintillescent, sensible, sharp, sharp-witted, shrewd, skilful, snazzy, soigné, spiffy, thoughtful, well-read, wise

AMUSING

arch, camp(y), cheering, cheery, cheesy, clownish, comedic, comical, corny, cuckoo, daffy, deadpan, diverting, droll, entertaining, facetious, farcical, fun, funny, goofy, hilarious, humorous, hysterical, ironic, irreverent, jokey, joking, joyous, kooky, merry, mirthful, mordant, playful, quick-witted, quipping, quirky, ribald, riotous, rip-roaring, risible, sarcastic, satirical, showboating, side-splitting, silly, slapstick, teasing, tongue in cheek, uproarious, waggish, wacky, whimsical, wisecracking, witty, wry, zany

APPEALING TO THE EMOTIONS

affecting, breathtaking, compassionate, diverting, dramatic, emotional, empathetic, endearing, engaging, exuberant, feeling, gripping, heartbreaking, heart-rending, heartwarming, idealised, infectious, inspiring, joyful, lachrymose, moving, noble, nostalgic, operatic, painful, poignant, romantic, rousing, rueful, sappy, satisfying, savage, sensitive, sorrowful, soulful,

spiritual, stirring, subjective, sweet, tear-jerking, tempestuous, tender, theatrical, touching, tragic, uplifting, upsetting, visceral, warmhearted, weepy, wholesome, wide-eyed, wistful, wrenching

WITH SERIOUS INTENTIONS

ambitious, artful, aspirational, aspiring, candid, challenging, contentious, courageous, daring, daunting, determined, didactic, difficult, dignified, disconcerting, disorienting, earnest, enterprising, esoteric, existential, forbidding, grandiose, gritty, gutsy, hardheaded, heartfelt, heartful, hell-bent, heroic, highbrow, highfalutin, high-toned, hopeful, idiosyncratic, incendiary, inflammatory, inscrutable, inspirational, kitchen-sink, loaded, lofty, old-fashioned, operatic, outré, passionate, patient, pedagogical, perplexing, pointy-headed, provocative, relentless, serious, serious-minded, sincere, slow-cooked, solemn, unique, unnerving, unsettling, well-intentioned

ACHIEVING HIGH INTENTIONS

accomplished, artful, assured, blue-ribbon, bravura, cerebral, civilised, classy, complete, consummate, controlled, cosmopolitan, cultivated, cultured, debonair, devastating, dignified, disturbing, edifying, educated, elegant, elegiac, elite, *épater les bourgeois*, erudite, esoteric, exacting, exciting, experienced, eye-opening, fine-spun, finished, glossy, graceful, gracious, high-end, high-minded, high-toned, humanistic, hushed, impeccable, instructive, intellectual, intense, landmark, lettered, literary, lyrical, maestro, masterful, masterly, memorable, neat, noble, noteworthy, perfectionist, personal, poetic, poised, polished, profound, pungent, quality, redolent, refined, remarkable, searing, shiny, skilful, skilled, sober, sophisticated, stimulating, stylish, sure-footed, tasteful, thought-provoking, upscale, virtuoso, vivid, weighty, well-bred, well-mannered, worthy

Achieving high intentions: person
arbiter, architect, artist, auteur, authority, cognoscente, connoisseur, craftsman, doyen, elder statesman, epicure, expert, genius, gourmet, maestro, master, maven, professional, sage, scholar, virtuoso, wizard

THOUGHT-OUT

analytical, assiduous, attentive, breezy, calm, canny, careful, clear-headed, clear-thinking, cogent, coherent, commonsense, confident, conscientious, considered, consistent, deliberate, dutiful, efficient, eloquent, focused, heedful, inventive, judicious, level-headed, listening, logical, lucid, manicured, measured, methodical, meticulous, observant, organised, painstaking, painterly, patient, prepared, prudent, quiet, rational, reasonable, reasoned, rigorous, ruminative, sane, scrupulous, sensible, shrewd, solicitous, sound, sure, sure-footed, thinking, thoughtful, tightknit, valid, well-calibrated, well-grounded, well-plotted, wise

Thought-out: nouns
clarity, clear-headedness, coherence, cohesion, common sense, congruity, consistency, discrimination, judgement, logic, lucidity, purity, rationality, reason, reasoning, sense, structure, symmetry, uniformity, unity

SUBTLE

artful, astute, cautious, circumspect, crafty, cunning, dainty, deft, delicate, devious, discerning, discrete, discriminating, elegant, elusive, ethereal, exquisite, fine, fine-grained, fine-spun, graceful, guarded, humble, inconspicuous, indirect, intimate, layered, light-handed, low-key, minimalist, modest, perceptive, precise, prudent, quiet, refined, reserved, restrained, reticent, retiring, select, self-effacing, sensitive, shrewd, shy, skilled, sly, sophisticated, suave, subdued, tactful, temperate, tenuous, textured, tranquil, tricksy, tricky, unassuming, understated, unfussy, unobtrusive, unostentatious, unpretentious, urbane

NEW

antic, archetypal, avant-garde, breakthrough, bridge-burning, budding, contemporary, curious, cutting-edge, daring, debut (n), different, distinct, distinctive, divergent, exotic, experimental, first, fresh, futuristic, germinal, hip, hot, incipient, initial, innovative, inventive, latest, left-field, mint, modern, neoteric, newbie, newfangled, novel, novice, odd, one-off, original, pilot, primary, pristine, protean, provocative, quirky, radical, refreshing, renovated, revamped, revolutionary, rising, seminal, startling, tyro, uncommon, unexplored, unfamiliar, unformulaic, unique, unprecedented, untried, unusual, virgin

PROMISING

able, auspicious, brilliant, capable, debuting, encouraging, endowed, favourable, gifted, hopeful, likely, mercurial, portentous, potent, precocious, pregnant, prodigious, rising, seminal, talented, thrusting, up-and-coming

Promising: person

debutante, first-timer, genius, newbie, newcomer, phenomenon, prodigy, prospect, protege, sensation, star, wonder, wunderkind

NOT STRAIGHTFORWARD

aberrant, abnormal, alien, anomalous, atypical, bent, bizarre, clandestine, coy, crafty, crooked, curious, deceptive, devious, eccentric, exceptional, extraordinary, fey, furtive, idiosyncratic, incongruous, individual, inexplicable, ironic, irregular, occult, odd, offbeat, off the wall, out of the blue, outlandish, outré, out-there, peculiar, playful, random, secret, self-conscious, shocking, sly, sneaky, startling, stealthy, strange, surprising, surreptitious, twisted, unanticipated, uncanny, uncommon, unconventional, underhand, unexpected, unforeseen, unorthodox, unpredictable, unusual, variable, wacky, weird, yo-yo

IMPORTANT OR POWERFUL

authoritative, blistering, cardinal, concussive, consequential, considerable, critical, crucial, decisive, distinguished, crucial, earth-shaking, earth-shattering, eminent, epochal, essential, fierce, full-throttle, fully equipped, fundamental, galvanising, hard-hitting, haunting, hefty, high-octane, high-wattage, historic, industrial-strength, influential, inspired, intense, invaluable, key, knockout, lasting, lingering, majestic, material, meaningful, memorable, mighty, militant, momentous, monumental, muscular, necessary, notable, noteworthy,

percussive, persistent, persuasive, pivotal, portentous, potent, powerful, priceless, prodigious, profound, prominent, puissant, remarkable, relevant, seminal, significant, strong, substantial, tectonic, valuable, virile, vital, vociferous, weapons-grade, weighty, world-shaking

BELIEVABLE

acceptable, actual, authentic, bona fide, candid, convincing, credible, damn-straight, dinkum, documented, echt, genuine, graphic, heartfelt, historical, honest, honest-to-goodness, kosher, legitimate, lifelike, likely, natural, persuasive, plausible, pragmatic, probable, real, realistic, representational, sincere, sound, swaying, true, true to life, truthful, unfeigned, valid, veracious, veridical, virtual, vivid, well-realised

COMPLETE

absolute, all-embracing, all-inclusive, all-out, ample, broad, cogent, completed, comprehensive, concluded, consummate, detailed, done, downright, effortless, entire, exacting, exhaustive, extensive, extreme, far-reaching, faultless, filled-out, finished, fleshed-out, flowing, from soup to nuts, full, full-blown, full-grown, full-scale, intact, out-and-out, overall, painstaking, perfect, plenary, pure, rank, realised, rounded, self-contained, standalone, sustained, sweeping, thorough, total, unbroken, undivided, unified, united, utter, whole, wholesale, wide-ranging, widespread

FULL

abounding, afloat, ample, awash, ballooned, beefy, brawny, brimful, brimming, broad, bulging, burly, bursting, chock-a-block, chock-full, clotted, coagulated, concentrated, congested, copious, crammed, crowded, dilated, elevated, engorged, extended, filled, flooded, freighted, gelatinous, glutted, gorged, heavy, hefty, heightened, imbued, intensified, inundated, jam-packed, jazzed up, laden, lined, loaded, overflowing, overrun, packed, plethorific, pneumatic, pregnant, pungent, ready to burst, redolent, replete, riddled, rife with, saturated, soaked, stiff, strapping, stuffed, supercharged, swarming, swollen, teeming, thick, well-fed

COMPLEX

abstruse, advanced, aureate, baroque, broad, busy, byzantine, complicated, composite, compound, convoluted, dense, detailed, difficult, elaborate, exaggerated, extravagant, fanciful, fancy, filigree (n), flamboyant, flash, florid, frou-frou, fussy, garnished, gilded, Gordian, guileful, hectic, hieratic, interlacing, interlinking, interlocking, interwoven, intricate, involved, knotty, labyrinthine, luxuriant, lyrical, maze-like, multifaceted, multifarious, multiplex, novelistic, obscure, operatic, opulent, ornamental, ornate, ostentatious, painterly, problematical, recondite, refined, rich, rococo, sophisticated, stylised, sumptuous, talky, tangled, theatrical, thorny, tortuous, tricksy, tricky, varnished

UNCOMPLICATED

apparent, articulate, artless, austere, certain, childlike, clean, clear, clear-cut, clear-headed, clear-thinking, comprehensible, crystal-clear, distinct, down to earth, easy, effortless, evident, explicit, faultless, guileless, humble, ingenuous, intelligible, intimate, jigsaw, logical, lucid, meek, minimal, modest, natural, naive, pithy, plain, pure, rational, reductive, regular, sheer, simple, slick, smooth, spare, straightforward, transparent, trenchant, unadorned, unambiguous, unassuming, unclouded, uncontaminated, undemanding, understandable, unequivocal, unfussy, unmistakeable, unpretentious, unsophisticated, unworldly, utter

REPUTABLE

admired, appreciated, authoritative, celebrated, decent, distinguished, esteemed, estimable, ethical, exalted, faithful, famed, high status, honourable, hushed, impressive, influential, loved, major, modest, moral, notable, prestigious, principled, prized, prominent, proper, proud, reliable, respectable, respected, restrained, revered, right, righteous, right-minded, significant, staunch, steadfast, trustworthy, uncompromising, upright, upstanding, valued, venerated, virtuous, well-regarded, well-thought-of

NOT GLOOMY

affirmative, blissful, blithe, bouncy, bright, buoyant, carefree, cheerful, cheering, cheery, chipper, chirpy, confident, content, convivial, delighted, devil-may-care, ecstatic, elysian, encouraging, euphoric, exhilarating, exultant, felicitous, freewheeling, gay, genial, glad, halcyon, happy-go-lucky, heartening, heartwarming, high-spirited, jaunty, jolly, jovial, joyful, lighthearted, lively, merry, on cloud nine, optimistic, perky, pleased, Pollyannaish, positive, relaxed, reviving, smiling, sparkling, spectacular, sunny, untroubled, unworried, up, upbeat, uplifting, vivacious

UNFLATTERING

UNFLATTERING: QUALITIES

apathy, awkwardness, clumsiness, confusion, contempt, cynicism, deceit, dishonesty, dullness, equivocation, flabbiness, gullibility, half-heartedness, ignorance, impatience, imprecision, incoherence, incompetence, inconsistency, laziness, lethargy, long-windedness, manipulation, mediocrity, messiness, naivety, predictability, pretension, schlock, schmaltz, sentimentality, snark(iness), squalor, stupidity, tastelessness, triteness, ugliness

HAVING FAULTS

average, awkward, below par, blemished, bloodless, bog-standard, broken, busted, damaged, damp, deficient, diffident, disappointing, faint, fair, faulty, flaccid, flawed, flimsy, forgettable, fragile, frail, grapeshot, imperfect, inconsistent, infirm, intermittent, lacklustre, limp, lukewarm, lumpy, manqué, marred, mediocre, minor, mixed, occasional, ordinary, overegged, pale, passable, perverse, puny, remedial, sapless, scarred, serviceable, shoddy, slack, slight, sloppy, spotty, soft, soggy, so-so, stained,

substandard, sullied, tainted, tarnished, thin, underbaked, unengaging, uneven, unexceptional, unfortunate, uninteresting, unmemorable, unreliable, unsatisfactory, unskilled, unsound, unspectacular, wan, watery, weak, wishy-washy

BAD

abysmal, appalling, atrocious, awful, callow, cloth-eared, clueless, corrupt, crappy, defective, deplorable, derided, dire, dishonourable, dismal, distasteful, distressing, dreadful, embarrassing, evil, excruciating, feeble, flyblown, foul, frightful, gamy, heinous, horrendous, incompetent, inconsequential, inferior, insubstantial, intolerable, lame, lamentable, laughable, lousy, low, low-life, ludicrous, mildewed, milquetoast, mouldy, naff, nauseating, no-good, nongish, painful, pathetic, peevish, pharisaical, pitiful, pointless, poor, puny, putrid, rancid, revolting, risible, rotten, sad, scant, second-rate, self-serving, shallow, sinful, sorry, spineless, splenetic, stale, stinky, terrible, tin-eared, unskilled, unwelcome, useless, valueless, vile, worst, worthless, wretched

Bad: nouns

chagrin, chore, complaint, condemnation, curate's egg, dejection, depression, disappointment, displeasure, dissatisfaction, drivel, drudge, duty, effort, failure, fiasco, fizzle, frustration, hokum, indignation, irritation, mistake, misfire, regret, task, trial, travesty, turkey

Bad: person

bad egg, blackguard, black sheep, bounder, bully, cad, charlatan, cheat, con artist, creep, criminal, crook, degenerate, felon, fraudster, goon, harridan, heavy, heel, hood, hoodlum, hooligan, jerk, knave, libertine, louse, lout, lowlife, mad dog, miscreant, mongrel, phony, rat, recidivist, reprobate, ruffian, scold, scoundrel, shrew, snitch, swindler, thug, trickster, villain, virago, vixen, witch

MANIPULATIVE

bathetic, bombastic, calculating, cloying, controlling, corny, cunning, devious, false-hearted, gooey, gushing, gushy, histrionic, hyperbolic, ingratiating, insidious, maudlin, mawkish, melodramatic, mushy, oversentimental, over-the-top, overwrought, pernicious, pulpy, saccharine, sappy, scheming, schlocky, schmaltzy, sentimental, sickly, slushy, soppy, sugar-coated, sugary, supercilious, surreptitious, syrupy, underhand, vomit-inducing, wet

STUPID

absurd, artless, asinine, backward, blockheaded, boneheaded, bonkers, brainless, bovine, cloddish, clot-headed, clueless, cockamamie, confused, cornball, crazy, cretinous, crude, daft, demented, dense, derelict, dim, dim-witted, directionless, doltish, dopey, dull, dull-witted, dumb, empty-headed, farcical, fat-headed, fatuous, feeble-minded, foolish, futile, gaga, goofy, gormless, half-witted, heedless, idiotic, ill-advised, ill-conceived, imbecilic, imprudent, inane, inept, injudicious, irrational, irresponsible, lame, lame-brained, laughable, lobotomised,

loopy, ludicrous, meaningless, mindless, mistaken, moronic, nitwitted, nonsensical, obtuse, outlandish, pointless, preposterous, pudding-headed, quarter-witted, rash, reckless, reductive, ridiculous, senseless, silly, simple-minded, simplistic, slow-witted, specious, suspect, thick, thick-skulled, thoughtless, tonto, troppo, unintelligent, unlettered, unreasonable, unthinking, unwise, witless

Stupid: nouns

absurdity, asininity, blooper, blunder, boo-boo, botch, brainlessness, buffoonery, bungle, density, dimness, error, fatuity, fault, faux pas, folly, foolishness, gaffe, hebetude, howler, idiocy, impropriety, lunacy, misapprehension, misstep, mistake, opacity, risibility, slip, solecism, thoughtlessness

Stupid: person

boor, buffoon, bumpkin, clot, cretin, dim bulb, dimwit, dolt, doofus, dope, dullard, dumbass, dummy, dunce, fool, halfwit, idiot, ignoramus, imbecile, jerk, moron, oaf, retard, schmendrik, schnook, simpleton, twit

UNTRIED

babyish, callow, childlike, credulous, dewy, dilettante, experimental, fledgling, fresh, green, guileless, gullible, hopeful, ignorant, immature, indecisive, inexperienced, inexpert, ingenuous, innocent, jejune, maiden, naive, nestling, new, newfangled, nobody, nonentity, parvenu, pristine, proto-, raw, recent, sophomoric, trendy, trusting, try-hard, unaccustomed, undergraduate, unfamiliar, unfledged, unknown, unpractised, unproven, unrefined, unseasoned, unsophisticated, untested, unworldly, vernal, wannabe, wet behind the ears, would-be, young

Untried: person

amateur, apprentice, beginner, dabbler, dilettante, freshman, greenhorn, ingénue, journeyman, neophyte, newbie, novice, sophomore, student, tyro, undergraduate, wannabe

NOT NEW

aged, ancient, antediluvian, anticipated, antiquated, antique, archaic, atavistic, banal, behind the times, blasé, boilerplate, bygone, clichéd, commonplace, conservative, conventional, creaking, dated, decrepit, demode, derivative, diagrammatic, dilapidated, dowdy, elderly, everyday, familiar, fogeyish, formulaic, fusty, garden-variety, hackneyed, has-been, humdrum, kitset (boil-in-the-bag, flat-pack, join-the-dots, colour / paint-by-numbers), mainstream, medieval, middle of the road, moribund, mundane, musty, obsolete, obvious, old, old-fashioned, old hat, old-school, old-time, ordinary, outdated, outmoded, out of date, passé, predictable, primaeval, primitive, quaint, quotidian, retro, retrograde, routine, schematic, sciolistic, shopworn, square, stale, standard, time-honoured, tired, traditional, unfashionable, unremarkable, unstylish, used, tumbledown, typecast, typical, vintage, washed-up, workaday, worn-out

Not new: nouns

assemblage, bromide, caricature, cliché, counterfeit, derivation, emulation, homage, imitation, nostrum, pablum, pastiche, piracy, plagiarism, platitude, rip-off, send-up, simulacrum, stereotype, take-off, typecasting

NOT SUBTLE

anticipated, artless, awkward, banal, blundering, bumbling, bungling, butterfingered, careless, clear, clichéd, clownish, clumsy, clunky, crass, cumbersome, embarrassing, expected, formulaic, foreseeable, fumbling, gauche, gawky, graceless, hackneyed, ham-fisted, heavy-handed, ill at ease, indelicate, indiscriminate, inelegant, inept, loud, lumbering, lurid, maladroit, obvious, ordinary, OTT, overbearing, overreaching, over-the-top, patent, patronising, plain, predictable, prosaic, see-through, sloppy, stale, strident, tactless, tired, tongue-tied, transparent, trenchant, trite, unambiguous, uncouth, uncritical, undemanding, unmistakeable, ungainly, unoriginal, unsubtle, unsurprising, unwieldy, visible, wooden

NOT CONVINCING

affected, arranged, artificial, bogus, calculated, cardboard, chimeric, confected, conniving, contrived, cooked-up, counterfeit, cynical, deceitful, deceiving, deceptive, diffident, dishonest, disingenuous, distorting, dummy, erroneous, ersatz, fabricated, facsimile (cod, faux, pseudo-, quasi-, sub-), fake, fallacious, false, far-fetched, faux, fictitious, fishy, forced, forged, fraudulent, fudged, half-hearted, hard-hearted, hokey, hypocritical, illusory, imitation, implausible, imposter, improbable, incorrect, indifferent, insincere, Janus-faced, made-up, make-believe, mannered, mechanical, misleading, misrepresentative, mistaken, mock, obdurate, operatic, pantomime, patronising, phoned-in, phony, Potemkin village, preposterous, pretend, put-on, replica, ripe, risible, sham, simulacrum, simulated, specious, staged, stage-managed, stagey, Stepford, stiff, stilted, stylised, suck-up, substitute, synthetic, theatrical, transparent, unbelievable, uncaring, uncertain, unconvincing, unimpressive, unlikely, unnatural, unpersuasive, unreal, unsuccessful, untrue, untruthful, vapid, wooden

POORLY THOUGHT OUT

accidental, anarchic, baffling, blind, brittle, brutal, careless, cartoonish, cavalier, chaotic, clumsy, cracker-barrel, disorderly, foolhardy, frivolous, green, half-arsed, half-baked, half-cocked, half-witted, haphazard, hasty, heedless, hurried, idealistic, ill-advised, ill-conceived, ill-considered, ill-judged, impractical, improvident, imprudent, impulsive, inconsiderate, indifferent, ineffective, ineffectual, injudicious, jerry-built, kitset (boil-in-the-bag, flat-pack, join-the-dots, colour / paint-by-numbers), lawless, misdirected, misguided, out of control, perfunctory, precipitous, premature, previous, rash, raw, reckless, regardless, rent-a-hack, romantic, rushed, shallow, shortsighted, simpleminded, slapdash, spontaneous, starry-eyed, superficial,

thoughtless, throwaway, trigger-happy, uncrystallised, undercooked, underripe, unfocused, unheeding, unintended, unplanned, unpredictable, unreflective, unripe, unruly, unthinking, unwise, unwitting, willy-nilly, woolly

NOT AMBITIOUS OR ACHIEVING AMBITION

adolescent, airheaded, airless, airy-fairy, amateurish, am-dram, anaemic, anodyne, antiseptic, asinine, banal, basic, benign, bland, boilerplate, bourgeois, bubblegum, by the numbers, callow, catalogue-like, cellophane, childish, colourless, complacent, confined, constrained, constricted, cramped, curated, daft, deodorised, derisory, dogmatic, earthbound, empty, evanescent, facile, faithful, featherweight, feeble, flat, flavourless, flimsy, flippant, fluffy, fossilised, frail, frothy, frumpy, futile, generic, glib, glitz, glossy, gossamer, hidebound, humble, inadequate, incommodious, infantile, inflexible, innocuous, insipid, insubstantial, jejune, juvenile, lacklustre, lazy, lifeless, light, lightweight, literal, lo-fi, lowbrow, low-rent, manufactured, meaningless, mechanical, middlebrow, milquetoast, mundane, namby-pamby, negligible, no-account, nugatory, pale, pallid, paltry, pedestrian, penny-ante, penurious, philistine, photonic, plain, plastic, pointless, poky, pragmatic, prim, proper, prosaic, puny, remote, restrictive, rigid, safe, sanitised, schematic, scrawny, senseless, skeletal, slender, slick, soft-pedalling, sophomoric, spartan, spectral, spiritless, sterile, suffocating, superficial, superfluous, tame, thin, threadbare, timid, tin-foil, tinny, tinsel, toothless, trifling, trite, trivial, twee, two-bit, unchallenging, uncultivated, unengaging, underpowered, unimaginative, uninspired, uninvolving, unquestioning, vapid, vaporous, vulgar, weak, whitebread, wide-eyed, wishy-washy, worthy

PRETENTIOUS

affected, artificial, arty, bombastic, conceited, condescending, conspicuous, exaggerated, faddish, flatulent, flowery, garish, glitzy, grandiloquent, grandiose, highfalutin, high-flown, high-sounding, histrionic, hoity-toity, hollow, humbug, hyperbolic, inflated, jumped-up, la-di-da, modish, ostentatious, overblown, pompous, portentous, posh, precious, pretend, sententious, showboating, show-off, showy, smug, snobbish, splashy, stagey, supercilious, superficial, superior, swollen, tony, try-hard, vacuous, vainglorious, voguish, wannabe, windy, would-be

BORING

anaemic, arid, banal, blah, bland, bloodless, blunt-edged, blurred, chaste, dead, desiccated, drab, dreary, dry, dull, flat, generic, glaucous, grey, heavy, ho-hum, humdrum, lacklustre, leaden, lethargic, lifeless, mind-numbing, monotonous, mousy, muted, no-frills, numbing, obtuse, pale, pedestrian, pithless, po-faced, prosaic, repetitive, sanctimonious, soporific, spineless, static, stultifying, tedious, tepid, thudding, tiresome, tiring, torpid, unexciting, unimaginative, uninspiring, uninteresting, uninvolving, vacuous, washed-out, wearisome

MUDDLED

addled, baffling, befuddled, bewildering, bitsy, blurry, broken, capricious, changeable, chaotic, clouded, cluttered, confused, confusing, contradictory, derelict, disconnected, discordant, discrepant, disjointed, disorganised, dissonant, enigmatic, erratic, fickle, foggy, fuddled, fuzzy, garbled, hazy, higgledy-piggledy, holus-bolus, ill-defined, illogical, impenetrable, inchoate, incoherent, incompatible, incongruent, inconsistent, inconstant, jumbled, mercurial, messed-up, mixed-up, muddleheaded, muffled, murky, muted, obscure, obtuse, opaque, pellucid, perplexing, pudding-headed, punch-drunk, purple, puzzling, scattered, schizophrenic, shambolic, slapdash, slap-happy, spasmodic, stodgy, temperamental, topsy-turvy, turbid, unclear, unpredictable, unstable, upside-down, vague, variable, volatile, whimsical, woolly, woolly-headed

NOT CONSISTENT

aberrant, ad hoc, adrift, amorphous, anomalous, arbitrary, broken, broken-down, capricious, changeable, choppy, conflicting, contradictory, desultory, deviating, dicey, digressive, discrepant, disjointed, dizzy, errant, erratic, fickle, fluctuating, fragmentary, half-hearted, half-pie, haphazard, herky-jerky, huckery, idiosyncratic, iffy, impetuous, imprecise, impulsive, incompatible, incomplete, incongruous, inconsistent, inconstant, irreconcilable, irregular, makeshift, mealy-mouthed, mercurial, mismatched, motley, paradoxical, partial, patchy, piecemeal, ragged, ragtag, rudimentary, saggy, scattershot, scrappy, shaky, shifting, sketchy, sporadic, spotty, staccato, stop-start, unbalanced, uncompleted, unequal, uneven, unfinished, unfixed, unpredictable, unreliable, unsettled, unstable, variable, volatile, wishy-washy, wonky

MISSHAPEN
adipose, adrift, aimless, amorphous, astray, awry, baggy, big-bellied, bloated, bow-legged, chaotic, contorted, contourless, corpulent, crooked, deformed, disfigured, disproportionate, distended, distorted, drooping, erratic, flaccid, flat-footed, flatulent, floppy, foggy, formless, gargoylish, gassy, gnarled, haywire, incoherent, indulgent, intemperate, lackadaisical, lax, leaky, limp, long-winded, lopsided, lumpen, malformed, maundering, messy, misbegotten, neglectful, negligent, obese, offhand, overblown, overgrown, overindulgent, overladen, overweight, paunchy, procrastinating, promiscuous, puffy, ragged, rambling, random, reckless, rickety, ropey, sagging, shapeless, shoddy, slack, slipshod, sloppy, slovenly, slurring, stodgy, sway-backed, swollen, truncated, twisted, unanchored, unsteady, untethered, untidy, vague, verbose, waffling, wandering, warped, wavering

TOO SLOW
apathetic, arse-dragging, backward, boring, complacent, constipated, crawling, creeping, dawdling, dilatory, distended, dragging, drawn-out, dreary, drowsy, exhausted, exhaustive, glacial, half-hearted, idle, inactive, indolent, inert, insipid, interminable, laborious, lacklustre, laggard,

languid, lax, lazy, leaden, lethargic, lifeless, limping, lingering, listless, loitering, long-winded, lumbering, mind-numbing, monotonous, moribund, obtuse, overlong, pedestrian, peristaltic, phlegmatic, plodding, ponderous, procrastinating, prolix, prolonged, protracted, retarded, rusty, sententious, shiftless, shilly-shallying, slack, slack-paced, sleepy, slothful, slow, slow-poke, sluggish, somnolent, soporific, stagnant, stodgy, tardy, tedious, tired, tiresome, torpid, treacly, uninteresting, unwilling, vacillating, verbose, waddling, wearisome, weary, wearying, windy, wishy-washy, wordy, work-shy

IRRITATING
aggravating, angering, annoying, bothersome, bruising, chafing, disagreeable, displeasing, distressing, disturbing, enraging, exasperating, frustrating, galling, grating, infuriating, irksome, jarring, maddening, nauseating, nettlesome, painful, peeving, perturbing, pesky, pestiferous, plaguesome, provoking, supercilious, tedious, tiresome, troublesome, troubling, trying, uncomfortable, vexatious, vexing, worrying

IN POOR TASTE
abnormal, ambiguous, ambivalent, anomalous, arguable, bourgeois, contestable, controversial, curious, debatable, disputable, doubtful, dubious, enigmatic, equivocal, evasive, fishy, forked, funny, high camp, imprecise, inappropriate, incongruous, indeterminate, kitsch, low camp, moot, odd, peculiar, philistine, polysemous, problematic, queer, questionable, rum,

rummy, shady, sick, strange, suspect, suspicious, uncertain, unconvincing, unengaging, unsavoury, unsuitable, unsure, untrustworthy, unusual, vague, vapid, vulgar

In poor taste: sexual person
adulterer, bimbo, catamite, dirty old man, flasher, floozy, harlot, hooker, hussy, hustler, jezebel, loose woman, nympho, panderer, pervert, philanderer, pimp, roué, scarlet woman, skirt-chaser, slapper, slattern, slut, sodomite, tart, tramp, trollop, whore

UNPLEASANT
abhorrent, abominable, bothersome, brutal, callous, disagreeable, disfigured, disgusting, distasteful, distressing, fetid, foul, ghastly, grisly, grotesque, harsh, heartless, hideous, horrible, horrid, insipid, irksome, loathsome, malicious, mean-spirited, merciless, nasty, objectionable, obnoxious, odious, offensive, off-putting, pitiless, repellent, repugnant, repulsive, ruthless, scrofulous, seedy, shabby, shocking, skanky, sordid, sour, spiteful, squalid, tawdry, ugly, unappealing, unappetising, unattractive, uncomfortable, unkind, unlikeable, unlovely, unsightly, unspeakable, unsympathetic, vicious, vindictive, wretched

OF LITTLE VALUE
adrift, aimless, barren, chaste, cheap, cheesy, common, crummy, directionless, empty, futile, good-for-nothing, hollow, impotent, inconsequential, inferior, in limbo, insignificant, insincere, irrational, irrelevant, lamentable, meaningless, meritless, miserable, negligible, niggardly, no-account, nothing, nugatory, otiose, paltry, picayune,

pointless, purposeless, rubbishy, second-rate, senseless, shabby, sterile, stillborn, superficial, superfluous, throwaway, trashy, trifling, trite, trivial, twopenny, unimportant, unprofitable, unrewarding, useless, vacant, vacuous, vain, valueless, void, wasted, worthless

Of little value: nouns
babble, balderdash, blather, bollocks, bumpf, bunch of arse, bunkum, claptrap, crap, dreck, drivel, dross, dud, error, flotsam, folderol, frivolity, gaffe, gibberish, glitch, hogwash, hooey, jetsam, mess, mistake, nada, nonsense, ordure, pants, picayune, prattle, shite, tomfoolery, trash, tripe, turkey, twaddle, zero, zilch, zip

DISREPUTABLE
amoral, base, brassy, cheap, cheating, chintzy, corrupt, crummy, cynical, deceitful, déclassé, depraved, devious, discredited, disgraceful, dishonest, dishonorable, dodgy, doubtful, flashy, garish, gaudy, gimcrack, heavy-handed, immoral, impertinent, infamous, in poor taste, insidious, louche, loud, meretricious, neanderthal, notorious, opportunist, questionable, rummy, scandalous, seamy, seedy, shady, sleazy, sordid, squalid, suspect, tacky, tasteless, tatty, tawdry, trashy, unethical, unprincipled, unscrupulous, wrong

HARMFUL
abusive, baneful, blistering, brutal, calumnious, catastrophic, contemptible, corrupting, counterproductive, cruel, damaging, dangerous, deadly, deceitful,

defamatory, degrading, deleterious,
denigrating, deplorable, depraved,
despicable, destructive, detestable,
detrimental, disadvantageous, dishonest,
dishonourable, distressing, disturbing, evil,
fraudulent, hateful, hurtful, ill-intentioned,
ill-willed, immoral, injurious, insidious,
invidious, libellous, malign, mischievous,
nasty, nefarious, negative, noxious,
painful, pernicious, poisonous, prejudicial,
punishing, risky, ruinous, scandalous,
sickening, slanderous, toxic, traumatic,
treacherous, underarm, underhanded,
unethical, unsafe, unscrupulous, unsuitable,
untoward, vicious, vile, wicked, wounding

NEUTRAL OR AMBIGUOUS

QUALITIES: NOUNS

abstraction, ambiguity, appearance,
bleakness, breadth, brightness, circularity,
complexity, depth, diffidence, fashion, fear,
gloom, homogeneity, largeness, linearity,
looseness, narrowness, obliqueness,
simplicity, slowness, smallness, speed,
tightness, weight, wideness, width,
sentiment, sex

MEANS OF DEFINING

analytical, categorical, cerebral,
constitutional, cultural, ecological,
epistemological, ethical, existential,
hypothetical, ideological, intellectual, legal,
logistical, metaphysical, methodological,
moral, ontological, organisational,
pathological, physical, physiological,
political, psychological, social, societal,
sociological, spatial, spiritual, structural,

technological, temporal, terminological,
theological, topographical

EVOKING OTHER STATES OF MIND

abstract, absurd, antic, apocryphal, astral,
baroque, bizarre, celestial, chimerical,
conceptual, curious, cyber, delirious,
disembodied, dizzying, dreamlike, dreamy,
drowsy, drugged, enchanted, esoteric,
ethereal, extraterrestrial, fanciful, fantastic,
futuristic, fey, gothic, hallucinatory,
heavenly, hypnotic, hypothetical, illusory,
imaginary, immaterial, incorporeal,
intoxicated, legendary, liminal, make-
believe, meditative, mesmeric, mesmerising,
metaphysical, mystical, mythical, narcotic,
nebulous, nocturnal, nostalgic, notional,
numinous, otherworldly, outlandish,
phantasmagoric(al), pretend, preternatural,
shadowy, spectral, spiritual, supernatural,
surreal, tranquillising, transcendental,
transporting, uncanny, unearthly, unreal,
unworldly, virtual, visionary, whimsical

Other states: nouns

allusion, apparition, daydream, delirium,
diorama, ecstasy, fallacy, fancy, hallucination,
illusion, imagination, insomnia, mediation,
nightmare, phantom, reverie, sedation, sleep,
stupor, surreality, trance, unreality, vision

Other states: figures

alien, apparition, banshee, bogeyman,
chimera, demon, doppelgänger, dybbuk,
eidolon, figure, ghost, ghoul, hallucination,
incubus, phantasmagoria, phantom,
poltergeist, spectre, spirit, spook, sprite,
succubus, wraith, zombie

SEXUAL

amorous, ardent, bawdy, blue, bodily, carnal, climactic, come-hither, coquettish, debaucherous, desirous, devious, earthy, edgy, erogenous, erotic, exotic, fetching, flirtatious, flirty, foxy, freaky, horny, hot-blooded, impassioned, intimate, juicy, kinky, lascivious, lecherous, lewd, libidinous, licentious, lubricious, lustful, naughty, nuptial, nymphomaniacal, passionate, perverted, physical, piquant, porny, potent, priapic, prurient, racy, randy, raunchy, ravishing, ribald, risky, risqué, rude, salacious, salty, satyric, scurrilous, seductive, sensual, sensuous, sexy, smutty, spicy, steamy, suggestive, sultry, sweaty, teasing, tempting, titillating, torrid, voluptuous

Sexual: person

call girl, casanova, comfort woman, concubine, courtesan, Don Juan, escort, flame, flirt, gigolo, lady-killer, Lothario, lounge lizard, madam, mistress, moll, nightwalker, playboy, player, porn star, prostitute, rent boy, sex worker, streetwalker, swinger, vamp, working girl

LOOSE

abstracted, amorphous, ample, anarchic, baggy, bohemian, carefree, casual, desultory, diffuse, digressive, discursive, drifting, easygoing, eccentric, eclectic, elliptical, extravagant, fleshy, free, free-and-easy, freeform, free-thinking, freewheeling, flowing, footloose, indulgent, informal, irregular, irrepressible, laissez-faire, lenient, liberated, libertine, loose-fitting, lubricated, meandering, natural, open-hearted, open-minded, organic, prolix, puffed-out, rambling, ramshackle, random, relaxed, roomy, roving, scrappy, scruffy, shifting, sociable, sprawling, straggly, straying, tenuous, tolerant, unbridled, unconstrained, unconventional, undeveloped, uneven, unfettered, ungainly, unkempt, unpredictable, unrestricted, unruly, unstructured, voluminous, wandering, wayward, well-fed, wild, woolly

NOT LOOSE

airtight, austere, circumscribed, clenched, clinging, clipped, close, close-fitting, compact, compressed, concise, condensed, confined, consistent, contracted, crisp, dense, efficient, elliptic, epigrammatic, exiguous, figure-hugging, firm, formal, hermetic, impenetrable, impermeable, impervious, laconic, limited, meagre, mingy, miserly, narrow, neat, niggardly, organised, parsimonious, pent-up, pinched, pointed, professional, pruned, rainproof, reserved, restricted, sealed, skimpy, sleek, slender, slick, slim, slimline, snug, sparing, spartan, staunch, stingy, stodgy, straitened, strict, stringent, succinct, taciturn, taut, tenacious, tense, terse, tight, tight-fitting, tight-lipped, trim, truncated, vice-like, waterproof, watertight, wound

LARGE

adipose, ample, astronomical, awesome, banner, big-boned, big-budget, boundless, bountiful, bulky, bumper, burly, capacious, chubby, chunky, colossal, comprehensive, considerable, copious, corpulent, diffuse, elephantine, enlarged, enormous, extensive, fat, gargantuan, generous, giant, gigantic, goodly, grand, great, handsome, healthy, heavy, hefty, heroic, hospitable, huge, hulking, humongous, immeasurable, immense, imposing, infinite, inflated, inordinate, jumbo, king-size, lavish, leviathan, liberal, mammoth, massive, monolithic, monster, monstrous, monumental, mountainous, munificent, muscular, numerous, outsize, overweight, portly, prodigious, profuse, prominent, queen-size, significant, sizeable, spacious, strapping, stupendous, substantial, sweeping, swollen, titanic, tremendous, turgid, unrestrained, vast, voluminous, wholesale, whopping, wide-ranging, widespread

Large: nouns

abundance, affluence, ampleness, bonanza, cornucopia, embarrassment, excess, extravaganza, glut, harvest, landslide, ocean, plenty, plethora, profusion, repertoire, shower, superfluity, surfeit, surplus, volume, welter

SMALL

atomic, bantam, bijou, claustrophobic, diminished, diminutive, dinky, dwarfish, elfin, humble, insignificant, itty-bitty, lilliputian, limited, little, low, lowercase, lowly, mean, micro, midget, mingy, miniature, minor, minuscule, minute, miserly, modest, negligible, paltry, pathetic, peanut, peewee, petite, petty, picayune, piddling, pocket-sized, puny, rarefied, reduced, runty, shrimpy, slender, slight, slim, small-scale, stingy, subatomic, svelte, sylphlike, teeny, tiny, undersized, wee, willowy, wispy

Small: nouns

breath, crumb, dash, drop, ghost, grain, hair, hint, inkling, iota, jot, mite, modicum, morsel, pittance, scintilla, scrap, shadow, shard, shred, skerrick, sliver, smidgeon, snippet, soupçon, speck, splinter, suspicion, tad, tinge, titbit, touch, trace, trickle, trifle, whiff, whisker, whisper, whit, wisp

EXTENDED OR WIDE

all-embracing, all-encompassing, all-inclusive, approximate, blanket, blistering, broad, capacious, commodious, deep, deliberate, demonstrative, drawn-out, effusive, elastic, elongated, encompassing, endless, expansive, extended, extensive, far-reaching, general, inclusive, inexact, lasting, lengthy, liberal, lingering, long, magnified, marathon, meaty, open, panoptic, patient, prolonged, pronounced, protracted, roomy, rough, sketchy, spacious, stretched-out, strong, substantial, sweeping, tolerant, wide-ranging

BRIEF OR NARROW

abbreviated, abridged, abrupt, barely (adv), blunt, brusque, close, compacted, compressed, concise, condensed, constricted, contracted, curt, defined, diminutive, disciplined, expeditious, fine, foreshortened, frugal, gruff, inflexible, laconic, lilliputian, limited, little, meagre, minute, particularised, pithy, precise, reduced, restricted, rigid, short, shrunken, slender, slight, slim, snappy, sparse, spartan, specialised, squeezed, stipulated, succinct, sufficient, tapered, terse, thin, tight, truncated, ungenerous,

FASHIONABLE

all-the-rage, au courant, avant garde, chic, chi-chi, contemporary, cool, current, designer, forward-looking, fringe, happening, hip, hot, in, in vogue, mod, modern, natty, now, popular, progressive, radical, snazzy, styley, stylish, swank, swish, tony, trendy, tricksy, tricky, twisted, up to date, voguish, with-it

Fashionable: nouns

charm, chic, élan, elegance, fashion, flair, froideur, panache, sang-froid, style, vogue

APPARENT

acknowledged, admitted, avowed, blatant, clear, concrete, confessed, conspicuous, corporeal, direct, disclosed, distinct, evident, eye-catching, flagrant, glaring, manifest, marked, noticeable, open, ostensible, overt, palpable, patent, perceptible, plain, public, recognisable, salient, seeming, self-evident, substantial, tangible, tell-tale, transparent, unconcealed, unequivocal, unhidden, unmasked, unmistakeable, visceral, visible

DISPASSIONATE

abstract, affectless, aloof, blunt, candid, calculated, cold-blooded, cool, detached, diffident, direct, disinterested, equitable, even-handed, forthright, hard-headed, heedless, impartial, impassive, impersonal, indifferent, insouciant, level-headed, lofty, meek, neutral, non-emotional, no-nonsense, obdurate, objective, Olympian, open-minded, ordinary, plain, plainspoken, po-faced, poker-faced, retiring, selfless, self-possessed, square-on, stand-offish, stoic, stony, straight, straightforward, stubborn, targeted, unassertive, unblinking, uncaring, uncompassionate, undeviating, unemotional, unfeeling, unilateral, unpenitent, unprejudiced, unromantic, unsure, unswerving, unsympathetic, unvarnished

NOT DIRECT

ancillary, angular, arcane, askance (adv), askew, backhanded, bent, biased, circuitous, circular, circumlocutory, crooked, curving, deviating, devious, diagonal, digressive, droll, eccentric, evasive, excursive, fey, freakish, freaky, geeky, implied, indirect, inferred, inverted, left-field, left-of-centre, meandering, nerdy, oblique, oddball, off-beam, off-centre, off-key, off-kilter, outré, out-there, perverse, rambling, roundabout, roving, sidelong, sideways, skew-whiff, slanted, sly, sneaky, spiral, surreptitious, swerving, tacit, tangential, tilted, topsy-turvy, tortuous, tricky, twisting, unconventional, veering, wayward, wandering, winding, wry, zigzag

EVOKING MIXED EMOTIONS

aigre-doux, ambiguous, ambivalent, antinomic, bittersweet, blended, double-edged, equivocal, ironic, layered, mingled, oxymoronic, paradoxical, poignant, schizophrenic, serio-comic, spicy, sting in the tail, sweet and sour, tart, tragicomic, undercut

CAUSING FRIGHT

alarming, blood-curdling, chilling, creepy, daunting, disquieting, distressing, disturbing, eerie, egregious, fearsome, forbidding, freaky, frightening, ghostly, hairy, harrowing, haunting, horrifying, intimidating, macabre, menacing, nasty, ominous, petrifying, scary, shivery, shuddery, sinister, spine-chilling, spooky, startling, terrifying, threatening, unsettling, upsetting, worrying

Causing fright: nouns

agitation, alarm, angst, anxiety, apprehension, awe, distress, dread, fear, fright, horror, nerves, nightmare, panic, phobia, shock, terror, trepidation

FAST OR ENTERPRISING

accelerated, active, adventurous, agile, aggressive, all-out, ambitious, ardent, assiduous, audacious, barrelling, blistering, breakneck, breathless, brisk, busy, dashing, diligent, double-quick, dynamic, eager, energetic, enthusiastic, exciting, expeditious, exponential, express, fast-paced, fleet-footed, frantic, galloping, hardworking, hasty, headlong, hectic, high-speed, hurried, hurrying, hustling, immediate, impetuous, indefatigable, industrious, jaunty, kinetic, lively, meteoric, nimble-footed, non-stop, precipitous, profligate, prompt, quick, rapid, rapid-fire, rattling, red-hot, riotous, rip-roaring, rocket-powered, scurrying, speedy, stroppy, swift, tireless, untiring, vigorous, vivacious, winged, yearning, zealous

SLOW OR CAREFUL

adagio, anal, apathetic, careful, cautious, crawling, dawdling, deliberate, didactic, dilatory, diligent, dilly-dallying, drawn-out, drowsy, easygoing, easy-paced, erudite, exacting, extended, fastidious, finicky, gentle, gradual, hesitant, hesitating, laggard, languid, leisurely, lethargic, long-play, measured, meticulous, painstaking, patient, pedantic, precise, prolonged, protracted, punctilious, relaxed, reluctant, rigorous, scrupulous, sleepy, slouching, slow-moving, tentative, time-consuming, unhurried, vigilant

SIMPLE

absolute, artless, ascetic, austere, authentic, bald, bare, bare-bones, basic, bread and butter, classical, clear, common, comprehensible, crystal-clear, cut-down, dinkum, elemental, elementary, essential, frugal, guileless, homely, household, humble, ingenuous, innocent, manageable, modest, natural, plain, plain-spoken, rudimentary, simplified, spare, sparse, spartan, stark, straightforward, subtle, succinct, unadorned, unadulterated, unalloyed, uncomplicated, undecorated, unembellished, unpretentious, unrefined, unsophisticated, unvarnished, verbatim

COMPLICATED

abstruse, advanced, baroque, busy, byzantine, complex, convoluted, dense, difficult, elaborate, extravagant, fancy, filigree (n), frou-frou, gilded, Gordian, guileful, hectic, hieratic, interwoven, intricate, involved, knotty, labyrinthine, maze-like, obscure, operatic, ornamental, ornate, ostentatious, pimped-out, recondite, serpentine, sophisticated, stylised, tangled, theatrical, tortuous, varnished

NOT ENTHUSIASTIC

averse, cagey, canny, careful, cautious, chary, circumspect, deliberate, diffident, disaffected, disinclined, dissenting, guarded, half-hearted, hesitant, ill-disposed, indisposed, involuntary, leery, leisurely, loath, lukewarm, mindful, non-committal, protesting, recalcitrant, reluctant, resistant, sceptical, shirking, shrinking, sulky, uneager, unenthusiastic, unsympathetic, unwilling, wary

GLOOMY OR BITING

acerbic, acid, acidulous, atmospheric, barbed, bitter, black, caustic, cutting, cynical, derisive, distrustful, doubtful, downbeat, glum, hard-boiled, harsh, ironic, lugubrious, melancholic, misanthropic, mocking, moody, mordant, negative, parodic, pessimistic, pointed, pungent, sarcastic, sardonic, satirical, saturnine, scathing, scornful, sour, stinging, strident, stringent, suspicious, trenchant, vehement, virulent, vitriolic, withering, wounding

BLEAK

apathetic, austere, black, blue, cheerless, chilling, claustrophobic, dark, defeated, dejected, depressing, desolate, despairing, desperate, despondent, discomforting, disconsolate, disheartening, dismal, dispiriting, dour, downcast, downbeat, downhearted, drab, dreary, forbidding, forlorn, funereal, futile, gloomy, glum, grave, grey, grim, harrowing, heartbreaking, hopeless, in the dumps, joyless, listless, lonely, melancholic, miserable, morbid, morose, nettlesome, sad, saddening, sorrowful, sour, sullen, tragic, uninviting, unwelcoming, woeful, wretched

NOT DULL

aglow, alight, beaming, blazing, blinding, bright, brilliant, burnished, cloudless, coruscating, dazzling, effulgent, flashing, flashy, fluorescent, glaring, gleaming, glinting, glistening, glittering, glossy, glowing, illuminating, incandescent, iridescent, lambent, lucent, luciform, luminous, lurid, lustrous, nacreous, radiant, reflective, refulgent, shimmering, shining, shiny, sparkling, sparkly, sunny, twinkling

USEFUL LANGUAGE

abase – (v) to degrade or humiliate

aberrant – (adj) departing from the norm

abeyance – (n) state of suspension or disuse, usually temporary

abhorrent – (adj) repellent, disgusting

abnegation – (n) act of giving something up

abrogate – (v) to cancel

abstemious – (adj) characterised by moderation in eating or drinking

abstinence – (n) practice of restraining (usually from sex or alcohol)

abstruse – (adj) hard to understand (similar:

esoteric, recondite)

academic – (adj) to do with learning, especially at university level; theoretical rather than of practical use, irrelevant

accentuate – (v) to emphasise or intensify

accolade – (n) expression of praise; award

acidulous – (adj) sour, biting

acquiescent – (adj) willing to do bidding of others without protest (verb: acquiesce)

acrimony – bitter animosity (adjective: acrimonious)

acuity – (n) sharpness of vision or intelligence

acumen – (n) ability to make accurate and quick judgements

adamantine – (adj) unyielding

adjure – (v) to earnestly appeal to

admonish – (v) to tell off or caution regarding one's behaviour (noun: admonition)

adulation – (n) excessive flattery (verb: adulate)

adulterate – (v) contaminate (noun: adulteration)

advocate – (n, v) one that supports a cause or pleads on behalf of another; to do so

aegis – (n) the protection or guidance of

aficionado – (n) dedicated enthusiast

agnate – (adj) on the father's side; related

alibi – (n) legal defence proving one was elsewhere

allay – (v) to relieve or lessen

allegory – (n) representation of principles or ideas through story or drama; such a story (adjective: allegorical; compare: fable, parable)

allusion – (n) indirect reference (compare: delusion, illusion)

altercation – (n) physical dispute

altruism – unselfish concern for others (adjective: altruistic)

ambience – (n) atmosphere or surroundings of place (adjective: ambient)

ambiguity – (n) uncertainty of meaning

ambit – (n) area of influence, scope

ambivalence – (n) the holding of conflicting views (adjective: ambivalent)

ambrosia – (n) food of the gods; something especially delicious

analogy – (n) comparison based on similar aspects

anathema – (n) that which is intensely disliked

ancillary – (adj) giving support; subordinate (similar: auxiliary)

anecdote – (n) short account, especially lively (adjective: anecdotal)

animus – (n) feeling of animosity or ill will (enmity = hostility; amity = friendship)

anodyne – (adj) bland, dull

anomaly – (n) deviation from norm

antebellum – (adj) before a war, originally the US Civil war

antediluvian – (adj) old-fashioned (meaning: before [biblical] flood)

antinomy – (n) fundamental contradiction between basic principles

antithesis – (n) direct opposite

aperçu – (n) discerning perception

apocryphal – (adj) unlikely to be true; mythical (noun: Apocrypha: disputed books of the Bible)

apogee – (n) culmination, ultimate point; furthest point of orbit of moon or satellite or moon from earth (opposite: perigee)

apoplexy – (n) extreme anger; stroke (adjective: apoplectic)

apostasy – (n) rejection of previous beliefs

apotheosis – (n) ideal embodiment

appease – (v) to pacify; to give concessions to

apposite – (adj) highly suitable or well chosen

arbitrary – (adj) determined by chance or capriciousness; exercised according to one's will rather than objective principles; the decision of a court or judge

arc – (n) part of a path; something that is curved

arcane – (adj) known or understood by select few, mysterious, hidden (compare: esoteric)

archetype – (n) original model; ideal

array – (n) display; collection of similar items

arrogate – (v) to claim for oneself without right

artefact – (n) a product of human conception

asperity – (n) harshness, especially of temper

asset – (n) valuable thing, person, or attribute (opposite: liability)

assiduous – (adj) careful and persistent

atavistic – (adj) of ancestors or genetic throwback; of previous behaviour that has returned

attenuated – (adj) diluted or weakened; tapered; thin

autodidact – (n) one who is self-taught

avatar – (n) embodiment; representation of self online

avocation – (n) sideline, hobby (avocate: to withdraw)

axiomatic – (adj) self-evidently true; aphoristic (noun: axiom)

bacchanalia – (n) joyful, often drunken celebration (similar: saturnalia)

backdrop – (n) background or setting of event; originally painted cloth at back of stage

backstory – (n) history or experiences of character before they appear on screen

badinage – (n) witty conversation

bailiwick – (n) one's area of authority, expertise (often literary or meant humorously)

bathetic – (adj) insincerely emotional; encouraging bathos

bathos – (n) insincere emotion; rapid descent from the serious to the trivial; triteness (compare: pathos)

bellicose – (adj) aggressive, warlike

bespoke – (adj) cut to individual's measurements, as of a suit; can be applied to other things made to specific requirements

boilerplate – (adj) predictable, as of a template

bolus – (n) a rounded mass, especially chewed food; large dose of drug

bombastic – (adj) characterised by high-sounded, exaggerated language (noun: bombast)

bonhomie – (n) cheerful friendliness; pleasant disposition (similar: geniality)

bootstrapping – (n) growing company without funding

braggadocio – (n) empty bragging; swaggering manner

bravura – (n) show of great spirit; brilliant performance

brio – (n) liveliness of spirit

bromide – (n) a trite and essentially meaningless phrase or platitude; a salt of hydrobromic acid, used in sedatives and photographic printing

bruit – (v) to spread widely, as in rumour

cabal – (n) small group of conspirators; secret plot

cachet – (n) quality conferring respect or admiration

cadaver – (n) body, corpse (adjective: cadaverous)

cadence – (n) the rise and fall in pitch of a voice; the beat or rhythmic flow of music or spoken words

calamity – (n) disaster that brings widescale distress (adjective: calamitous)

calculus – (n) method of computation, calculation; reasoning

caliginous – (adj) dark and misty

calumnious – (adj) discrediting and harmful, especially of statements

camouflage – (n) means of disguise

canard – (n) unfounded or false report, rumour

canon – (n) collection of work by writer, etc., considered bona fide or indicative

carapace – (n) a shell, especially metaphorically

caricature – (n) exaggerated representation

catharsis – (n) emotional relief by way of intense experiences or release of pent-up thoughts and feelings

cavil – (v) to make petty objections

censor – (n, v) an official who grades publications or artworks for public consumption, etc.; to do so

censorious – (adj) finding fault

censure – (n, v) harsh criticism; to severely criticise

charade – (n) pretence or travesty

chiaroscuro – (n) the technique and effect of using light and shadow, or of being partly in shadow (compare: silhouette)

chimeric – (adj) highly improbable or fanciful (noun: chimera)

chorus – (n) in drama, one who comments on action; part of song; body of singers

cinematic – (n) like cinema, so strong on visual stortelling; relating to filmmaking

circumlocution – (n) 'beating about the bush' (fancy: periphrasis)

circumspect – (adj) cautious, often respectfully

cliché – (n) overfamiliar expression or idea

climax – (n) highest point or culmination; turning point in drama

clutch – (n, v) group (similar: bevy, slew); to grip

coalesce – (v) to come together

coda – (n) passage at end of work of art or music

codify – (v) to classify, organise into a system

coeval – (adj) contemporary; one of the same age or epoch

cognate – (adj) of same family or nature

cognomen – (n) familiar name, nickname (similar: moniker, sobriquet)

composition – (n) artwork; combining of parts into whole

conceit – (n) an elaborate metaphor or theme in literary or dramatic work; excessive pride

conflate – (v) to merge (texts, characters, etc.) into one

conjunction – (n) a joining or occurring together; joining element of grammar

construct – (n, v) conception, interpretation; to build

contretemps – (n) awkward clash

conundrum – (n) difficult or insoluble problem; traditionally, a riddle that may be answered by a pun (see Common and Occasional Confusions, page 77)

convention – (n) widely accepted technique; generally agreed practice

corollary – (n) statement or proposition that follows naturally from previous proven one

corpus – (n) collection of writings on a subject

coruscating – (adj) more generally, dazzling or brilliant; glittering or sparkling

costive – (adj) constipated; miserly; slow to speak

covert – (adj) secret, disguised (similar: clandestine, stealthy, surreptitious, underhand)

covey – (n) a small flock of birds

criteria – (n) plural form of criterion, a standard on which decision is based

crux – (n) critical point

cue – (n) signal to change; hint

curio – (n) unusual object

curlicue – (n) decorative curl in a signature or similar

cynosure – (n) the centre of attention, or point of guidance

dandle – (v) to bounce (usually child) on knee

deathless – (adj) undying, though often carrying an ironic charge

debut – (n) first public appearance

décolletage – (n) low neckline on a woman; cleavage

deleterious – (adj) dangerous, harmful

delusion – (n) false belief or understanding (compare: allusion, illusion)

demagogue – (n) unprincipled mob leader

demimonde – (n) marginally respected group of society

démodé – (adj) out of fashion

demotic – (n) ordinary people's language

dénouement – (n) final part of story, especially in which problems are resolved

deprecate – (v) to express disappoval of; to belittle (noun: deprecation)

derisory – worthy of ridicule; expressing derision

derogatory – (adj) negative remarks, particularly about individual (similar: disparaging)

derrick – (n) type of crane or oil well framework, from surname of 1600s English hangman

desecrate – (v) to treat contemptuously something that is sacred or deeply respected (noun: desecration)

desiccated – (adj) dried up; lifeless

desultory – (adj) jumping from one thing to another

détente – (n) lessening of tensions, especially between countries

diadem – (n) royal authority, from headband worn

dialogue – (n) conversation for two; exchange of ideas

diatribe – (n) abusive critical attack

dichotomy – (n) division into two, particularly elements that are contradictory or exclusive (see Common and Occasional Confusions, page 77)

dictum – (n) authoritative announcement

didactic – (adj) intended to instruct; preachy

digression – (n) a wandering from the main subject (adjective: digressive; fancy: divagation) dilatory – (adj) intended to waste time or delay

dilemma – (n) choice between two options, both of which seems equally unfavourable; a difficult choice (see Common and Occasional Confusions, page 77)

diminution – (n) act of reduction; the resulting decrease

disclaimer – (n) denial of knowledge; statement denying legal responsibility

disingenuous – (adj) not truthful; pretending to be unsophisticated

dissemble – (v) to hide the truth; feign; disguise

dissolute – (adj) given to indulging in immoral pleasures

distaff – (adj) on the female side of a family

ecclesiastical – (adj) relating to the church or its clergy; suitable for use in a church

ecumenical – (adj) relating to the union of the different branches of the Christian church

effete – (adj) weak; decadent; effeminate

effigy – (n) crude likeness of person, especially to be burnt as symbol of dislike

effloresce – (v) to burst into flower (noun: efflorescence)

effusive – (adj) highly enthusiastic (noun: effusion)

eidetic – (adj) of memory or mental image, extremely clear and vivid (eidetic memory = photographic memory)

elliptical – (adj) marked by extreme economy of expression so as to be unclear; relating to the shape of a regular oval

emancipation – (n) the act of freeing someone or something, especially from slavery

embrocation – (n) skin lotion; act of applying such

émigré – (n) emigrant, particularly political exile

emissary – (n) person sent on a mission, usually for government or higher authority

endemic – (adj) specific to a country, area or people

enigma – (n) something with a hidden meaning, such as a puzzle or riddle (adjective: enigmatic; see Common and Occasional Confusions, page 77)

ensemble – (n) group of musicians, actors, etc. who regularly perform together; (adj) such a group without clear lead or leads

entourage – (n) attendants to person of importance

ephemeral – (adj) lasting a short time, fleeting

epiphany – (n) sudden deep perception, particularly in mundane circumstances (adjective: epiphanic)

epistemology – philosophical study of the origin and nature of knowledge (compare: ontology)

epistolary – (adj) of or associated with the writing of letters

epitome – (n) thing or person that typifies wider subject or idea (similar: exemplar, ideal)

equanimity – (n) even-mindedness, composure

equipoise – (n) balance or counterbalance

equivocate – (v) to avoid making explicit or committed statement

ersatz – (adj) substitute or fake

escapade – (n) wild or reckless adventure (plain: lark)

esoteric – (adj) intended for or understood

by special group, secret, not for general consumption (compare: arcane)

espionage – (n) spying, the use of spies

etiolated – (adj) pale, originally from lack of sunlight

euphonic – (adj) pleasing to the ear (noun: euphony)

eviscerate – (v) to disembowel, to gut

exculpatory – (adj) clearing of guilt or blame

exegesis – (n) critical interpretation (adjective: exegetical)

exigent – (adj) demanding, urgent

exiguous – (adj) excessively scanty

existential – (adj) relating to one's existence or purpose in life; relating to individual experience and moral choice with regard to view that life is meaningless or absurd

exposition – (n) part of work that explains its meaning or intent; in-depth explanation or the act of doing so

expunge – (v) to eliminate

extemporise – (v) to speak or do without preparation (noun: extemporisation; compare: impromptu)

fable – (n) short fictional tale making moral point, often supernatural and with animals (compare: allegory, parable)

facet – (n) aspect or phase

fallacy – (n) mistaken notion

farrago – (n) hotch-potch

fastidious – (adj) particular (often excessively); easily disgusted

favela – (n) Brazilian slum

fealty – (n) fidelity, especially to feudal lord or monarch

febrile – (adj) feverish

fecund – (adj) fertile

filigree – (n) delicate ornamentation

finagle – (v) to swindle, cheat

finesse – (v, n) to make better; quality of having skill or fine control, especially in sporting endeavours

fixture – (n) something that is attached, as in a dwelling; regular event; something or someone permanently located in a place

folderol – (n) foolishness; meaningless refrain in songs

foray – (n) sudden advance or raid

formula – (n) prescription or recipe; established method; representation of compound or equation (adjective: formulaic; plural: formulae or formulas)

fractious – (adj) irritable; hard to manage (noun: fractiousness)

frisson – (n) momentary thrill

froideur – (n) coolness of manner (compare: sang-froid)

frou-frou – (adj, n) extravagantly ornamented; fussy ornamentation; rustling sound, as of shiny material

fugue – (n) psychological loss of identity; style of composition, particularly music, in which a theme is repeated and developed

fulminate – (v) to angrily criticise

fungible – (adj) interchangeable

gambit – (n) opening move in game

gamut – (n) the full extent of, range

gimcrack – (adj) showy but poorly constructed

gimmick – (n) device or scheme used to attract attention

gist – (n) essence (similar: nub, thrust)

gnomic – (adj) aphoristic; cryptic; of special knowledge

halcyon – (adj) peaceful and happy; prosperous

harbinger – (n) indication of something to

come (from one who used to travel ahead to arrange lodgings for army or royal party)

hauteur – (n) haughtiness

hedonistic – (adj) devoted to pleasure (noun: hedonism; similar: sybaritic)

hegemony – (n) powerful influence of group or state over another

hellion – (n) troublesome young person (historical)

hermetic – (adj) airtight; impervious to external influence

hiatus – (n) a gap, especially in something that should be continuous

homage – (n) display of respect to artistic superior or predecessor, especially through an artwork

hubris – (n) excessive confidence, often misplaced, cockiness (adjective: hubristic)

hybrid – (n) something of mixed origin; car running on petrol and electricity

hymn – (n) song of praise, especially to a god

hyperbole – (n) fanciful exaggeration (adjective: hyperbolic)

idiom – (n) phrase whose meaning can not be ascertained from the literal meanings of its components, such as 'having a ball' (adjective: idiomatic)

illusion – (n) trick, deception or misapprehension; fantasy; impression or appearance (compare: allusion, delusion)

imbue – (v) to fill or pervade

impasse – (n) situation without immediate possibility of progress; road blocked or with no exit (compare: stalemate)

impetus – (n) momentum

impinge – (v) encroach, intrude

imprimatur – (n) official approval or mark of such

impromptu – (adj, adv) spoken or performed with no or little preparation (compare: extemporise)

improvident – (adj) lacking care, especially financial (noun: improvidence)

inchoate – (adj) not entirely formed; at the earliest stage of development

incognito – (adj, adv) without recognition; disguised

incommunicado – (adj, adv) without the ability or willingness to communicate

indictment – (n) a formal accusation; a condemnatory criticism

indolent – (adj) lazy (noun: indolence)

ineffable – (adj) too great to be uttered in words

infrangible – (adj) not capable of being separated into parts

innuendo – (n) derogatory hint(s) or insinuation(s)

insidious – (adj) stealthy and harmful

insinuate – (v) to imply or suggest something, particularly of a negative nature; to manoeuvre oneself into a position

insouciance – (n) casual unconcern

integrity – (n) quality of adhering to principles

interlude – (n) period between events

internecine – (adj) mutually destructive

interpolate – (v) to insert (often unfairly), to fill in a series

interpretation – (n) explanation of work of art

interregnum – (n) pause, particularly time between monarchs

inure – (v) to accustom

invective – (n) bitter accusatory language;

such expression or discourse

inveigle – (v) to win over by flattery, wheedle

invidious – (adj) enviable; causing envious dislike

involution – (n) act of involving, state of being involved, complexity (also has medical, grammatical, mathematical definitions)

jeremiad – (n) lengthy tale of lament or that which prophesies doom

juxtaposition – (n) act of setting things side by side; state of such

kismet – (n) destiny or fortune

lacrymal – (adj) relating to tears or crying

lacuna – (n) gap or hiatus, especially in printed text (plural: lacunae)

lascivious – (adj) lewd or lecherous (similar: salacious; fancy: lubricious)

laud – (v) (adjective: laudatory; compare: plaudit)

legatee – (n) recipient of a legacy

Levant – (n) Middle East (adjective: Levantine)

levitation – (n) ability to rise in defiance of gravity, especially without obvious means (verb: levitate)

levity – (n) lightness of manner or spirit

liability – (n) legal financial obligation; opposite of asset, in both financial and figurative terms, especially when applied to a person

lineage – (n) ancestry (compare: provenance)

linear – (adj) of or resembling a straight line

litany – (n) long, tedious list; in Christianity, series of prayers with responses

liturgy – (n) prescribed form for public religious worship

locus – (n) place where thing is located; centre of activity

longueur – (n) tedious passage in work of art or literature; period of extreme boredom

louche – (adj) disreputable, of questionable morality or taste, decadent

lucrative – (adj) profitable

ludicrous – (adj) absurd

lugubrious – (adj) excessively mournful or gloomy

magnanimous – (adj) generous of spirit

manifesto – (n) public declaration of principles

manqué – (adj) having not quite achieved ambition, particularly individual (word order: follows noun)

maquillage – (n) makeup; the art of applying it

maunder – (v) to speak quickly and incessantly, often in a low voice, especially about unimportant matters; to wander

maxim – (n) saying that expresses a general truth

meme – (n) an idea or behaviour that spreads easily

mendacity – (n) tendency to be untruthful

meretricious – (adj) superficially attractive or sincere

metamorphosis – (n) transformation

meticulous – (adj) extremely careful or precise, sometimes excessively

métier – (n) person's specialty (similar: forte)

miasma – (n) negative atmosphere or influence; foul, thick vapour

milieu – (n) social or artistic environment; general ambience

milquetoast – (adj, n) timid (said of person)

mimesis – (n) imitation or representation

of art; providing example as opposed to explanation; mimicry in nature (adjective: imitative)

modicum – (n) small or token amount

mollify – (v) to calm; lessen in intensity

momentum – (n) impetus

monologue – (n) long solo speech

mordant – (adj) sharply sarcastic, biting and incisive

moribund – (adj) lacking vitality, dying

myopic – (adj) shortsighted or narrow-minded

nadir – (n) the lowest point, especially of despair; point on the celestial sphere directly below an observer (opposite: zenith)

narrative – (n) account of events

nebulous – (adj) vague, lacking defined form; hazy or cloudy

nefarious – (adj) wicked

neoteric – (adj) modern, of recent origin

nexus – (n) point of connection

niggardly – (adj) miserly (person: niggard)

nihilism – (n) rejection of moral and religious principles (adjective: nihilistic)

nimbus – (n) luminous halo or mist around saint, etc.

noisome – (adj) causing nausea, putrid

nostrum – (n) cure-all; solution, especially for political ills (compare: pablum, panacea, platitude)

nuance – (n, v) subtle variation or distinction; to attempt to achieve this

nugatory – (adj) of little or no importance

nullify – (v) declare invalid, annul

nullity – (n) state of non-existence

obdurate – (adj) impassive to feeling or humanity; difficult to change, especially morally

obeisance – (n) act or expression of obedience or respect, such as a bow (verb: obey)

obfuscate – (v) to make dark, confused or obscure (noun: obfuscation)

obstreperous – (adj) defiant, noisy and hard to control (noun: obstreperousness)

oeuvre – (n) the life work of an artist

oleaginous – (adj) oily, slippery (similar: unctuous)

omnipotence – (n) the quality of being or seeming to be all-powerful (adjective: omnipotent; compare: ubiquity)

ontology – study of the nature of being (compare: epistomology)

onus – (n) responsibility, often disagreeable

opsimath – (n) person who studies or learns late in life (compare: polymath)

orthogonal – (adj) statistically or thematically unrelated

ostracise – (v) to shun or expel

otiose – (adj) without function or purpose, especially of word or expression

overtone – (n) hinted meaning (undertone = implied tone; colour under another)

pablum – (n) trite or oversimplified ideas

pabulum – (n) basic food; insipid intellectual nourishment

palate – (n) sense of taste; roof of mouth

palette – (n) range of colours in painting, film, etc.; range of skills used by non-visual artist; board of painter

palimpsest – (n) something that still bears traces of its original use

palpable – (adj) able to be easily perceived or noticed; obvious

panacea – (n) universal remedy (compare: nostrum)

panoply – (n) splendid array

parable – (n) short allegorical tale illustrating moral or spiritual point (compare: allegory, fable)

paradox – (n) proposition that appears to contradict itself or be absurd, but which may be true (see Common and Occasional Confusions, page 77)

parlay – (v) to turn something to one's advantage; to stake winning on a subsequent bet

parley – (v) to discuss peace terms with the enemy

parody – (n) a humorous imitation of a better known artwork or person (verb: to 'send up')

parse – (v) to examine (speech, etc.) closely by breaking it up into its component parts

parsimonious – (adj) excessively frugal, stingy (noun: parsimony)

partisan – (adj, n) strongly supportive of one side or another, especially politically; person holding such a position

parturient – (adj) about to give birth

pastiche – (n) imitation of other's work, especially satirical (similar: send-up, spoof, take-off)

pathos (n) – quality of art that evokes sympathy, pity, etc.; the feeling evoked (compare: bathos)

patina – (n) fine finish on surface gained with age; coating (similar: sheen)

paucity – (n) scarcity, lack

pecuniary – (adj) relating to money

pensée – (n) thought, especially written down

penurious – (adj) miserly; poor

perdition – (n) damnation, hell

peremptory – (adj) putting an end to debate; urgent; dictatorial

perfidious – (adj) treacherous

peripatetic – (adj) in a manner that moves from place to place

perspicuous – (adj) easily understandable, as of speech or writing

pertain – (v) relate, have relevance or belong to

phantasmagorical – (adj) characterised by fantastic images and unlikely juxtapositions; surreal

picaresque – (adj) of a story about a loveable rogue, often in loosely connected episodes

picayune – (adj) of little value; mean

placate – (v) to appease, allay anger of

plangent – (adj) loud and plaintive, especially of a sound or voice

platitude – (n) remark that is obvious or trite, especially when made as if important or has deep meaning (compare: nostrum, pablum)

plaudit – (n) expression of approval (compare: laud)

plenary – (adj) complete, especially of a meeting attended by all members

polemic – (n) argument that fiercely attacks an idea; this kind of writing or speech (polemics = the art or practice of verbal debate)

polymath – (n) one who is learned at more than one subject (compare: opsimath)

precipitate – (adj, v) rushed or rash, especially decisions; to bring about without delay

précis – (n) concise summary

predicament – (n) plight

predilection – (n) preference, often with negative overtones

prelapsarian – (adj) of a carefree time in the

past (meaning: before the [biblical] fall of Adam and Eve)

premise – (n) basic proposition (premises = land and buildings)

prevarication – (n) use of deliberately vague or evasive language; dishonest conduct

primordial – (adj) rudimentary, first-formed

probity – (n) uprightness or honesty

problematic(al) – (adj) difficult, causing problems

procrastination – (n) the putting off to a later time of something that should be done (see: vacillation)

profligate – (adj) irresponsibly extravagant

prolix – (adj) needlessly wordy

propaganda (n) – political misinformation, or such material

propagate – (v) to spread or make common, as in ideas; to grow or multiply

propensity (n) tendency or natural inclination (similar: predisposition, proclivity)

propitious – (adj) favourable

prose – (n) ordinary language of writing that is not poetry

proselytise – (v) recruit to a religion or belief

protagonist – (n) main character in literary work (antagonist = adversary)

protean – (adj) able to take different forms, variable

prototype – (n) rudimentary working model

provenance – (n) documented history of something, especially an artwork (compare: lineage)

proviso – (n) condition or stipulation

prurient – (adj) unusually interested in sexual matters

psychosomatic – (adj) showing physical symptoms that arise from the mind or emotions; imaginary; relating to that which links the body and mind

punctilious – (adj) attentive to details or correct behaviour

purblind – (adj) poorly sighted; lacking discernment; obtuse (pronounced PIR-bly-nd)

purdah – (n) state of social isolation, from Hindu and Muslim practice of segregating sexes

pusillanimous – (adj) lacking courage (noun: pusillanimity)

putative – (adj) generally considered such, supposed, alleged

putsch – (n) sudden change of government or attempt to overthrow existing one (similar: coup, coup d'état)

quiddity – (n) essence of person or thing; trivial point of contention

quiescent – (adj) being quiet or at rest (similar: latent, dormant; noun: quiescence)

quintessential – (adj) most typical, core (noun: quintessence)

quixotic – (adj) naively idealistic or chivalrous

quotidian – (n) commonplace (similar: mundane)

rationale – (n) fundamental reasons

rhapsody – (n) exaggeratedly emotional work; state of bliss; improvised musical work

recalcitrant – (adj) reluctant (noun: recalcitrance)

recherché – (adj) rare; sought out; pretentious

recondite – (adj) difficult to understand for ordinary people; little known or hidden recusant – (n) one who refuses to submit to authority

redolent – (adj) fragrant; strongly suggestive (noun: redolence)

refrain – (v, n) to hold oneself back; repeated phrase in song or poem, or the music for it; repeated utterance

refute – (v) to prove wrong; to deny (similar: rebut; reject might be preferred to avoid confusion if no proof is evidenced)

regnant – (adj) ruling, widespread

reify – (v) to make abstract thing real or concrete

renaissance – (n) any serious revival in culture or learning, after the European Renaissance

repertoire – (n) the range of roles or styles in which an artist has performed or written before

reportage – (n) writing that attempts to describe events and facts precisely rather than offer interpretation or opinion; collecting and reporting of current events through the media

requited – (adj) returned, particularly feelings of love (verb: requite; opposite: unrequited)

resonant – (n) strong and deep in tone; having significance or an enduring effect; evocative or bringing to mind (noun: resonance)

retinue – (n) followers or attendants to important person

rhetoric – (n) the art or technique of speaking or writing well to persuade others; particularly when preceded by 'empty', language that is ostentatious and intended to impress but meaningless

riposte – (n) retort, verbal retaliation

rubric – (n) set of rules or categories

ruse – (n) plan intended to deceive

sabotage – (n, v) malicious damage or disruption, especially for political, military or commercial reasons; to carry out such an act

salacious – (adj) characterised by lust

salient – (n) striking; outstanding; protruding (noun: salience)

sang-froid – (n) composure, particularly under pressure (compare: froideur)

scenario – (n) outline for series of events

schematic – (adj) symbolic, simplified or formulaic

schism – (n) division of group into opposing groups; the groups thus formed (adjective: schismatic)

scrupulous – (adj) painstaking

scrutiny – (n) close and careful study (verb: scrutinise)

sedulous – (adj) diligent, painstaking

segue – (n, v) transition from one idea or theme to another, whether seamless or noticed; to do this (pronounced SEG-way)

semantic – (adj) relating to meaning, especially of words (semantics: study or word meaning; more casually, academic quibbling over meaning)

sensibility – (n) mental and emotion perception

sententious – (adj) given to expressing maxims, aphorisms, or moralising (compare: tendentious)

sequester – (v) to isolate, as in a jury; to store, as in carbon dioxide; to seize as security against legal claims

serendipity – (n) accidental discovery of

something fortunate or advantageous (adjective: serendipitous)

shirk (v) – to avoid work or responsibility

shirr – (v) to draw together along parallel lines, especially cloth; to bake unshelled eggs until set

sidereal – (adj) relating to stars or constellations

signally – (adv) notably (adjective, noun: signal)

silhouette – (n) filled-in outline of face or recognisable shape of person or thing (compare: chiaroscuro)

simulacrum – (n) representation; a weak semblance of something or trace (plural: simulacra)

sinecure – (n) paid job involving little or no work; ecclesiastical position not requiring spiritual duties

skein – (n) tangle; coil of wool or thread; flock of geese

sobriquet – (n) nickname (similar: moniker, cognomen)

soigné – (adj) well groomed

solace – (n) comfort in times of distress or misfortune (fancy: solatium)

solipsism – (n) theory that self is only reality

sophistry – (n) use of false arguments

sophomoric – (adj) youthfully pretentious, as of a US second-year university student, a sophomore

specious – (adj) seemingly plausible but actually false

spruik – (v) to publicly talk something up

stalemate – (n) stage in proceedings from which no party can move, from chess (similar: deadlock, draw; compare: impasse)

stasis – (n) state of slowdown or inactivity

stereotype – (n) overgeneralised representation

stigma – (n) shame or discredit; originally a brand left in the skin

stipend – (n) regular income, salary

stratagem – (n) trick or plan to gain advantage

Stygian – (adj) gloomy, as in hell

suborn – (v) bribe (someone) to commit crime

subterfuge – (n) a deceptive trick

sybaritic – (adj) devoted to pleasure or luxury (person: sybarite; similar: hedonistic)

synopsis – (n) outline or abstract

synthesis – (n) a combination of elements that form a whole

talisman – (n) charm

tantalising – (adj) arousing desire but remaining just out of reach (verb: tantalise)

temerity – (n) recklessness

tendentious – (adj) biased; partisan (compare: sententious)

tenet – (n) a principle or doctrine

tessellated – (adj) checked like a mosaic

thesis – (n) a proposition or line of argument (compare: antithesis, synthesis)

tirade – (n) strongly critical and protracted speech (fancy: philippic)

topos – (n) in literary theory, a traditional theme or element in a story, such as the prodigal son (plural: topoi)

tract – (n) pamphlet, often political or religious, intended as propaganda, or metaphorically, work that serves similar purpose; substantial area of land or water

traduce – (v) to shame by making false

statements

tragedy – (n) drama that features calamitous events and ending

trait – (n) characteristic or quality of individual

transcript – (n) written or typed copy

travesty – (n) grotesque and undignified imitation

treatise – (n) formal written account

trenchant – (adj) vigorous or incisive

trepidation – (n) state of apprehension; trembling

troika – (n) group of three, especially of equal power; Russian vehicle pulled by three horses abreast

trope – (n) word or phrase used figuratively, common theme or style, four main types being metaphor, metonymy, synecdoche and irony (see Terminology, page 118)

ubiquity – (n) quality of being or seeming to be everywhere; extreme availability (adjective: ubiquitous; compare: omnipotence)

umbrage – (n) sense of slight or offence

usurp – (v) to take the place of; to seize for oneself, usually illegally

utopia – (n) perfect society; depiction of it, often meant dismissively (opposite: dystopia)

uxorious – (adj) – relating to a husband's extreme fondness for his wife (noun: uxoriousness; opposite: maritorious)

vacillation – (n) wavering; inability to make a decision

vapid – (adj) lacking importance; without flavour

vehement – (adj) forceful, emphatic

veneer – (n) external appearance, especially deceptively attractive; any thin surface layer

verbatim – (adj, adv) 'word for word'

verbose – (adj) excessively wordy

veridical – (adj) corresponding with reality or future events

verisimilitude – (n) the quality of seeming a true likeness

vernal – (adj) characteristic of spring; young and fresh

vestige – (n) trace, the remains (often in plural; adjective: vestigial)

vicissitude – (n) change of fortune (often in plural)

vignette – (n) short film or literary scene; page design in book, often incorporating vine leaves; illustration with indefinite border

vindication – (n) the state of being proven correct (verb: vindicate)

vista – (n) distant view

vitiate – (v) to spoil, render defective

winsome – (adj) charming in a childlike way

whitebread – (adj) dull or conventional (similar: Milquetoast)

zeitgeist – (n) the spirit of an age; the attitudes and outlook of a specific period or generation

zenith – (n) the highest point; astronomical point on the celestial sphere directly above the observer (opposite: the nadir)

FANCY LANGUAGE

abiogenesis – (n) theory of living matter coming from non-living

abrogate – (v) to put aside, appeal, annul

accismus – (n) an affected refusal; feigned disinterest

accrete – (v) to grow together or into one

adipose – (adj) fatty

admonitory – (n) containing a scolding or warning

adumbrate – to give outline of, foreshadow

agio – (n) currency exchange charge, so agiotage

alacritous – (adj) fast and enthusiastic

aleatory – (adj) subject to chance, as in the throw of a dice

alexiteric/-pharmic – (adj) countering poison, contagion

altazimuth – (n) telescope

amusia – (n) tone deafness

anagnorisis – (n) in Greek drama, the point at which the hero emerges from ignorance and realises his true situation

anamnesis – (n) recollection

anechoic – (adj) sound-absorbent, without an echo

antic – (adj) ludicrously odd behaviour or action

aperçu – (n) illuminating comment; short synopsis

apophenia – (n) seeing patterns in random things or data (similar: pareidolia)

aposematic – (adj) having warning colours

apotrope – (n) talisman to ward off evil, such as holy water, garlic or a crucifix

appurtenant – (n) accessory, equipment (plural: appurtenances)

arche – (n) in Greek philosophy, the initial, fundamental principle of the world

argute – (adj) sharp or shrill

aristarch – (n) severe critic

assay – (v) to test, examine

atavism – (n) reversion to a primitive type

aureate – (adj) excessively ornamented

autochthonous – (adj) indigenous (of flora, fauna or people); in psychology, of ideas coming into the mind unrelated to a person's train of thought

bacciferous – (adj) berry-producing

barbate – (adj) bearded

barmecide – (n) one who offers an imaginary or disappointing benefit

bloviate – (v) to speak or write pompously

breviary – (n) collection of Christian prayers, hymns, etc.

brumous – (adj) foggy

cabotage – (n) coastal navigation and trade

cachinnation – (n) loud laughter (verb: cachinnate)

caliginous – (adj) dark or misty

calumny – (n, v) slander, false accusation (verb: calumniate)

calvous – (adj) bald

calx – (n) remains of metal or mineral after high heat

campestral – (adj) relating to uncultivated fields; rural

caravanserai – (n) traditional inn in eastern countries with room for caravans; used metaphorically for long and colourful groups of people and vehicles

catabolic – (adj) destructive breakdown of complex elements into simpler ones, especially in body, involving large amounts of released energy catadromous – (adj) living in fresh water but travelling to seawater to breed

cataract – (n) waterfall; eye disease

cecity – (n) blindness

chance-medley – (n) action with element of chance

charientism – (n) pleasantly disguised insult

charivari – (n) noisy mock serenade to married couple

chatoyant – (adj) with changing lustre like cat's eye

cibarious – (adj) edible, relating to food

clamant – (adj) vociferous; demanding attention

claque – (n) a group that is hired to clap; fawning admirers

clinquant – (adj) glittering with gold or tinsel

clou – (n) main idea or point of interest

coeval – (n, adj) contemporary in time

colloid – (adj) gelatinous

concatenate – (v, adj) to link together

concinnity – (n) elegant harmony in artwork, particularly music

convocate – (v) to assemble

copacetic – (adj) extremely satisfactory

coprolalia – (n) uncontrolled swearing

cordwainer – (n) shoemaker (archaic)

corybantic – (adj) frenzied, as in dancing

cozenage – (n) fraud

crenate – (adj) scalloped

crenellated – (adj) having repeated square indentations

crepuscular – (adj) dark, as of twilight

cynosure – (n) focus of admiration; a guiding star

deipnosophy – (n) art of dinner conversation

deliquesce – (v) to dissolve, melt

démarche – (n) political step, particularly new

dendriform – (adj) in the shape of a tree

desuetude – (n) state of disuse, inactivity

détraqué – (n) psychopath

discalced – (adj) of religious orders, barefoot or sandalled

divagation – (n) wandering off subject (useful: digression)

ecdysiast – (n) striptease artist

echt – (adj) authentic

éclat – (n) successful effect

edentulous – (adj) toothless (noun: edentulism)

effulgent – (adj) radiating light

elute – (v) to extract a substance (noun: elution)

encomium – (n) a tribute; warm and glowing praise

eonism – (n) adoption of clothes or manners of opposite sex, especially by a man; transvestism

epicene – (adj) effeminate, androgynous, asexual

epigamic – (adj) that which attracts a mate

epigone – (n) mediocre imitator, follower of known artist

erythrism – (n) redness in complexion or hair colour

euhemeristic – (adj) explaining myths using history

exequy – (n) funeral procession or rites

exiguous – (adj) very small; scanty (noun: exiguity)

exsiccate – (v) to dry up; make dry

extempore – (adj) impromptu

extirpate – (v) to root out, destroy

extrinsic – (adj) being not an inherent part of something

faisandé – (adj) affected, theatrical

fascicle – (n) a bundle (anatomy: muscle fibres; botany: leaves, etc.; literary: a serialised story)

fatidic – (adj) prophetic

fecundate – (v) to fertilise

filigree – (n) delicate or intricate ornamentation

fimbriate – (adj) fringed (similar: laciniate)

flagitious – (adj) wicked; heinous

frass – (n) excrement of insect larva

fugacious – (adj) lasting a brief time

fulminate – (v) to utter a strong condemnation or verbal attack

fustian – (n) pretentious, exaggerated speech (useful: bombast)

glair – (n) egg white; a glaze made of egg white

gnar – (v) to growl

guichet – (n) ticket office, etc. with grille

hamatia – (n) in Greek tragedy, a character's fatal flaw

hebetude – (n) stupidity; dullness of mind

hedonic – (adj) devoted to pleasure (noun: hedonism)

hieratic – (adj) highly stylised or formal, as in traditional Egyptian or Greek art

homiletic – (adj) preaching, as in a homily or sermon

hortatory / hortative – (adj) strongly encouraging

humectant – (n) a substance that reduces the loss of moisture

hyaloid – (adj) transparent

hypergolic – (adj) igniting on impact

hypnopompic – (adj) of the state just before waking

ichor – (n) substance in veins of gods

illeist – (n) one who refers to self in the third person

illocution – (n) an action that is carried out by writing or saying something (compare: locution, perlocution)

imbrication – (n) overlapping

imbrue – (v) to stain

imprimatur – (n) official mark or guarantee; a licence to print a book

inamorato – (n) male lover (inamorata: female lover)

inane – (adj) empty, worthless

incarnadine – (adj) flesh-coloured or blood red

inosculate – (v) to join closely

interdict – (v, n) to prohibit; a prohibition

interlocutor – (n) one who takes part in a conversation

interpellate – (v) to formally question an official

janissary – (n) an elite devoted follower

jejune – (adj) not interesting, meagre, dull

je ne sais quoi – (n) an indefinable quality

jentacular – (adj) relating to breakfast

juvenilia – (n) works produced in artist's youth

laciniate – (adj) fringed (similar: fimbriate)

lachrymose – (adj) causing tears; given to tears

lagniappe – (n) regional term for small gift given to customer at time of purchase

lapidary – (adj) accurate, formal and condensed; sharply delineated; related to the cutting of precious stone or monumental inscriptions

legerdemain – (n) slight of hand; deception

limn – (v) to describe or depict

limnetic – (adj) of a body of fresh water, in the deeps away from the shore

lineament – (n) distinctive feature,

especially of face

littoral – (adj) of the seashore or beach

locution – (n) style of speech (compare: illocution, perlocution)

loquacious – (adj) talkative, chatty

lubricious – (adj) slippery; tricky; characterised by lust (useful: salacious, lascivious)

ludic – (adj) playful

lustrate – (v) to purify through ceremony

lychnobite – (n) one who works at night and sleeps in the day

maculated – (adj) spotted; defiled

manumit – (v) to free from slavery

marmoreal – (adj) like marble, so cold, white, smooth

matériel – (n) available means; materials and equipment, especially of armed forces

micturate – (v) to urinate

minatory – (adj) threatening

miscible – (adj) capable of being mixed, especially in chemistry

moil – (v, n) to toil; drudgery

moloch – (n) powerful object requiring sacrifice

mordacious – (adj) biting, especially of sarcasm

mulct – (v) to swindle (someone)

nacreous – (adj) iridescent

nictitate – (v) to wink or blink

noesis – (n) the mental process

noetical – (adj) relating to the intellect, purely intellectual

nosism – (n) use of royal or editorial 'we' in assertions of private opinion

nugacity – (n) triviality

nutation – (n) nodding (verb: nutate)

obtenebrate – (v) to cast a shadow over

orison – (n) prayer

oscitant – (adj) yawning, inattentive (noun: oscitancy)

osculate – (v) to kiss

ossify – (v) to become rigid, like bone

ostiary – (n) doorkeeper, of church or similar

otiose – (adj) pointless; idle

oubliette – (n) dungeon with single trapdoor in ceiling

paean – (n) a song of praise

panegyric – (n) elaborate formal public expression of praise (similar: encomium)

pareidolia – (n) ascribing significance or meaning to a random pattern or natural occurrence (similar: apophenia)

parisology – (n) the use of ambiguous words

paseo – (n) a stroll

patronymic – (n) a name derived from the name of the father

pavid – (adj) fearful

peccant – (adj) sinning; erring; unhealthy

pelage – (n) fur, hair or wool covering of mammals

pelagic – (adj) of the open sea

pellucid – (adj) translucent, clear

periphrasis – (n) 'beating around the bush' (similar: circumlocution)

perlocution – (n) persuasive speech (compare: illocution, locution)

philippic – (n) speech of strong and bitter condemnation (similar: tirade)

piliferous – (adj) having or producing hair

plangent – (adj) loud, resounding; plaintive

plenipotentiary – (n) one invested with complete powers

plexus – (n) a network formation

plumose – (adj) feathered

pococurante – (n, adj) an indifferent person;

indifference

poetaster – (n) inferior poet

pollex – (n) thumb

polysemous – (adj) having many meanings

pother – (n) a commotion or state of nervous activity

praetorian – (adj) lacking in integrity, corruptible

prandial – (adj) relating to dinner or lunch

premorse – (adj) broken off

proneur – (n) one who flatters

propinquity – (n) nearness in time, place, relation or nature

propitiatory – (adj) that which renders favourably to appease or ingratiate

puissant – (adj) having great power or influence

pusillanimous – (adj) cowardly

quiddity – (n) the essence of a person or thing

quidnunc – (n) a gossip

quietus – (n) the receipt of a final payment; a release from life

quondam – (adj) former

rebarbative – (adj) repellant

recision – (n) the act of cutting back

recreant – (adj, n) cowardly or disloyal; unfaithful person

recusant – (n) one who refuses to submit, often to religious dictates

repine – (v) to fret

riparian – (adj) of or by a riverbank

rodomontade – (adj) boastful

saccade – (n) rapid eye movement, as when reading

sacerdotal – (adj) priestly; claiming undue authority for the presthood

sanctum – (n) private retreat

sapience – (n) deep wisdom; aping wisdom

satrap(y) – (n) tyrannical ruler

schadenfreude – (n) glorying in another's misfortune

sciolistic – (adj) demonstrating superficial knowledge of or interest in; amateurish (pronounced SI-olistic)

scissile – (adj) easily cut or split

sennit – (n) braided rope or plant material, as used in Polynesia

serotine – (adj) happening or flowering late

sesquipedalianism – (n) the practice of using long words

sessile – (adj) without a stalk; permanently attached

soi-disant – (adj) self-styled, would-be

solatium – (n) compensation for injured feelings; related to solace

soubrette – (n) a girlish flirtatious role, such as maidservant, in theatre or opera

souteneur – (n) a pimp

souterrain – (n) an underground chamber or passage

splanchnic – (adj) visceral, of the intestines

stochastic – (adj) random; governed by the laws of probability

sub rosa – (adj) secretly communicated

sudoriferous – (adj) sweaty

sulcate – (adj) deeply grooved

supererogation – (n) in Roman Catholic tradition, good works and prayers done beyond duty that can be put to use by others; action beyond the call of duty

supernal – (adj) of a higher world

susurration – (n) soft whispering or rustling

suzerain – (n) a state that controls another but allows the subject state autonomy over domestic affairs

sward – (n) area of short grass

sybaritic – (adj) fond of sensuous pleasure

syzygy – (n) alignment, especially in astronomy

tenebrous – (adj) gloomy

terpsichorean – (adj) pertaining to dancing

testaceous – (adj) having a shell; reddish-brown

thaumaturge – (n) a magician or a worker of marvels

threnody – (n) lament in song or ode

tocsin – (n) a warning signal

toper – (n) serious drinker, drunkard

tortious – (adj) wrongful

tractable – (adj) docile

tumbrel – (n) cart carrying victims to guillotine

ukase – (n) an arbitrary decree; a legal edict of Tsarist Russia

ultramontanism – (adj) in Roman Catholicism, favouring supremacy of pope over local authorities

umbrageous – (adj) shaded; said of a person, suspicious, likely to take offence

usufruct – (n) legal right to the use and enjoyment of another's property

vatic – (adj) prophetic

veridical – (adj) corresponding with fact or reality

vernissage – (n) private viewing to start art exhibition

vertiginous – (adj) pertaining to vertigo; (casual: extremely high)

vesicant – (adj) causing blisters

vibrissa – (n) whisker (plural: vibrissae)

vilipend – (v) to disparage

viridity – (n) greenness

voluptuary – (n) sensualist (similar: hedonist, sybarite)

PLAIN LANGUAGE

VERBS

abet, abide, addle, adopt, adore, adorn, air, amass, ambush, answer, argue, arrest, attack, avenge, avoid, avow, bait, bake, bark, barter, bash, bask, batter, baulk, bawl, bellow, belt, bicker, bide, billow, bilk, bite, blare, bleach, bleat, bleed, bless, bloat, blot, blush, bode, bore, borrow, bother, brace, breach, bribe, bridle, bristle, broach, bruise, buckle, bumble, burrow, bury, caress, carve, chant, cheat, chide, chime, chisel, choke, churn, cite, clash, cleave, clench, cling, clog, clout, coax, cobble, covet, cower, cradle, cram, crank, crave, creak, creep, cringe, croak, crouch, cull, curse, dally, defy, delve, deny, drain, drench, drone, droop, dwindle, eke, exit, fade, falter, fault, fester, fix, flail, flex, flutter, fondle, forage, fret, frisk, froth, fumble, gape, gaze, goad, gorge, grab, grate, grieve, grovel, gush, gust, haul, heave, heed, hinder, huddle, hurtle, irk, jerk, jest, jolt, jostle, juggle, knit, leech, linger, loom, lumber, lurk, map, mar, melt, mingle, moan, moot, nick, nudge, obey, oust, pamper, parch, pierce, plead, plough, plunder, plunge, poke, quell, quench, rage, reckon, rig, rile, root, rue, scold, scour, scowl, scupper, seep, seethe, shatter, shred, shrink, shrivel, shun, skulk, snare, sneer, sob, spawn, splinter, spur, squander, squash, stain, stall, startle, steal, stifle, stoop, stow, straddle, straggle, strain, stray, stride, strive, struggle, stump, stumble, sully, surge, sulk, swallow, sway, swell, swelter, swill, swindle, swoon, swoop, tamper, tarnish, thrive, throttle, thwart, toil, trample, trawl, tremble, trickle, vent, vex, vie, vow, wane, weep, weld, wield, wilt, wince, wither, woo, yank, yearn, yield, yoke

NOUNS

abuse, acorn, agony, aisle, alarm, alert, alien, altar, ambush, anger, answer, aroma, array, ash, awe, bait, balm, bane, bark, barrow, barrel, bastion, battle, bauble, beacon, beast, belly, binge, birth, bite, blade, blame, blanket, blare, blast, blaze, blemish, blight, blimp, bliss, blister, blot, blush, bluster, bore, bother, bout, brace, brawl, breach, bribe, brim, brink, bruise, brunt, brute, bulge, chaos, cheek, chore, chorus, circus, clan, clash, claw, clout, coma, corpse, cradle, cramp, cringe, crook, curse, drain, droop, dust, echo, exit, fade, fault, flank, flesh, fluke, flurry, fork, fray, froth, furrow, gaze, germ, ghost, gist, glimpse, gloom, glory, glow, glut, grave, grime, grit, gush, havoc, heel, heft, hoax, huddle, hurdle, hurt, hymn, itch, jest, jewel, joke, junk, kernel, knot, knuckle, lark, leech, linger, louse, map, maze, mesh, mint, mire, mirth, niggle, noose, notch, oaf, oath,

omen, onus, plunder, plunge, poke, purge, rage, riddle, rift, ripple, rival, root, ruin, ruse, sake, scar, sheen, shelter, shred, siege, slur, smother, snort, spark, spawn, spell, splinter, spree, squall, stain, sting, stink, storm, strain, strand, strife, struggle, stumble, suck, surge, swallow, swirl, thaw, thorn, thrall, threat, thrill, throng, thrust, tinge, toil, trickle, trough, truth, tumult, tussle, vow, wane, wilt, yield, yoke

ADJECTIVES

able, adult, alive, alone, aloof, ample, awkward, bald, barren, bent, bitter, bland, blank, bleak, blind, blithe, blunt, brave, brittle, brute, coy, crook, curt, daft, deaf, fallow, false, idle, mute, pagan, pale, rival, rosy, rude, stale, steep, stern, stiff, stray

CONJUNCTIONS

albeit, although, and, as, because, but, for, if, nor, not, or, so, than, though, unless, when, whereas, whether, while, yet

PREPOSITIONS

about, after, against, along, among, around, at, before, behind, below, beneath, beside, between, beyond, but, by, circa, despite, down, during, except, for, from, in, inside, into, like, near, of, off, on, out, outside, over, past, since, through, throughout, till, to, toward, under, underneath, until, up, upon, vis-a-vis, with, within, without

COLOURFUL LANGUAGE

ACTION

bamboozle, barrack, billow, bubblewrap, bungle, canoodle, caterwaul, chuckle, crackle, dragoon, dunk, dwindle, finagle, flicker, frolic, gallivant, gambol, gargle, glom, gurgle, hobnob, hustle, mingle, mumble, murmur, pummel, quarrel, rustle, schmooze, scrimp, simmer, slather, slither, sneak, sneeze, snooze, splinter, swaddle, tangle, teeter, tremble, trumpet, wander, wither

AMOUNT

batch, block, brace, bunch, chunk, clod, clump, cluster, clutch, dollop, dose, gob, handful, harvest, heap, host, hunk, knot, load, lump, mass, measure, modicum, mound, nugget, number, packet, parcel, pile, portion, quantity, quantum, raft, ration, screeds, shitloads, slew, smattering, splodge, stack, sum, swag, tally, total, umpteen, volume, wad

BIG DEAL

aggrandisement, array, ballyhoo, blurb, burlesque, circus, cornucopia, hoohah, hoopla, hullabaloo, hyperbole, lollapalooza, panoply, parade, pomp, razzmatazz, smorgasbord, spectacle, spotlight, whirlygig, whoopee

CONFUSION

argy-bargy, boggle, bouillabaisse, brouhaha, cacophony, clutter, conundrum, discombobulate (v), farrago, fiasco, fracas, frenzy, gallimaufry, hotchpotch, hubbub, imbroglio, impasse, jumble, kerfuffle,

malarkey, mangle, mayhem, melange, melee, menagerie, mess, mish-mash, morass, palaver, pandemonium, pickle, quandary, quagmire, rigmarole, ruckus, shambles, shenanigans, skirmish, squabble, tumult, wrangle

EQUIPMENT

accoutrements, apparatus, appendages, appurtenances, dingus, dongle, doodah, doohickey, gadget, gear, gizmo, gubbins, innards, jigger, junk, kit, paraphernalia, thingamajig, toggle, utensil, watchyamacallit, widget

FUTURE

coda, dénouement, destiny, dharma, doom, fate, finale, fortune, future, happenstance, karma, kismet, luck, moksha, nirvana, predestination, providence, resolution, samsara, serendipity, the breaks, the wheel of fortune, the will of heaven

GREETING CARD

always, angel, announce, baby, beauty, best, bird, birthday, bless, bliss, brave, bright, butterfly, care, celebrate, condolence, cute, dawn, day, desire, dove, dream, eyes, face, faith, family, flower, forever, forgive, friend, fun, gift, giving, goodness, goodwill, hands, happy, health, heart, heaven, holiday, home, hope, inspiration, invite, joy, kiss, kitten, know, laughter, life, light, love, luck, marriage, memory, moon, more, mystery, nature, night, partner, patience, peace, prayer, proud, puppy, release, remember, rest, rose, sleep, smile, soul, star, strength, strong, success, sun, sweet, sympathy, thank, true, truth, up, virtue, wealth, well, win, wish, wonder

HIGHEST POINT

acme, apex, apogee, apotheosis, brow, ceiling, cloud nine, crescendo, crest, crown, heights, lodestone, meridian, ne plus ultra, paragon, peak, pinnacle, prowess, roof, seventh heaven, summa cum laude, summit, zenith

HUMAN WEAKNESS

blunder, blurt, flummox, foible, funk, glower, guzzle, harangue, hassle, hijack, hubris, hustle, kowtow, malinger, mollycoddle, pillory, quiver, ransack, rubberneck, shrivel, simper, skulduggery, skulk, snivel, strangle, stumble, swindle, tremble, tussle, wallop, wallow

LOWEST POINT

bedrock, bupkis, cipher, fundament, *nada*, nadir, nethermost, nil, nix, nobody, nothing, nought, nowhere (boondocks, Timbuktu, the wop-wops), perigee, the pits, rock bottom, rump, sod-all, third-class, third-rate, underbelly, void, zero, Z-grade, zilch, zip

MATHEMATICS

abacus, addition, algebra, algorithm, arithmetic, binary, calculus, circumference, coordinate, diameter, division, equation, factor, function, geometry, hypotenuse, integer, isosceles, linear, mean, median, minimum, mode, multiplication, norm, numeral, obtuse, parabola, permutation, perpendicular, pi, polygon, prime, probability, quadratic, quadrilateral, quota, radius, random, statistics, subtraction, trigonometry, vector

NEGATIVE

abuse, abyss, agony, blood, burn, casualty, chaos, corpse, crepuscular, crucifixion, cruel, crumble, cry, curse, darkness, death, demise, despair, destruct, dilapidated, disease, doom, draconian, end, enemy, eternal, evil, exit, expire, fake, fall, false, fatal, fear, fester, final, ghoul, grave, greed, grief, hate, heartache, heartbreak, hell, kill, last, leave, lies, lose, malign, mortal, mourn, murder, orphan, pain, perish, poison, ruin, sadness, scourge, shadow, silence, sin, skull, slay, stigma, strife, suffer, suicide, tears, terminal, tragedy, ugly, violence

NONSENSE

balderdash, baloney, blah, blather, bollocks, bunkum, clanger, claptrap, cockamamie, codswallop, dodginess, doggerel, drivel, eyewash, fiddle-faddle, flimflam, flummery, folderol, gibberish, gimcrackery, gobbledygook, gunk, hogwash, hokum, hooey, humbug, mumbo-jumbo, pabulum, piffle, poppycock, prattle, shonky, tomfoolery, trumpery, twaddle, waffle

OVERBLOWN TALK

banality, blah-blah, blarney, blather, bombast, bromide, bunk, cant, chatter, chinwag, chitchat, claptrap, claver, cliché, commonplace, flannel, fustian, gab, gossip, hearsay, hot air, hyperbole, innuendo, insinuation, jabberwocky, jargon, motto, nostrum, pabulum, platitude, ramble, rumour, scuttlebutt, slogan

REMAINS

bilge, carcass (entrails, flesh, guts, innards, offal, spleen), chaff, compost, debris, detritus, discards, dregs, drool, dross, embers, faeces, flotsam, fossil, frass, garbage, jetsam, junk, lees, refuse, residue, rot, rubbish, rubble, scum, sediment, silt, slag, sludge, smithereens, sweepings, trash, vestiges

SCIENCE

abstract, acceleration, adhesive, alphabet, amphibian, amplitude, antenna, articulation, assembly, astronomy, asymmetry, atmosphere, atrophy, attribute, automatic, ballistics, buoyancy, calibration, cantilever, circulatory, combustion, compass, condensation, conductivity, consistency, contraction, convection, corrosion, counterweight, diffusion, displacement, distillation, dynamo, effervescence, efficiency, encryption, entropy, equilibrium, evaporation, friction, functionality, fuselage, gravity, hardware, harmonic, hibernation, horizontal, hypothesis, impetus, incandescence, inertia, insulation, interpretation, irrigation, kinetic, latitude, locomotion, longitude, lubrication, magnetism, mechanism, metabolism, momentum, motion, navigation, nomenclature, obsolescence, oscillation, parallax, parameter, peripheral, perpendicular, precipitation, propulsion, prototype, quantum, rational, reciprocation, refraction, resistance, resonance, rotation, sanitation, spacial, static, stimulus, synthetic, termination, terrestrial, theorem, traction, transmission, turbine, velocity, viscosity

SMALL AMOUNT OR THING

bagatelle, bauble, blink, bobble, crumb, dash, diddums, flicker, fragment, frippery, gleam, glimmer, hint, inkling, iota, molehill, morsel, pittance, scintilla, shadow, shard, shimmer, shred, skerrick, sliver, smattering, smudge, snippet, soupçon, splinter, tad, tassle, tchotchke, trace, trifle, trinket, tuppence, whit

SMART TALK

aphorism, badinage, banter, blarney, bon mot, comeback, dis, epigram, impromptu, jibe, josh, kid, patter, persiflage, quip, raillery, razz, rebuttal, rejoinder, repartee, rib, riposte, wisecrack, witticism

WEAK

anaemic, brittle, effete, colourless, dicky, doddery, faded, fallow, feeble, fragile, gutless, insipid, jaded, jejune, lacklustre, lily-livered, listless, mealy-mouthed, pallid, puny, rickety, sagging, sallow, shaky, shrivelled, sickly, sissy, spineless, tired, torpid, vanilla, vapid, wan, watered down, weak-kneed, weary, wilting

WITH ENTHUSIASM OR
TO EXCESS

aflame, agog, ardent, bacchanal, carousal, choleric, crazed, debauchery, demonic, dotty, ebullient, exuberant, fervent, fevered, feverishly, frantic, frenetic, gaga, gung-ho, hedonistic, hot-blooded, hotheaded, nutty, orgy, rabid, rhapsodic, wassail, wild-eyed, woo-woo, zealous

WITHOUT ENTHUSIASM
OR CARE

bedraggled, decrepid, desultory, expeditious, faff (around), feckless, foolhardy, half-arsed, half-pie, haphazard, harum-scarum, heedless, higgledy-piggledy, holus-bolus, madcap, meandering, precipitous, ramshackle, slapdash, slipshod, slovenly, tumbledown, wanton

PHONETICALLY
INTERESTING WORDS

EUPHONIC ENDINGS

-bble words

babble, bobble, bubble, cobble, cribble, dabble, dibble, drabble, dribble, fribble, gabble, gobble, grabble, hardscrabble, hobble, hubble, kibble, knobble, mabble, nibble, nobble, nubble, pebble, pubble, quibble, rabble, rubble, scrabble, scribble, squabble, stubble, wobble

-ckle words

buckle, cackle, chuckle, cockle, fickle, freckle, hackle, heckle, honeysuckle, pickle, prickle, ramshackle, ruckle, shackle, sickle, spackle, speckle, stickle, strickle, suckle, swashbuckle, tackle, tickle, trickle, truckle

-ddle words

addle, befuddle, caboodle, coddle, cuddle, diddle, doddle, faddle, fiddle, fuddle, griddle, guddle, huddle, meddle, middle, muddle, noddle, paddle, peddle, piddle, puddle, quiddle, raddle, reddle, riddle, ruddle, saddle, skedaddle, straddle, swaddle, toddle, twaddle, twiddle, waddle

-ffle words

baffle, coffle, duffle, faffle, gaffle, kerfuffle, muffle, piffle, raffle, riffle, ruffle, scuffle, shuffle, skiffle, snaffle, sniffle, snuffle, souffle, truffle, waffle, whiffle

-gger words

bigger, bragger, bugger, dagger, digger, hugger, jigger, ligger, logger, mugger, rigger, shagger, slugger, snigger, stagger, swagger, swigger, Tigger, trigger

-ggle words

bedraggle, boggle, boondoggle, daggle, gaggle, giggle, goggle, haggle, hornswoggle, jiggle, juggle, niggle, smuggle, snuggle, squiggle, straggle, struggle, toggle, waggle, wiggle, wriggle

-llow words

allow, bellow, billow, callow, fallow, fellow, follow, hallow, hollow, marshmallow, mellow, pillow, sallow, shallow, swallow, tallow, wallow, yellow

-pple words

apple, cripple, dapple, fipple, grapple, hopple, nipple, pineapple, ripple, stipple, supple, tipple, topple, whipple

-ttle words

battle, bottle, brittle, cattle, cuttle, dottle, fettle, kettle, little, mettle, mottle, nettle, pottle, prattle, rattle, scuttle, settle, shuttle, skittle, spittle, tattle, throttle, wattle, whittle

-zzle words

bedazzle, bezzle, dazzle, drizzle, embezzle, fizzle, frazzle, frizzle, grizzle, guzzle, mizzle, muzzle, nozzle, nuzzle, pizzle, puzzle, razzle, schemozzle, sizzle, sozzle, swizzle

HYPHENATES

airy-fairy, argy-bargy, arty-farty, blah-blah, bric-a-brac, chit-chat, creepy-crawly, dilly-dally, easy-peasy, flim-flam, flip-flop, fuddy-duddy, gang-bang, goody-goody, hanky-panky, happy-clappy, helter-skelter, higgledy-piggledy, hocus-pocus, ho-hum, hoity-toity, holus-bolus, hotch-potch, hugger-bugger, hugger-mugger, hunky-dory, hurly-burly, hush-hush, itsy-bitsy, jiggery-pokery, knick-knack, lickety-split, mish-mash, mumbo-jumbo, namby-pamby, never-never, nitty-gritty, okey-dokey, pell-mell, ping-pong, pooh-pooh, razzle-dazzle, riff-raff, rinky-dink, roller-coaster, roly-poly, rumpy-pumpy, shilly-shally, sing-song, so-so, teeny-weeny, tittle-tattle, topsy-turvy, touchy-feely, toy-boy, tut-tut, willy-nilly, wishy-washy, yin-yang

Energetic hyphenates

can-do, cop-out, do-over, get-go, go-ahead, go-getter, go-to, heave-ho, know-how, look-in, look-see, must-see, quick-smart, run-in, say-so, shoo-in, whim-wham, yo-yo, zip-zap

WORD DUOS

above and beyond, assault and battery, beck and call, bed and breakfast, better or worse, bits and bobs, black and blue, black and white, bread and circuses, breaking and entering, brickbats and bouquets, bricks and mortar, by and large, cat and mouse, cats and dogs, cause and effect, cease and desist, chalk and cheese, chapter and verse, cheap and cheerful, checks and balances, cheek by jowl, chicken and egg, clear and present, come and go, common or garden, crime and punishment, curds and whey, cut and dried, cut and run, damn and blast, dead and buried, done and dusted, doom and gloom, do or die, dribs and drabs, ebb and flow, fast and loose, fits and starts, flesh and blood, flotsam and jetsam, friend or foe, front and centre, fun and games, give and take, hammer and tongs, hard and fast, heart and soul, heaven and hell, hell or high water, here and now, here and there, high and mighty, hither and thither, hither and yon, hit or miss, home and dry, home and hosed, hue and cry, huff and puff, hustle and bustle, kicks and giggles, king and country, kiss and tell, kith and kin, law and order, loathe and despise, meet and greet, milk and honey, null and void, odds and ends, out and about, past and present, pay and display, peace and quiet, pen and ink, pillar to post, pins and needles, pride and joy, pure and simple, the quick and the dead, rack and ruin, rise and shine, rock and roll, room and board, root and branch, sackcloth and ashes, safe and sound, salt and pepper, short and sweet, sink or swim, skin and bone, Sodom and Gomorrah, song and dance, spick and span, stand and deliver, smoke and mirrors, stuff and nonsense, suited and booted, terms and conditions, thick and thin, time and tide, tips and tricks, tongue and groove, touch and go, up and coming, up and running, wait and see, wine and dine

FIGURATIVE LANGUAGE
One-word
A-M

albatross, alchemy, ambrosia, antidote, anvil, apocalypse, armada, armageddon, avalanche, axle, backdrop, bastion, bedlam, bedrock, behemoth, bloodshed, blueprint, boycott, brainstorm, bulwark, byword, camouflage, carnage, cauldron, cavalcade, chaos, charade, checkmate, chimera, cipher, circus, citadel, crescendo, crucible, crusade, curse, deluge, departure, devil, doldrums, domino, drift-net, echelon, edifice, eddy, elixir, embargo, equation, exile, exodus, fodder, fossil, friction, fringe, fulcrum, furnace, fusillade, gamut, gauntlet, genuflect, gesture, gristle, halcyon, haven, headwind, homework, honeymoon, horizon, hurdle, impasse, inferno, jeremiad, jigsaw, juggernaut, jungle, keelhaul, kernel, keystone, labyrinth, lair, landslide, laurel, limelight, limpet, linchpin, litmus, lodestar, logjam, loophole, maelstrom, mainstay, mask, masterstroke, maw, mayhem, milestone, millstone, minnow, miracle, mirage, mothball, mountain, muscle, mutiny

N-Z

nemesis, nightmare, noose, nucleus, ocean, offshoot, omen, pageant, panacea, pantheon, parachute, parapet, pawn, phalanx, picnic, pigsty, pivot, placebo, plague, portents, prism, prison, pulpit, Pyrrhic, quarantine, quest, quicksand, residue, revolt, roulette, Rubicon, rupture, sabotage, salvage, salvo, scourge, shackle, shibboleth, shortcut, showdown, sideshow, sinew, skeleton, smokescreen, snapshot, sounding board, spectre, stagnate, stalemate, stampede, steerage, stonewall, summit, sunrise, sunset, swansong, taboo, tailwind, tempest, tendril, tether, thicket, thunderbolt, timebomb, touchstone, treadmill, treason, trigger, trough, tsunami, tyranny, universe, vanguard, vendetta, veneer, venom, verdict, vigil, voodoo, vortex, Waterloo, watershed, whirlpool, whirlwind, whitewash, windfall, yardstick, zoo

Two-word

Achilles' heel, Bermuda triangle, bête noire, black sheep, blue moon, chardonnay socialist, circuit-breaker, dark horse, devil's advocate, dog's bollocks, dry run, eager beaver, elbow grease, fault line, fig-leaf, firing line, fool's errand, girl Friday, good Samaritan, gravy train, hobby horse, Holy Grail, humble pie, killer app, laughing stock, long shot, loose cannon, Mary Celeste, paper tiger, philosophers' stone, red carpet, roller-coaster, Rosetta stone, show pony, silver lining, silver spoon, snake oil, stalking-horse, Trojan Horse, white elephant, white knight, wild card

EUPHEMISMS
Alcohol or drugs

high, impaired, inebriated, intoxicated, out of it, substance abuser, tired and emotional, wet one's whistle

Body and functions

faeces = ca-ca, night soil, poop; cleavage = bosom, bust, décolletage; bum = derrière, behind, bottom; crotch = groin, loins; masturbation = onanism, self love; sweat = perspiration; urination = answer the call of nature, micturation, powder one's nose, see a man about a dog, spend a penny, take a leak

Death
breathe one's last, buy the farm, cash one's chips, Davy Jones's locker, Elysian Fields, depart this life, fragged, go the way of all flesh, kick the bucket, pass away, pass on, push up daisies, River Styx, shuffle off this mortal coil, six feet under, sleep with the fishes, taken

Disability
differently abled, hard of hearing, of restricted growth, learning difficulty, mentally challenged, physically challenged, prosthesis, special child, visually impaired

Fat
baby fat, big boned, chunky, curvy, festively plump, fleshy, heavy set, large, muffin top, of ample proportions, plus-size, round, stout, voluptuous, well-fed, well-upholstered, womanly

Pregnancy
a happy event, baby bump, bun in the oven, eating for two, expecting, in a delicate condition, in the family way, knocked up, up the duff, with child

Sex
the beast with two backs, the birds and the bees, bonk, doctors and nurses, doing the wild thing, exchanging bodily fluids, giving head, horizontal mambo, how's your father, putting from the rough, tipping the velvet; chastity: abstinence, saving oneself for marriage; prostitution: turning a trick, the world's oldest profession; associated roles: comfort woman, escort, gigolo, john, madam, midnight cowboy, pimp, rent boy, street walker, trick, woman of easy virtue, working girl

Gayness
breeders, batting for the other team, friend of Dorothy, longtime companion, lover of Barbra Streisand (or Kylie Minogue, Liberace, Madonna, Liza Minnelli, Oscar Wilde), uphill gardener

War
body count, collateral damage, conflict, friendly fire, incontinent ordinance, peace process, police action, post-traumatic stress syndrome following shell shock and battle fatigue, preemptive strike, soft target, surgical strike

Work
between jobs, disestablished, gardening leave (paid leave while working out a contract), inventory shrinkage (theft by staff), lay off, rightsize, streamline, surplus to requirements, wanting to spend more time with the family

Other
appropriate (steal), colour (blush), economical with the truth (lying), capital punishment (death penalty), Dear John letter (one that tells recipient they are being left for someone else), ethnic cleansing (expulsion, unlawful imprisonment or genocide of ethnic minority), incident (a crash, accident or disaster), jumped the

shark (when an ongoing TV show is past its best), losing one's lunch (vomiting), reduced circumstances (poor), sanitation engineer (rubbish collector), shooting blanks (male infertility), smallest room in the house (the toilet), social disease (venereal disease)

Real-estate language

access to motorway, amenities, boutique, careful attention to detail, charming, chic, close to everything, compact, concept plans available, conveniently located, cosmopolitan, cute, desirable location, diamond in the rough, discerning buyer, easy on the pocket, entertaining space, exceptionally presented, exposed brick, fixer-upper, freshly painted, frontage, gazump, gazunder, handyman's delight, hideaway, incomparable, incomplete refurbishment, intimate, irresistible, lifestyle choice, lively, look no further, low-maintenance, luxurious, modern, modest, natural light, needs finishing touches, needs updating, no onward chain, north- / south-facing, numerous options, open plan, owners going overseas, prestigious, private, quaint, rarely available, reduced, refined, renovated, retro, rural, rustic, secluded, short distance, sophisticated, spacious, starter home, stunning, stylish, sunny, tranquil, tree-lined, unique, up and coming, urban, vacant possession, walking distance, water view, well-proportioned

SPECIALIST TERMS

Pertaining to

agriculture – agrarian, geoponic
apes or monkeys – simian
argument – elenctic
authors – auctorial

barbers – tonsorial
belief or opinion – doxastic
black magic – goetic
branches – rameal
breakfast – jentacular
bristles – setiform
chin – genial
church unity, worldwide (Christian) – ecumenical
clay – argillaceous
conjecture; involving random variable – stochastic
coughing – tussicular
dancing – terpsichorean
desires – orectic
dinner or lunch – prandial
dreams – oneiric, morphean
drinking – potatory
duty; obligation – deontic
ear – otic, aural
face – prosopic
fermentation; infection – zymotic
fig-shaped – caricous
fish – piscine
fishing – halieutic
flogging – vapulation
fruit bearing – frugiferous
fruit eating – frugivorous
gardens – horticulture
glass; a thin transparent membrane – hyaloid
grass – gramineous
hair – tricho-
hand – chiro-
hearing; ear – aural
hospital – nosocomial
ill health; invalidism – valetudinarian
infection; fermentation – zymotic
intellect – noetical

invalidism; ill health – valetudinarian

jaw – maxillary

kissing; mouth – oscular

knee – genual

lakes, dwelling in – lacustrine

laughter – gelastic

left side – sinistral

lips; vulva – labial

live young, bearing – viviparous

lunch or dinner – prandial

marriage – connubial, conjugal

marshes – paludal

membrane, thin and transparent; glass – hyaloid

mouth; kissing – oscular

obligation; duty – deontic

opinion or belief – doxastic

pain – algesic

palaces – palatine, palatial

penis, penis-shaped – phallic

prophecy – fatidic

priesthood – sacerdotal, hieratic

puberty – hebetic

rain – pluvial

random variable, involving; conjecture – stochastic

ribs – costal

right side – dextral

self – auto-

sexual activity involving three or more people (especially homosexual activity) – spintrian

skin – cutaneous

snow – nival

sound; speech – phonic

stars – sidereal

sun – helio-, solar

sweat – sudorific

tail: having a tail, tail-like, towards the

tail – caudate (caudal)

thinness – lepto-

thought, reasoning – dianoetic

throat – gular

touch – haptic

tree growing – silvacultural

twilight – crepuscular

uncle – avuncular

vertigo – vertiginous

vulva; lips – labial

windows – fenestral

wisdom or studying – palladian

worms – annelidous

wrist – carpal

Medical terms

ablation – removal of body part or tissue

abscission – removal of body tissue by cutting

abulia – inability to make decisions, often after brain damage

acidosis – excess acid in blood

acritochromacy – colour blindness

acromegaly – a growth hormone disorder, often occuring in middle age, initially involving swelling of hands and feet

ageusia – the total loss of taste

akathisia – a condition characterised by inability to keep still

alactasia – the inability to digest (sugar in) milk

alexia – an inability to read

amaurosis – loss of vision

anomia – form of aphasia involving loss of specific words or names

anosmia – inability to detect smells

anxiolytic – anti-anxiety (drugs or therapies)

aphasia – loss of ability to speak or

understand speech

apnoea – cessation of breathing

apoptosis – programmed cell death

ataxia – the inability to control voluntary movement, especially gait

atretic – relating to abnormal closure of bodily opening

auscultation – listening to sounds through a stethoscope

axilla – armpit

bariatrics – field of medicine dealing with excessive body weight

betacyanin – a chemical in beetroot that turns urine and faeces red

blepharitis – eyelid inflammation

blepharospasm – eyelid spasm

bregma – frontal and parietal bone join in skull

bruxism – teeth grinding

bufotenin – psychoactive chemical released from *Bufo* genus of toads, sometimes licked by humans for the effects

bursitis – a painful inflammation of synovial fluid sacs

cachinnation – laughter

capsulitis – frozen shoulder

cicatrix – scar tissue over a wound that has healed

comedo – blackhead

deglutition – swallowing

diaphoresis – sweating, particularly excessively

diaphysis – shaft of bone (epiphysis = end of bone)

disulfiram – chemical used to treat chronic alcoholics

docosahexaenoic acid – fatty acid in seafood believed to aid brain development

dorsal – relating to the back

dyscalculia – difficulty with numbers

dysgraphia – difficulty with writing

dyslexia – difficulty with words

dyspareunia – painful intercourse

dysphagia – difficulty swallowing

dysplasia – the imperfect development of an organ

dyspnea – difficulty with breathing

dyspraxia – difficulty with co-ordination

dystonia – a disfiguring muscle contraction

ectopic – of a pregnancy, occurring outside the uterus

edentulism – toothlessness (adjective: edentulous)

embololalia – a disorder in which nonsense sounds are inserted into speech

encopresis – soiling oneself

enuresis – wetting oneself

episiotomy – cut to perineum between vagina and anus to ease childbirth

epistaxis – nosebleed

erythrism – redness in complexion or hair colour

fistula – an abnormal passageway between organs or vessels

flabella – the muscle one frowns with

fomite – an inanimate object that can transmit germs (e.g. coin)

gular – relating to the throat

halitosis – bad breath

hepatic – pertaining to the liver

hyoid – a bone in the throat

hypochondria – a morbid preoccupation with health

hypoxia – shortage of oxygen

iatrogenic – caused by medical treatment, such as complication or infection

idiopathic – in cases of disease, of unknown cause

imbrication – an overlapping, especially of layers of tissue

ischaemia – a lack of blood to a part of body

kyphosis – outward curvature of spine (lordosis = inward curvature)

laparo- – abdomen, abdominal wall; flank; loin

levator ani – a pelvic floor muscle

lienal – pertaining to the spleen

luminol – a chemical used by police to detect blood traces as it reacts with iron

lycopene – a chemical in tomatoes, said to help guard against prostate cancer

mamilla – the nipple on a woman's breast

maxillary – pertaining to the jaw

meconium – first faeces of newborn

methyl mercaptan (asparagusic acid/ chlorophyll) – a chemical in asparagus that makes urine smell and turn green

metopic – pertaining to the forehead

myelic – pertaining to the spinal cord

necrosis – unprogrammed cell death

nephric – pertaining to the kidneys

neutropenia – having low resistance to infection

nocebo – a dummy drug that has a negative effect

nociception – the process of sensing pain

nosology – classification of disease

oscitancy – the act of yawning

otic – pertaining to the ear

palpebral, blepharo- – pertaining to the eyelid

paregoric – (that which) lessens pain

parietal – of body cavities

pediculosis – lice infestation

pellagra – a vitamin deficiency disease

causing rough skin and other problems, often seen in alcoholics

philtrum – groove beneath the nose

phimosis – the inability of the foreskin to retract

placebo – a dummy drug with a positive effect

plantar – pertaining to the sole of the foot

pollex – thumb

prodrome – an early symptom of disease

prognosis – forecast of a disease's course

prosopagnosia – the inability to recognise faces

pruritus – itching

pulmonary – pertaining to the lungs

rachidian – pertaining to the spine

renal – pertaining to the kidney

resveratrol – in grapes, a chemical said to aid the heart

rhinoplasty – nose job

rhinorrhea – runny nose

rhinotillexomania – extreme nose-picking

sciatic – pertaining to the hip or ischium bone of pelvis

sequela – condition resulting from previous injury or disease

sternutation – sneezing

styptic – able or tending to contract tissues, especially to stop bleeding

superciliary – pertaining to the eyebrow

syn-popanethial-s-oxide – the substance in onions that triggers tears

teratogenic – causing congenital malformations

veisalgia – a hangover

vernix – the white 'cheesy' substance covering newborn babies

vesical – pertaining to the bladder

PREFIXES AND COMBINING FORMS

Common

ante – before: antenatal

anti – against: anti-abortion

circum – around: circumnavigate

counter – against, in opposition to: counterintuitive

dis – opposite: disagreeable

dys – abnormal: dystopia

epi – upon, beside: epicentre

extra – outside, beyond: extraterrestrial

hyper – above: hyperactive

hypo – under, deficient: hypodermic

inter – between: international

intra – among, within: intravenous

macro – large-scale: macroeconomics

mega – large: mega-mall

meta – of a different order, transcending: metamorphosis

micro – small-scale: microeconomics

mis – wrong(ly) or bad(ly): misunderstand

multi – many: multinational

non / un – not: non-aligned, unwilling

over – beyond, over, exceeding: overexcited

para – beyond, beside: paranormal

peri – around, about: periscope

poly – many: polygamy

post – after: postnatal

pre – before: premature

praeter / preter – outside the range of: preternatural

proto – first, earliest, in the making: prototype

pseudo – phoney: pseudo-scientific

quasi – seemingly: quasi-religious

retro – previous, backwards: retrospective

semi – half: semicircular

sub – beneath: subcutaneous

super – directly above or higher: supercilious

supra – above, transcending: supranational

trans – across: transnational

uber – highly superior: uber-cosy

ultra – beyond or extreme: ultra-orthodox

Occasional

anthropo – man: anthropomorphic

archaeo – ancient: archaeology

biblio – book: bibliography

crypto – secret: cryptography

cyber – of the internet or digital worlds: cyberspace

ecto – outside: ectoplasm

endo – inside: endoscopy

gastro – stomach: gastroenteritis

haemo – blood: haemophiliac

hetero – different: heterosexual

hydro – water: hydroponic

lipo – fat: liposuction

litho – stone: lithograph

nano – microscopic: nanotechnology

necro – death: necromancy

omni – all, everywhere: omnipotent

ortho – straight, correct: orthography

perma – permanent: permafrost

phago – eating or destroying: phagocyte

pheno – visible: phenology

phono – sounds: phonograph

photo – light: photosynthesis

physio – physical: physiotherapy

phyto – plant: phytogenesis

ur – primitive or original: ur-religion

xeno – strange or foreign: xeno-transplant

SUFFIXES AND TERMINATIONS

-ability, -aceous, -age, -algia, -androus,
-archy, -arium, -athon, -atory, -biosis,
-centric, -cide, -cracy, -cycle, -cyte, -derm,
-ectomy, -escence, -esque, -etic, -fication,
-ful, -gate, -genesis, -genic, -gram, -graphy,
-hood, -ia, -iatric, -ible, -ibility, -ic, -id,
-ify, -illion, -isation, -ise, -ish, -ism, -ist,
-itis, -ity, -kin, -kinesis, -less, -like, -ling,
-lisis, -logy, -loid, -lyse, -mancy, -mania,
-manship, -ment, -morph, -nomy, -ogenic,
-ome, -onym, -onics, -opia, -orama, -osis,
-otomy, -ous, -path, -pede, -phile, -philia,
-phobe, -phobic, -phone, -phore, -plasm,
-plasty, -plex, -pod, -polis, -ric, -scape,
-scope, -ship, -some, -stan, -stasis, -taxis,
-therm, -thon, -tion, -tron, -trophy, -tropy,
-tude, -ular, -urgy, -urous, -valent, -ville,
-vorous, -war, -ward, -wear, -wide, -wise,
-worthy, -zygous

Suffix-based coinages

-aholic, -holic — extreme devotee or addict, after alcoholic

bookaholic, chargeaholic, chocoholic,
danceaholic, golfaholic, saveaholic,
sexaholic, shoeaholic, shopaholic,
soupaholic, sugarholic, wordaholic,
workaholic

-arian — advocate

disciplinarian, fruitarian, futilitarian,
libertarian, totalitarian, trustafarian
(slacker or counterculture adherent who
lives on a trust fund, after Rastafarian)

-ati — like-minded elite or specialist group

digerati / technorati (those in the IT /
internet know), glitterati (celebrities and
the wealthy crowd), letterati (those who
frequently write letters to media), literati
(literature and publishing intellectuals),
illiterati (those who take pride in
not knowing about much), twitterati
(knowledgeable fans of Twitter)

*-gate — scandal, after Richard Nixon's
Watergate Hotel conspiracy*

Irangate (after 1986/7 Iran–Contra
arms trade scandal involving Reagan
Administration), nannygate (actor
Rob Lowe's problem with a nanny),
paintergate (NZ PM Helen Clark's
signing of an auctioned painting),
troopergate (sexual allegations around
Bill Clinton), wardrobegate (Sarah Palin
clothing allowance problems)

-ista — arbiter

fashionista / stylista (fashion arbiter),
Guardianista (stereotypical liberal left
reader of the *Guardian*), recessionista (chic
bargain hunter)

*-itis — physical or slight mental affliction, after
ailments such as arthritis*

bankeritis (strange behaviour after
working as banker), senioritis (tendency
to take it easy in last year of schooling),
third-term-itis (jitters over third term
in political office), Wiiitis / Nintenditis
(pain in arms following play with Wii/
Nintendo video game)

-ivist — active supporter, after activist

actorvist (an actor who promotes social
causes), lactivist (one who promotes
public breast feeding), slacktivist (lapsed
or rhetorical activist)

*-nik — one who espouses a cause, after the era
of the Russian spacecraft Sputnik*

beatnik (from Beat generation), neatnik,
nudnik (Yiddish = nag), peacenik
(protester for peace), refusenik (those who

refuse to serve in Israeli armed forces, or things such as honours and awards more generally)

-onomics – economics-based study of a subject or shrewd purchasing plans

chic-onomics (being fashionable at a low price), cruise-onomics (boat cruises), emotionomics (marketing based on customer emotion), freakonomics (unrevealed economic findings about society), open source-onomics (open source computing)

-orexia / -orexic – obsession, particularly involving weight, after anorexia

alcorexia (drinking rather than eating), bigorexia (obsessive body building), manorexia (male extreme slimming), tanorexia (tanning), yogarexia (yoga)

JOURNALISM

Tabloidese

agony, angel, axe, babe, bag, ban, beast, beating, beauty, bizarre, blast, boozy, brace, brave, break-up, bully, bungle, bust-up, carnage, cash, celeb, champ, cheat, chilling, chop, clinch, cock-up, collapse, confession, cover-up, crim, crisis, curse, dash, deadly, deal, deny, dream, dump, erupt, exclusive, explosion, expose, fab, fail, fan, farce, fave, fear, feud, fiend, fight, fire, fix, flaunt, flutter, fortune, foxy, frosty, fury, gag, gong, goss, gran, guilty, heaven, hefty, hell, hero, hike, hols, horror, hot, hunk, hurtle, idol, inferno, inside, jibe, lash, loom, loser, massacre, miff, miracle, monster, mum, nasty, nightmare, op, outfit, pal, peek, pic, plea, potty, probe, racy, rags, rampage, rant, raunchy, rehab, reveal, rip-off, risk, rocked, romp, row, ruckus, run-in, saucy, scandal, scramble,

secret, sexy, shame, shock, shot, sink, sizzle, skirmish, slam, smash, snap, sneak, snipe, snub, sordid, sour, split, spoof, spy, star, stoush, strife, stunning, suspect, sweep, terror, thrash, thrill, thug, tip, tot, toxic, tragic, trial, truth, tussle, vanish, victory, vid, vow, wacky, warning, whopping, wild, winner, wonder

Short headline words

act, add, after, away, back, ban, battle, beef up, before, best, bet, beware, bit, border, boss, brand, build, built, burn, buy, call, cap, case, cash, chief, choke, clash, clobber, close, closer, creep, crept, deal, dealt, deny, dig, die, droop, drop, duck, earn, embrace, end, eye, face, fall, fan, fear, feel, felt, fight, find, fine, finish, fire, fired, fit, fix, flock, force, found, gain, game, gave, gift, give, given, get, glimmer, got, grab, grew, grow, hand, hear, heard, hell, hex, hit, hop, hope, hurt, icing, jail, jest, job, junk, keep, kept, know, leak, lean, leave, left, line, link, local, look, loom, lose, loss, made, make, mar, move, name, nod, nose, odds, off, on, open, paint, past, pay, peak, pick, place, plan, pledge, plunge, profit, progress, prompt, punish, rage, ran, rap, rate, recipe, refuse, repent, rib, rid, ride, right, rip, rise, risen, risk, road, rob, rode, rose, rough, rub, run, sack, sale, sat, save, savvy, scrap, search, sell, send, sent, set, shelf, shelve, shine, shuffle, sit, slow, slur, smoke, sold, sound, space, spanner, speak, splash, stake, stand, stint, storm, sue, survive, take, taken, talk, tap, target, tease, tell, test, thrust, tip, toe, told, toll, took, top, tow, track, trim, trip, try, tumble, turn, united, up, want, war, warn, watch, win, wing, wink, won, work, worst, write

Introduction verbs

argue, ask, check out, comes up with, discover, dissect, eavesdrop, examine, explore, fear, find, get (gain, grab, obtain), give, grill, has (boasts, possesses), have, hear, interrogate, interview, investigate, is (finds oneself, remains), look (at), meet, mull, observe, peek, peer, ponder, profile, provide, question, quiz, remember, report, say, speak to, spy, unearth, visit, wonder

FOREIGN TERMS IN ENGLISH

FRENCH TERMS

à deux – for two, so intimate or romantic

agent provocateur – one who attempts to provoke others to act

aide-mémoire – thing intended to jog the memory

à la carte – selected individually from the menu, so can be applied to other items bought separately, rather than as a package

à la mode – fashionable

amour propre – self-esteem

ancien régime – political and social systems in place before French Revolution; outmoded system (old rule)

au contraire – to the contrary, usually used in a humorous or literary sense

au fait – familiar [with]

au naturel – raw or without dressing as applied to food; naked

au pair – young (and often foreign) person who minds children and house-keeps in exchange for lodging

avant-garde – using the latest artistic ideas; boundary-pushing

belles-lettres – literature valued for aesthetic nature rather than content

bête noire – thing or person that irritates above all else

bien pensant – right-thinking (people)

bon vivant – person who enjoys good food, wine and company

canard – hoax, deliberately misleading story

carte blanche – unrestricted freedom to act or organise matters as one wants

cause célèbre – issue or legal case that continues to cause controversy or debate

chacun à son goût – literally 'to each his/her own taste', used to note difference in another's choice

clou – central point of interest or idea

comme il faut – in accordance with convention; genteel, proper

cordon bleu – of cooking, first class

cordon sanitaire – barrier or buffer zone in place for medical or political reasons

coup de foudre – astonishing and unexpected event such as love at first sight; 'bolt from the blue'

coup de grâce – any final, decisive blow

coup d'état – overthrow of a government, usually violent

crème de la crème – the very best, as in people of society or other superlative example

de haut en bas – in a condescending manner

déjà vu – feeling that a moment has been already experienced at an earlier point in time

demi-monde – marginal group; prostitutes

démodé – out of fashion

de rigueur – socially required

dernier cri – the latest fashion

de trop – excessive or superfluous

double entendre – remark with two meanings, often with one being sexually suggestive

du jour – the latest fashion, often pejoratively, as in 'the car du jour'

en bloc / en masse – together, in a group

enfant terrible – troublesome but talented person

entrepôt – import–export sea port

épater les bourgeois – to shock the 'middle classes', especially with an artwork that breaks convention

esprit de corps – team spirit, group morale

faît accompli – done deal; something that is done or set in motion and not able to be altered

faux pas – misstep, especially in a social sense

femme fatale – attractive but ultimately destructive woman

fin de siècle – end of century

folie à deux – madness in which two associated people share same delusion

force majeure – in law, unexpected event that provides an out to not fulfil the terms of an agreement; force that is impossible to resist

gauche caviar – 'champagne socialist' or 'limousine liberal'

haute couture – the most exclusive and expensive ranges of tailored fashions from the top designers

haut monde – high society

idée fixe – an obsession or fixation

je ne sais quoi – an undefinable quality [in person or thing], usually positive

joie de vivre – upbeat mood or happiness (literally 'joy at being alive')

laissez-faire – policy of non-interference, often applied to variety of capitalism with minimal government intervention

lèse-majesté – treason; affront to another's dignity

maître d' – short for maitre d'hotel, the person in charge of front of house at a restaurant

ménage à trois – a relationship or sexual encounter involving three people

née – refers to a woman's maiden name, Jane Brown, née Green

noblesse oblige – idea that those of rank or wealth have wider social obligations

nom de guerre – pseudonym, alias, alter ego

nom de plume – pseudonym of an author

nouveau riche – person who has recently come into money, but who possibly lacks social graces

objet d'art – artwork considered to be of artistic merit; a small decorative object

outré – unconventional; challenging

pièce de résistance – outstanding item or accomplishment

pied-à-terre – small flat kept for secondary accommodation

plus ça change – abbreviation of phrase 'plus ça change, plus c'est la même chose', meaning that despite change, much remains the same

prêt-à-porter – clothes that are ready to wear off the rack as opposed to tailored

raison d'être – key purpose

récherché – rare; sought out; pretentious

risqué – sexually suggestive to point of rudeness or indecency

savoir faire – knowledge of how to act in any situation; tact

soi-disant – self-proclaimed, so-called

succès d'estime – critical rather than

financial success

succès de scandale – artwork that achieves success because of its link to scandal rather than its artistic merits alone

succès fou – a wild success

tour de force – exceptional artistic achievement; standout work of artistic career

trompe l'œil – technique or other visual medium that tricks the eye

volte-face – sudden and total change in opinion

GERMAN TERMS

angst – anxiety, apprehension, often with depression

bildungsroman – novel detailing figure's development

blitzkrieg – sudden large military offensive

doppelgänger – person's double; can be supernatural

drang nach osten – eastern expansion policy

ersatz – replacement; fake

fingerspitzengefühl – fine discrimination in language or other complex area of culture

gastarbeiter – guest-worker

gestalt – in the arts, describes that whole of structure is greater than the parts; psychological theory of mind

götterdämmerung – violent collapse of a society or regime, literally 'twilight of the gods'

kaput – broken

katzenjammer – unpleasant noise; hangover

realpolitik – politics based on practical factors rather than principle

Reinheitsgebot – ancient purity of beer regulation, now superseded

schadenfreude – enjoyment of other's

misfortune

sprachgefühl – a good ear for the correct use of language

verboten – forbidden

wanderjahr – time of travel before settling down

wanderlust – irresistible yearning to travel

Wehrmacht – WWII German armed forces

weltanschauung – comprehensive world view

weltschmertz – world weariness

wunderkind – child prodigy; hugely successful young person

zeitgeist – spirit of an age; the attitudes and outlook of a specific period or generation

LATIN TERMS

ab initio – from the beginning

addendum – thing to be added

ad hoc – improvised

ad hominen – against the person, as in abuse

alma mater – university one studied at

alumnus – male former student of a specific educational institution, usually university (alumna = female; alumni = plural)

bona fides – now taken to be the plural form of a person's credentials

carpe diem – seize the day, encouraging the enthusiastic enjoyment of the present while it lasts

caveat emptor – let the buyer beware

circa – approximately, referring to a date

compos mentis – of sound mind, having one's wits about one

de facto / de jure – according to the way things are / the law

de gustibus – shortened form of phrase stating that there is no point challenging people's preferences

de profundis – from the depths (Psalms)

deus ex machina – a literary device in which something unlikely is introduced to resolve matters in the plot

dramatis personae – the cast of characters in a work

erratum – error (plural = errata)

exempli gratia – e.g., meaning for example (i.e. = id est, or 'that is')

ex parte – legal term meaning from one side only

ibidem – in books, abbreviated to ibid., refers to last source cited

in absentia – used when someone is absent, particularly accused in a trial

infra dig – beneath one's dignity

in loco parentis – in the place of the parent

in medias res – beginning in the middle of a story

in partibus – abbreviated term meaning 'in the land of the unbelievers'

in petto – in secrecy, especially of Roman Catholic appointments

inter alia – among other things

in utero – in the womb

in vino veritas – 'truth in wine', a reference to the manner in which alcohol lowers inhibition and discretion

ipso facto – by that very fact; meaning that something is the case as a direct result of something else: We have moved on from a world in which mother-in-laws are, ipso facto, funny

ipso jure – by law

lapsus linguae / lapsus calami – slip of the tongue / pen

mala fide – in bad faith

mea culpa – admission that 'I am to blame'

memento mori – object that serves as a reminder of the inevitability of death

mens rea – guilty mind, used when discussing accused

mirabile dictu – wonderful to relate

note bene – NB, note this well

parti pris – formed opinion without good evidence

passim – term used in footnotes, etc., to refer to an item that appears frequently throughout a text

per diem – for each day, particularly a person's expenses

persona non grata – unwelcome person

prima facie – term for evidence that suggests but doesn't prove guilt

pro bono – term for work done by lawyer for free, such as public good cases

pro tempore – for the time being

quid pro quo – equivalent or replacement

quod erat demonstrandum – which was to be shown, often abbreviated to QED

sic – thus, meaning quoted as in the original, with errors intact

sine qua non – an essential part of a whole

SPQR – abbreviation for the Roman Republic

sub rosa – secretly

suggestio falsi – positive misrepresentation

sui generis – unique, of its own kind (especially legislation)

summa cum laude – the highest distinction that can be achieved by US college student

tabula rasa – blank slate

tempus fugit – time flies, noted as an imperative to hurry

terra incognita – unknown territory

terra nullius – land belonging to no one

vade mecum – something regularly carried; ready reference book

vox populi – popular opinion, particularly as through media vox pops with people on the street

INDIAN TERMS

ahimsa – doctrine of non-violence, in Hinduism, Buddhism, Jainism

bapu – spiritual father (Hindu)

chakra – the centres of spiritual energy in the body, according to yoga principles

desi – someone (else) from the Indian subcontinent, particularly when abroad

Devanagari – alphabet used by Indian languages

dharma – duty, eternal law, proper conduct of living (Hindi)

gora – slang term for white male (female = gori) (Hindi)

gurdwara – place of worship for Sikh

guru – teacher, spiritual guide

jalebi – fried flour sweets

karma – acts and deeds that influence samsara

pukka – first class, genuine

puri – type of deep-fried bread

mandala – sacred symbol used in meditation etc.

mantra – chant, slogan

nirvana – release from lifecycle, idealised place

rakshasa – Hindu evil spirit

samsara – cycle of life

suttee – Hindu practice of widow throwing herself on husband's funeral pyre

titli – Hindi term for butterfly

JEWISH/YIDDISH TERMS

Ashkenazim – Jews of central or northern Europe origin

azyme – Passover cake

blintze – filled pancake

bris / brit malah – eighth-day circumcision

Chanukah – winter festival

dreidel – a top-like toy for Chanukah game

genizah – room attached to synagogue

golem – clay figure that is brought to life in folklore; a servant who carries out a command with literal exactness

goy(ische) – something or someone not Jewish

kibitz – banter, offer unwanted advice

kippah / yarmulke – skull cap

kvell – to exclaim joyfully, burst with pride

Manischewitz – US kosher goods brand, especially relating to wine

megillah – long, tediously detailed account

mensch – honorable, dependable person

meshuga – crazy

Mishnah – oral law

mohel – official who circumcises (rhymes with oil)

nebbish – timid or ineffectual person

nudnik – boring pest

Sanhedrin – high council of Jewish judges

schlep – to take one's time; to lug; tedious or slow trip

schlub – clumsy oaf

schlump – a slovenly person

schmaltz – sentimental sweetness

schmendrik – foolish, naive person

schmuck – idiot, dimwit

schnook – gullible, naive person

schnorrer – someone who takes advantage of others' generosity

shaatnez – relates to rules about not

interweaving wool and linen

Shekina – manifestation of God's female aspects

shiksa – non-Jewish woman (often mock pejorative)

shmatte – tattered clothing, junk

shtetl – Jewish community in East European country

shtick – performer's gimmick

shul – Yiddish word for synagogue

tallis / tallit – prayer shawls

Talmud – collection of rabbinical, oral traditions

tefillin – boxes with strap worn during morning prayer

tikkun olam – concept in Judaism, Hebrew for 'healing the world'

Torah – first five books of Tanakh, the Hebrew Bible

verklempt – overcome with emotion

yenta – a gossipy person

yeshiva – institution for study of Torah and Talmud

zaftig – attractively plump

JAPANESE TERMS

bushido – the Samurai code of honour

depachika – food halls in basements of department stores

honne – one's true feelings

inro – historical small case for carrying objects

kaiseki – multi-course haute cuisine meal

karoshi – death from overwork

kawaii – playfully cute

keikogi – a martial arts uniform

keiretsu – an interrelated group of companies

kimono – a traditional Japanese garment

koban – a community policing post

minshuku – a traditional family-run inn

netsuke – a carved toggle for securing inro to obi

nisei – child of Japanese immigrants

obi – sash worn with kimono or *keikogi*

rikishi – a sumo wrestler

sarariman – an office worker

seppuku – self-disembowelment

shinju – group suicide; the double suicide of two lovers

soroban – a Japanese abacus

sumo – Japanese wrestling (top ranks: yokozuna, ozeki, sekiwake, komusubi, maegashira)

tatemae – one's public face

yakuza – Japanese mafia

yukata – informal summer kimono

MUSLIM / ARABIC TERMS

akhirah – afterlife

Azrael – angel of death

burka – a dark robe worn by Muslim women, especially in Afghanistan

cadi – a judge

caliphate – a Muslim-ruled area

fatwa – ruling, edict

Hadith – account of Muhammad's deeds

halal – permissible

haram – forbidden

harem – wives and concubines, women's quarters

hijab – Islamic dress code for women

imam – the leader of prayers in a mosque

intifada – 'shaking off', an insurrection, particularly applying to Palestinian struggles

jibbah – a long coat

jihad – a struggle or holy war

marabout – a hermit or monk

mosque – a place of worship

muezzin – caller to prayer

mufti – a priest or expounder of law

Mughal – a member of the Indian subcontinent Muslim dynasty

mullah – a mosque leader

muwalladun – historical non-Arab converts to Islam

nabob – an official under the Mughal emperors

schmata – Arab headdress

seraglio – historical harem in a Muslim palace

shahada – a declaration of faith

shariah – a code of religious law

sherif – a leader; a descendant of Mohammed

shroff – money changer

softa – theological student

ulema – clerical establishment

umma – the community of Allah

ARABIC-ORIGINATED WORDS

admiral, alchemy, alcohol, algebra, algorithm, alkali, almanac, amalgam, apricot, assassin, checkmate, coffee, cork, cotton, elixir, ghoul, giraffe, jar, lemon, loofah, magazine, mattress, monsoon, nadir, rook (chess piece), safari, sugar, tariff, typhoon, zenith

MISUSE OF LANGUAGE

COMMON AND OCCASIONAL CONFUSIONS

abstruse – (adj) hard to understand

obtuse – (adj) blunt; slow to understand

accede (to) – (v) to agree; to take office

exceed – (v) to go beyond

succeed – (v) to achieve or do well; to take office after someone

accept – (v) to approve, generally agree upon; to receive

except – (v) to leave out

except – (prep, conj) excluding, only

adduce – (v) to show as evidence or proof

deduce – (v) to infer or judge based on what one knows

adverse – (adj) unfavourable (as in conditions)

averse – (adj) opposed or strongly disinclined to

affect (n) – in psychology, a feeling or emotion (stress on first syllable)

affect (v) – to change; to pretend to have or feel something (stress on second syllable)

effect (n) – an outcome (stress on second syllable)

effect (v) – to bring about (stress on first syllable)

alimentary – (adj) relating to digestion or food

elementary – (adj) basic

allusion – (n) an indirect reference

delusion – (n) an irrational mistaken belief

illusion – (n) an incorrect perception or belief

aloud – (adv) audibly

allowed – (v pp) permitted

alternate – (v, adj, n) to do by turns;
  occurring in turns; substitute (for adjective
  and noun: stress on the third syllable)
alternative – (n, adj) the other of two
  things; not mainstream

ambit – (n) area of influence, scope
gambit – (n) the opening move in a game
  or manoeuvre
gamut – (n) the full extent of, range

amused – (adj, v pp) occupied pleasantly
bemused – (adj) confused, preoccupied

anal – (adj) of the anus
annal – (n) historical record (usually in
  plural)
annul – (v) to declare invalid
anterior – (adj) to the front
posterior – (adj) to the back
ulterior – (adj) in the background; beyond
  what is obvious

antithesis – (n) opposition or contrast of
  ideas
synthesis – (n) converging or unification of
  ideas
synopsis – (n) a summarising view
thesis – (n) argument

appraise – (v) to estimate the worth of, to
  check
apprise (of) – (v) to inform (often oneself)

approbation – (n) approval
opprobrium – (n) public disgrace or that
  which brings it
probation – (n) a supervised non-jail period

for offenders; a trial period for new
employees
privation – (n) the condition or result of not
  having (usually, lacking basic necessities)

arbitrage – (n) practice of taking advantage
  of price differential, usually in financial
  markets
triage – (n) medical sorting of patients'
  needs

arrant – (adj) completely, without
  qualification
errant – (adj) wandering; in a state of error

ascend – (v) to climb
ascent – (n) a climb
assent – (v) to express agreement
consent – (v, n) to agree to; agreement

ascribe – (v) to attribute (to)
describe – (v) to give account of in words
inscribe – (v) to mark with signature or
  words; to engrave; to informally dedicate
prescribe – (v) to recommend or formally
  advise; to establish officially
proscribe – (v) to prohibit
subscribe – (v) to receive as a result of
  regular payment; to believe, as in a theory
transcribe – (v) to write out in full from
  notes or another medium; to convert or
  rearrange from one form to another

assure – (v) to give confidence
ensure – (v) to make sure
insure – (v) to undertake insurance

bare – (v, adj) to strip off, disclose; naked

bear – (n, v) animal; to carry

bearing – (n) demeanour

batten – (n) strip of timber used in construction or joinery

baton – (n) light shaped stick; truncheon

bazaar – (n) marketplace

bizarre – (adj) weird

begin – (v) to start, often after a period

start – (v, n) to begin, often for first time (must be used for machines and vehicles); to jump or shy in surprise; beginning

bequest – (n) the act or substance of giving by way of a will

inquest – (n) legal investigation, especially by coroner into death

request – (n, v) ask for, demand; the act of asking for

bloc – (n) grouping of nations, etc. for common purpose

block – (n, v) mass of stone or wood; to prevent

born – (v pp, adj) having been given birth to; having from birth (He was born on a Friday; a born star)

borne – (v pp) past participle of verb 'to bear' (She has borne seven children)

borrow – (v) to obtain temporarily ('I borrow something *from* you')

lend – (v) to allow the use of temporarily ('I lend something *to* you'); to impart (it lends the house a certain charm)

loan – (n, v) something lent; to lend (but never means to impart)

bought – (v pp) past tense of buy

brought – (v pp) past tense of bring

cache – (n) hiding place or stores hidden; temporary computer memory (pronounced kash or kaish)

cachet – (n) something that confers prestige (pronounced kash-ay)

cantankerous – (adj) quarrelsome

rancorous – (adj) having deep-seated resentment

careen – (v) to lurch or swerve while in motion; to rush without care; to tilt a boat (for cleaning, etc.)

career – (v, n) to move at full speed; the course of one's chosen profession

cellulose – (n) a carbohydrate that forms most plant cell walls

celluloid – (n) a plastic substance; figuratively, motion pictures

cellulite – (n) a fatty deposit that causes a dimpling effect on the skin surface

censor – (n, v) an official who grades publications or artworks for public consumption; to do so

censorious – (adj) finding fault

censure – (n, v) harsh criticism; to severely criticise

chintzy – (adj) cheap and/or poor quality

ditzy – (adj) scatterbrained

glitzy – (adj) shiny, show-off

kitschy – (adj) in bad taste, said of art

klutzy – (adj) clumsily, of a klutz

ritzy – (adj) luxuriously elegant

cinch – (n, v) something easy; to tighten
  like a belt

cliché – (n) a hackneyed expression

clinch – (n, v) an embrace; to hold securely

climactic – (adj) to do with climaxes

climatic – (adj) to do with climate

coarse – (adj) rough, uncouth

course – (adj) path, channel

complement – (v, n) to add features or
  variety to; something that completes or
  combines to make a whole

compliment – (v, n) to praise; expression of
  praise

complementary – (adj) adds to total

complimentary – (adj) free as part of
  service; conferring praise

compound – (v, n, adj) to make worse or
  greater; a mixture; consisting of more than
  one thing

impound – (v) to confine

propound – (v) to suggest

confidant – (n) one you confide in

confident – (adj) having confidence

confusion – (n) disorder

infusion – (n) a liquid solution prepared by
  soaking or steeping

profusion – (n) an abundance or great
  flowing

conspire – (v) to plot with others

expire – (v) to cease living

inspire – (v) to arouse someone to action,
  through emotional response or by example

perspire – (v) to sweat

transpire – (v) to give off water; to happen

continual – (adj) continues with breaks

continuous – (adj) continues without breaks

conundrum – (n) difficult or insoluble
  problem; traditionally, a riddle that may
  be answered by a pun

dichotomy – (n) division into two,
  particularly elements that are
  contradictory or exclusive

dilemma – (n) the choice of two, equally
  unfavourable options; a difficult choice

enigma – (n) something that is mysterious
  or that has a hidden meaning (such as a
  puzzle or riddle)

paradox – (n) a statement that seems to be
  contradictory but which may still be true

convince – (v) to persuade

evince – (v) to make evident

evoke – (v) to bring forth

invoke – (v) to call on someone (often a
  higher power) for help

creak – (v) make noise

creek – (n) small stream

credible – (adj) believable

creditable – (adj) trustworthy, praiseworthy

credulous – (adj) gullible

cronyism – (n) patronage of friends with no
  regard for their qualifications

favouritism – (n) inclination to partiality

nepotism – (n) patronage of relatives

parochialism – (n) a local, narrow or
  similarly resticted outlook

crotch – (n) the gap between the legs

crutch – (n) a support

curb – (v) to restrain or check

kerb – (n) border between road and
  footpath

currant – (n) dried seedless grape, raisin

current – (n, adj) flow; contemporary

cymbal – (n) a percussion instrument

symbol – (n) a sign

daze – (v, n) to confuse; confusion

faze – (v) to unsettle or disconcert

phase (in/out) (v, n) – begin/cease to use; a
  period

raise – (v) to lift

raze – (v) to burn or level to the ground

decent – (adj) respectable; pleasant and
  obliging

descent – (n) process or action of going
  downward; ancestral lineage

declaim – (v) to deliver a formal speech; to
  speech vehemently

disclaim – (v) to deny or renounce claim to

proclaim – (v) announce officially or
  publicly

defer – (v) to put off until later; to give way
  to

demur – (v) to object

deny – (v) to reject

deter – (v) to turn away or try to prevent

delude – (v) to deceive

include – (v) to take in

preclude – (v) to prevent beforehand

denounce – (v) to publicly accuse or
  condemn

pronounce – (v) to articulate upon or pass
  judgement

denunciation – (n) public accusation or
  condemnation

enunciation – (n) clear articulation of
  speech; a formal declaration

pronunciation – (n) speech pattern as
  moderated by stress, inflection, cadence,
  intonation, etc.

dependant – (n) someone who is reliant
  upon another

dependent – (adj) reliant upon

descendant – (n) issue of a forebear

descendent – (adj) downward-moving

determinedly – (adv) with determination

deterministically – (adv) from determinism,
  the idea that every event, including
  human action, has a cause that is outside
  of human will

determinately – (adv) having precise limits

diligence – (n) hard work

indigence – (n) poverty

indolence – (n) laziness

mendacity – (n) tendency to be untruthful

discomfit – (v) to disconcert

discomfort – (n, v) lack of comfort; to make uneasy

discreet – (adj) judicious or unobtrusive (noun = discretion)

discrete – (adj) distinct or separate (noun = discreteness)

disinformation – (n) information designed to put the recipient on the wrong track

misinformation – (n) incorrect information

disinterested – (adj) dispassionate, indifferent; impartial

uninterested – (adj) not interested

disinterest – (n) lack of interest

diuretic – (adj, n) that which encourages urination

emetic – (adj, n) that which encourages vomiting

laxative – (adj, n) that which encourages emptying of bowels

divert – (v) to effect a change of course; to amuse; to deflect

invert – (v) to flip, reverse, or turn inwards

pervert – (v) to divert towards the illicit or abnormal

subvert – (v) to undermine or overthrow

doubtful – (adj) unlikely; causing or experiencing or raising doubts

dubious – (adj) raising suspicion; causing doubts

draft – (n, v) preliminary sketch; money order; US conscription; to draw up an outline

draught – (n) air current; serving of alcohol

dual – (adj) having two

duel – (adj) fight between two persons

eclipse – (n, v) obscuring of one planet, moon or star by another; to surpass and so put someone or something in one's shadow

ellipse – (n) in geometry, an oval shape

ellipsis – (n) in text, three dots indicating words left out; in figurative language, a sentence structure in which words are omitted but understood

elicit – (v) to draw out or bring forth

illicit – (adj) not legal or socially permitted

emaciated – (adj) very thin, wasted

emancipated – (adj) free from social, political or legal restraint; to be less inhibited by social or moral convention

emasculated – (adj) castrated or made of reduced effectiveness

eminent – (adj) prominent

immanent – (adj) inherent; subjective

imminent – (adj) about to occur

emission – (n) that which is emitted or given out

omission – (n) that which is omitted or left out; act of leaving out

remission – (n) an abatement, especially of cancer

enquiry – (n) a question

inquiry – (n) an official investigation

entomology – (n) study of insects

etymology – (n) study of word origins

ersatz – (adj) inferior, substitute

erstwhile – (adj) former

evoke – (v) to call forth

invoke – (v) to call upon

provoke – (v) to incite, challenge

revoke – (v) to withdraw or reverse

exercise – (v, n) to train; a task

exorcise – (v) to get rid of, e.g. evil spirit

expatiate – (v) to speak or write about at length; to wander

expatriate – (n, v) a citizen who lives abroad (= expat); to expel or remove oneself from one's native country

patriot – (n) one who loves a fatherland

expeditious – (adj) marked by efficiency or speed

expedient – (adj) marked by self-interest rather than principle

exponent – (n) one who expounds or interprets

proponent – (n) one who proposes

prosecutor – (n) one who initiates criminal action

defendant – (n) one who is defending, often in court

febrile – (adj) feverish

fecund – (adj) fertile; intellectually productive

feeble – (adj) weak, hopeless

fertile – (adj) rich in resources; capable of breeding

fragile – (adj) easily broken

feign – (v) to pretend

feint – (n, v) a deceptive move; to make such a move

faint – (v, adj) to swoon; weak

filial – (adj) of a son (sometimes of a daughter)

philately – (n) stamp collecting

floe – (n) flat segment of pack ice

flow – (v, n) to move freely, circulate

flounder – (v) to stumble, subside

founder – (v) to fail

flout – (v) to ignore (pronounced flowt)

flaunt – (v) to show off oneself or one's possessions arrogantly

foreword – (n) preface of a book

forward – (adj, adv, v) ahead; to send on, promote

fraught – (adj) causing anxiety; laden or burdened

wrought – (adj) worked into shape, as with metal

gaff – (n) a fishing hook; a nautical spar; slang for home or a trick

gaffe – (n) a mistake

gaffer – (n) the chief electrician on a film set; slang for old man

genteel – (adj) well-bred

gentile – (adj) not Jewish

gentle – (adj) mild of disposition

hackle – (n) hair on back and neck, usually of dog, often in plural

heckle – (v) to harass a (usually stage) performer with comments and interjections

hermetic – (adj) sealed airtight, or free from outside influences

heuristic – (adj, n) involving learning or problem-solving; such a method or practice

hermeneutics – (n) the theory and study of interpreting texts (hermeneutic: explanatory)

hoi polloi – (n) common people; 'the' in front is common and correct in English usage

home (in) – (v) to get closer to

hone – (v) to make sharper, improve

horde – (n) group of people

hoard – (n, v) a store; to amass

hew – (v) to carve out

hue – (n) shade of colour

idle – (adj) lazy; without work

idol – (n) image of a god; a false god; someone who is adored

imply – (v) I imply something in what I say

infer – (v) you infer something from what I said

incredible – (adj) hard or impossible to believe; amazing

incredulous – (adj) sceptical, disbelieving

insidious – (adj) beguiling but harmful and spreading

invidious – (adj) causing resentment, especially if unfair

lead – (v) to guide from front; leash; most important (pronounced leed)

lead – (n) metallic element (pronounced led)

led – (v pp) guided

lighting – (n) effect of lights

lightening – (n) making lighter

lightning – (n) electricity bolt from cloud

loose – (adj) not secured or tight

lose – (v) opposite of to win

lucrative – (adj) profitable

ludicrous – (adj) absurd

lugubrious – (adj) gloomy, often excessively so

salubrious – (adj) healthy or wholesome

linen – (n) bed / table coverings only

crockery – (n) plates, cups, etc.

cutlery – (n) knives, forks, etc.

mantel – (n) mantelpiece

mantle – (n) cloak; figuratively, cloak of responsibility; interior layer of planet

marital – (adj) of marriage

martial – (adj) of war

miasma – (n) a noxious or unhealthy atmosphere

milieu – (n) social or artistic environment; general ambience needling – (n) a provocation or irritation, especially deliberately so

wheedling – (n) sly negotiating using flattery

overweening – (adj) excessive; overbearing

wean – (v) to detach from; to accustom to an alternative

pablum – (n) trite or oversimplified ideas

pabulum – (n) basic food; insipid intellectual nourishment

pain – (n) an ache, physical anguish

pane – (n) a sheet of glass

pair – (n, v) a set of two; to group into twos

pare – (v) to trim

palate – (n) sense of taste; the roof of the mouth

palette – (n) range of colours in painting, film, etc.; range of skills

pallet – (n) portable platform for moving freight

peak – (n) summit, both literal and figurative (i.e. 'in peak fitness')

peek – (v, n) to take small look; such a look

pique – (v, n) to excite interest in or to hurt someone's pride; wounded pride

pedal – (v, n) to push levers on bicycle; such levers

peddle – (v) to sell

pontificate – (v) to pronounce upon

prevaricate – (v) to be deliberately ambiguous

procrastinate – (v) to put something off until later

prognosticate – (v) to foretell

poor – (adj) without money or possessions

pore – (n, v) skin passage; pore over = to study intently

pour – (v) to flow out

posterity – (n) future generations

prosperity – (n) general wealth and success

precede – (v) to go before

proceed – (v) to go ahead

proceeds – (n) money produced

preclude – (v) to deliberately leave out; to make impossible

principal – (n, adj) the head of school; the highest in rank

principle – (n) fundamental truth; a fundamental source or element

prise – (v) to lever open or out

prize – (v, n) to value; a reward or trophy; to prise (US)

prodigy – (n) young person of genius

progeny – (n) offspring

prone – (adj) lying face downwards; disposed to

prostate – (n) a gland in male mammals

prostrate – (adj) lying stretched out, often in submission

supine – (adj) lying face upwards

rain – (n) precipitation

reign – (v, n) to rule over; such rule

rein – (v, n) to pull back; horse's straps

rebut – (v) to argue against

refute – (v) to disprove

repudiate – (v) to deny or disclaim

reek – (v) to smell strongly and often unpleasantly of

wreak – (v) to inflict (upon)

right – (adj, adv, v, n) correct; not left; to correct; entitlement

rite – (n) ceremonial observance

wright – (n) maker or repairer (usually in compounds)

write – (v) to make letters or words; create software

rort – (n, v) dishonest scheme or fraud; to defraud

taut – (adj) under tension

tort – (n) a civil wrong

torte – (n) type of cake

scald – (v) to injure with hot liquid

scold – (v) to tell someone off

scrimp – (v) to be sparing, especially in spending

skimp – (v) to do or supply insufficiently

sententious – (adj) given to expressing maxims, aphorisms, or moralising

tendentious – (adj) biased, partisan

deleterious – (adj) dangerous, harmful

simulate – (v) to mimic

stimulate – (v) to excite

site – (n) a place

sight – (n) vision

solecism – (n) a minor mistake in grammar, expression or etiquette

solipsism – (n) view that self is only knowable thing

stanch – (v) to stop the flow of

staunch – (adj) firm, steadfast, determined

stationary – (adj) standing still

stationery – (n) writing materials

their – (pron) of them

there – (adv) not here

they're – (v) contracted form of 'they are'

throes – (n) spasms (in the throes of = struggling with)

throws – (v) hurls

tire – (v) get weary

tyre – (n) the rubber outer rim of a wheel

trooper – (n) mounted soldier, US state policeman

trouper – (n) experienced, dependable person

vain – (adj) proud of appearance

vein – (n) blood vessel

valid – (adj) well grounded, convincing, correctly deduced

vapid – (adj) dull, lacking liveliness

vicious – (adj) brutal; dangerous

viscous – (adj) sticky; having a thick glutinous consistency

wage – (n, v) regular payment for work; to engage in an activity, such as war wager – (n, v) bet; to make such a bet

waive – (v) to give up thing have rights to

waiver – (n) an agreement not to pay or
abide by

waver – (v) to show or feel doubt; to sway

weather – (n) atmospheric conditions

wether – (n) castrated ram

whether – (conj) if, in case

while – (prep, v) during; to pass time

wile – (n) cunning, usually plural

CLICHÉ 'STREETS'

Arab St – the Arab world

Civvy St – civilian everyday life

Easy St – the good life

Fleet St – British newspapers

Grub St – literary hacks, particularly
British ones

High St – generic city shopping precinct

K Street – home of US government lobby
groups in Washington DC

Madison Avenue – US advertising world

Mahogany Row – corporate boardrooms

Main St – generic city business centre

Massachusetts Ave – US thinktanks

Queer St – in debt or difficulty

Skid Row – a state of extreme financial
hardship; a squalid area

Struggle St – everyday hardship

Tin Pan Alley – place of popular music
production

Wall St – US stock exchange and financial
centre

FREQUENTLY MISSPELLED

aberrant, abscess, absence, acceptable,
accolade, accommodate, accumulate,
acquaintance, affidavit, aficionado,
algorithm, annihilation, anomalous,
apostasy, auxiliary, beleaguered,
benefited, bouillon, caffeine, caipirinha,
camouflage, Caribbean, cemetery,
census, chameleon, chamomile, chilblain,
collateral, colossal, commiserate,
confectionery, conscientious, consensual,
coruscate, curriculum, deceased, decrepit,
dénouement, desiccated, desperately,
dilapidated, dilettante, disastrous, ecstasy,
effervescence, embarrassment, emissary,
euthanasia, exhilaration, expat(riate),
exuberant, facetious, fiery, fluorescent,
focusing, fusillade, gauge, genealogy,
genuflect, glamorous, governor, guarantee,
haemorrhage, heinous, hierarchy, hindrance,
humorous, hypocrisy, idiosyncrasy,
incandescence, indigenous, indispensable,
indictment, innocuous, inoculate,
intercede, inure, irascibility, irresistible,
leisure, manoeuvre, mayonnaise, medieval,
millennium, minuscule, mischievous,
misspelled, moccasin, necessary,
obsolescence, obstreperous, odyssey,
paraphernalia, pastime, pejorative, perennial,
perseverance, pretence, privilege, profited,
propaganda, propagation, psychiatrist,
pyrrhic, renaissance, rheumatism, rococo,
rhyme, rhythm, saccharine, sacrilege,
sacrilegious, separate, sergeant, skulduggery,
squalor, succumb, supersede, symmetrical,
threshold, toboggan, tourniquet, woollen,
yacht, yield

SECTION 2
CHARACTERISATION

'It is true that ordinarily her voice was shrill, her face hard and sharp as a hatchet, her figure lumpy and her intentions selfish. The softer self came into possession only once or twice a week, and then, ordinarily, in the evening.' — *John Steinbeck,* Tortilla Flat

People are a collection of aspects, physical, mental, spiritual. They can be labelled by their appearance, their occupation, their relations to others, their resemblance to others, real or fictional. They exist in various states, and they act, react and interact. A person or character wears certain clothes, has certain mannerisms and a specific accent, is of a certain class. Their types have been mapped before, in many cases, by great writers.

CHARACTER TYPES

POSITIVE

auteur, bon vivant, cherub, connoisseur, consort, daredevil, doyen, dreamboat, genius, goddess, gourmand, guiding light, guru (sage, swami), hard-body, heart-throb, hero(ine), highbrow, hotshot, hunk, iconoclast, leader, looker, maestro, magnate, master, maven, mentor, messiah, patriot, prodigy, prophet, protégé, raconteur, saviour, scholar, sexpot, showman, sophisticate, stalwart, titan, torchbearer, truth-teller, valentine, virtuoso, warrior, whistleblower, wizard, yummy mummy

NEGATIVE

assassin, blabbermouth, blackguard, blowhard, bludger, bootlegger, bore, bozo, braggart, brute, buffoon, bumpkin, cad, charlatan, chav, cipher, con man, couch potato, crackpot, crank, creep, criminal, crybaby, culprit, cur, curmudgeon, deadbeat, degenerate, delinquent, demagogue, desperado, despot, dink, drudge, dunce, egghead, femme fatale, fiend, foe, fogey, fool (buffoon, idiot), frat-boy, fugitive, gadfly, ganglord, gangster, gasbag, geriatric, ghoul, glutton, gold-digger, goon, greenhorn, gringo, grouch, guerrilla, harpy, harridan, hausfrau, hillbilly, hitman, hoodlum, hooligan, hothead, hustler, hypocrite, infidel, ingénue, interloper, junkie, kidult, killjoy, know-it-all, kook, larrikin, libber, loser, Lothario, lounge-lizard, lunatic, mafioso, malingerer, maneater, maniac, marauder, minion, minx, miscreant, miser, misfit, misogynist, moll, naïf, narcissist, neanderthal, nerd, nincompoop, no-hoper, oaf, obsessive, oddball, opponent, outlaw, pariah, patsy, philanderer, philistine, pimp, pointy-head, popinjay, psychopath, puppet, quack, rabble-rouser, rake, rapscallion, rascal, rebel, redneck, renegade, reprobate, rogue, rookie, roustabout, rubbernecker, ruffian, scoundrel, shirker, show pony, shrew, shyster, simpleton, sissy, slacker, slave, smarty-pants, snitch, snob, sociopath, spinster, spoilsport, sticky beak, stoner, stooge, sycophant, thief, thug, toady, tosser, traitor, trophy, truant, turncoat, twerp, tyrant, villain, voyeur, vulgarian, weirdo, whippersnapper, witch, wretch, yeoman, yob, yokel, yuppie, zealot

DESCRIPTIVE

accomplice, acolyte, activist, adversary, aesthete, aficionado, agnostic, alter-ego, alumnus, amazon, ancestor, aristocrat, artisan, atavist (genetic throwback), avatar, banshee, barfly, beau, belle, boffin, bohemian, bookworm, breadwinner, burgher, cadaver (corpse, stiff), chatterbox, citizen, cohort, collaborator, colleague, companion, compatriot, débutante, dilettante, dissident, diva, divorcee, dowager, everyman, exile, expatriate, fiancé(e), figurehead, firebrand, flirt, foreigner, friend (ally, buddy, chum, cohort, mate, pal), geek, grandee, hippie, hipster, homesteader, husband, impresario, incumbent, innocent, jock, kingpin, libertine, mannequin, martyr, maverick, mistress, neighbour, neophyte, nomad, orphan, outcast, outsider, passenger, patriarch, patron, pauper, peacenik, peasant, peer, penitent, pensioner / senior citizen, pilgrim, playboy, pragmatist, predecessor, pundit, ragamuffin, recluse, refusenik, ringleader, salary man, scion, sheik, sibling, sidekick, singleton, sissy, socialite, soulmate, stickler, sugar daddy, suitor, surrogate, survivor, suspect, swashbuckler, tomboy, underdog, veteran, victim, volunteer, waif, wife

Male

adolescent, bachelor, beau, bloke, boy, boyfriend, brother, chap, cousin, dude, father, fellow, friend, gent(leman), grandfather, guy, herr, husband, kid, lad, lover, man, master, mate, nephew, partner, patriarch, sibling, son, squire, teen(ager), toyboy, uncle, youngster, youth

Female

adolescent, aunt, bachelorette, belle, chick, cousin, damsel, daughter, frau, fraulein, friend, girl, girlfriend, grandmother, kid, lady, lass, lover, madam, maiden, mate, matriarch, milf, miss, mother, nan, niece, partner, sibling, sister, teen/ager, tomboy, wife, woman

Young person

adolescent, babe, baby, boy, child, daughter, girl, hellion, infant, juvenile, kid, lad, lass, minor, newborn, nipper, offspring, preschooler, prodigy, schoolchild, son, teen/ager, toddler, tween, tyke, urchin, youngster, youth, wunderkind

OCCUPATIONS

academic, accountant, administrator, adviser, agent, analyst, architect, artist, assistant, athlete, attendant, author (writer), banker, beggar, boss, broker, buccaneer, builder, bureaucrat, careerist, celebrity (personality, public figure, star), civil servant, cleaner, clerk, coach, con artist, consort, consultant, contractor, courtesan, crew, critic, croupier, curator, custodian, customer, designer, developer, diplomat, doctor, driver, editor, emissary, employee, employer, engineer, entertainer, entrepreneur, escort, executive, exporter, farmer, financier, follower, gatekeeper, guard, guide, henchman, host, hunter, importer, industrialist, instructor, interpreter, interrogator, inventor, investigator, investor, labourer, landlord, lawyer, leader, magnate, manager, mandarin, manufacturer, marketeer, master, mediator, medic, mercenary, merchant, messenger, model, musician, nanny, negotiator, nurse, officer, operator, organiser, philanthropist, planner, politician, prostitute, publisher, pundit, referee, representative, retailer (trader, vendor), scientist, servant, sex worker, shaman, slave, soldier, sportsperson, spy, statesman, student, teacher, teammate, technician, technologist, therapist, thespian, tradesman, trainer, tutor, tycoon, wheeler-dealer, wonk, worker

CHARACTER TYPES: UNUSUAL

agent provocateur (troublemaker), amanuensis (dictation secretary), anchorite / autarkist (hermit), anorak / trainspotter (obsessive geek), apparatchik (an unquestioningly loyal subordinate), arriviste (an ambitious or recently successful person), autodidact (self-taught person), Brahmin (highly cultured person), brigand (one of band of robbers), Bunbury (imaginary person, used as an excuse to do something), carpetbagger (an outsider who presumptuously seeks an important local position), charlatan (one who falsely claims professional expertise), chatelaine (madame of large house), chorine (chorus girl), clochard (vagrant), coxcomb (fool), dandy / fop (man preoccupied with his vanity), deipnosophist (one skilled in dinner conversation), denizen (person inhabiting particular place), doppelgänger (double of living person, originally ghostly), éminence grise (person of great influence without official position), enfant terrible (unorthodox but talented individual), epigone (mediocre imitator, follower of known artist), factotum (multitasking person), famulus (personal attendant), farceur (a writer or actor of farce, joker), flâneur (an aimless stroller), flibbertigibbet (scatterbrained chatterer), frondeur (political rebel), giglet (a rude person; a giggly girl), hegemon (paramount leader), janissary (elite devoted follower), jobsworth (lowly official who follows rules to the letter), legatee (recipient of a legacy), lotus-eater (a lazy pleasure seeker), malefactor (wrongdoer), majordomo (head of household), mensch (honorable, dependable person), nabob (wealthy or influential person), niggard (stingy person), oligarch (one of small ruling faction), opsimath (person who studies or learns late in life), panjandrum (a powerful or self-important person), Pantaloon (fool), pariah (social outcast), parvenu (recent arrival

to higher social class), pasha (one of high rank), pettifogger (a petty untrustworthy lawyer), philistine (one with no interest in or appreciation of higher arts), pilgarlic (bald-headed person), polymath (one who is learned at more than one subject), quidnunc (nosy person or gossip), quisling (one who aids an enemy), roué (debauched man given to drinking and womanising), scallywag (rascal), swain (lover or young country man), swami (Hindu religious teacher or mystic), trustafarian (slacker of inherited wealth, especially in Britain), *Übermensch* (superior person or demi-god), valetudinarian (person excessively concerned with their ill health), virago (a fierce woman), vizier (senior officer in Muslim government), wallah (person responsible for particular duty)

CHARACTER TYPES: HISTORICAL

Caesar, centurion, conquistador, dragoman (formerly an interpreter in Arabic or Middle Eastern countries), emperor, haruspex (one who predicted the future by way of animal entrails), pasha (officer in Turkey and north Africa), pharaoh, viceroy, tartar

STOCK CHARACTERS

absent-minded professor, antihero, born loser, boy next door, casanova, charmer, cheerleader / prom queen (evil, kind-hearted, originally ugly, overconfident), chosen one / messiah, cop (rule-breaker, stickler), dodgy geezer / wideboy, double agent, enforcer, jock (dumb, evil, kind-hearted), drill sergeant (evil, kind-hearted), fall guy, final girl (last on screen in horror film), gangster / hood, geek / nerd, geek girl (socially inept, secret beauty), hero / heroine (flawed, offbeat), idiot savant, loose cannon, loveable rogue, naysayer / Eyeore, oddball, outsider (genius, kind-hearted, rich, troubled), plain jane (bad hair, braces, glasses, unibrow, secretly beautiful), rebel / troublemaker, rookie (fast-learning, moral), sidekick (annoying, clumsy, foolish, incompetent, likeable, specifically talented), stoner (wise), wise fool

CHARACTER TYPES BY TRAIT

Antihero: Terry Malloy from Elia Kazan's film *On the Waterfront*, James diGriz in the Harry Harrison series of *Stainless Steel Rat* sci-fi novels, Jim Stark from the film *Rebel Without a Cause*, Henry Dorsett Case from William Gibson's novel *Neuromancer*

Charming troublemaker: Bart Simpson from *The Simpsons* TV series, Ferris Bueller from John Hughes' film *Ferris Bueller's Day Off*

Constructed reality: Truman Burbank from Peter Weir's film *The Truman Show*, Neo (Thomas Anderson) in the Wachowski brothers' film *The Matrix* and sequels, Henry Dorsett Case from William Gibson's novel *Neuromancer*

Female action hero: Buffy, Ellen Ripley from the *Alien* film series, Sarah Connor from film *Terminator 2*, Sydney Bristow from the *Alias* TV series, Trinity from *The Matrix* film series, Lara Croft from the *Tomb Raider* games and movies, Wonder Woman from the comic and TV series, Xena from the TV series

Faustian hero: Barton Fink from Coen brothers' film of the same name, Harry Angel from film *Angel Heart*, Johnny Blaze from film *Ghost Rider*, Manfred from Lord Byron's poem of the same name, Seymour Krelborn from the play and film *Little Shop of Horrors*, Stanley Moon from the film *Bedazzled*, Dorian Gray from Oscar Wilde's novel *The Picture of Dorian Gray*

Infidelity: Molly Bloom from James Joyce's novel *Ulysses*, Madame Bovary in Gustave Flaubert's novel of the same name

Joie de vivre: Falstaff from Shakespeare

Mad scientist: Professor Barnhardt from the film *The Day the Earth Stood Still*, Doc Brown from the *Back to the Future* film series, Victor Frankenstein from Mary Shelley's novel *Frankenstein*, Dr Strangelove from Stanley Kubrick's film of the same name

Machiavellian: Dr Gregory House in the TV programme *House MD*

Madness: King Lear, Bertha Mason (mad woman in attic in Charlotte Brontë's *Jane Eyre*), RP McMurphy from Milos Forman film *One Flew Over the Cuckoo's Nest*

Male action hero: Bruce Lee in his kung fu movies, D'Artagnan from *The Three Musketeers*, Jack Bauer from the *24* TV series, Indiana Jones, James Bond, Jason Bourne, John McClane from the *Die Hard* film series, Luke Skywalker and Han Solo, Neo from *The Matrix* film series, Robin Hood, Tarzan, Zorro

Moral hero: Lawyer Atticus Finch from Harper Lee's novel *To Kill a Mockingbird*, Marshall Will Kane in the western film *High Noon*, Captain James T Kirk from the *Star Trek* TV series

Obsequiousness: Uriah Heep in Charles Dickens' novel *David Copperfield*, Reverend William Collins in Jane Austen's novel *Pride and Prejudice*, the high-end retailer Mr Hollister in Garry Marshall's film *Pretty Woman*

Paranoiac: Jerry Fletcher from the film *Conspiracy Theory*, Brill from the film *Enemy of the State*

Power behind the throne: Grima Wormtongue in *The Lord of the Rings*

Rebel: Holden Caulfield from JD Salinger's novel *The Catcher in the Rye*, Jim Stark from the film *Rebel Without a Cause*

Seducer: Don Juan, Casanova, Cleopatra, James Bond, Marquis de Sade, Mata Hari, the sirens from Greek mythology

Tomboy: Calamity Jane from books and films about the historical frontierswoman's life, George from Enid Blyton's *Famous Five* series of children's novels, Jo March from Louisa May Alcott's novel *Little Women*, Laura from *Little House on the Prairie*, Scout from Harper Lee's *To Kill a Mockingbird*

Tortured hero: Heathcliff from Emily Brontë's novel *Wuthering Heights*

Unquestioning obedience: Mr Parsons in George Orwell's novel *Nineteen Eighty-Four*

Villain: Nurse Mildred Ratched from Milos Forman's film *One Flew Over the Cuckoo's Nest*, Abanazar from *Aladdin*, HAL-9000 in the film *2001: A Space Odyssey*

Wallflower: Laura Wingfield in Tennessee Williams play *The Glass Menagerie*

HUMAN DESCRIPTIONS

POSITIVE

adaptable, adventurous, affable, affectionate, alert, ambitious, animated, ardent, articulate, astute, attentive, brainy, brawny, calm, candid, capable, charming, chaste, cheerful, chivalrous, clucky, compassionate, confident, competent, congenial, consistent, contrite, cooperative, cordial, courteous, crafty, creative, cunning, curious, decisive, dedicated, defiant, demure, devoted, devout, dexterous, diligent, dogged, doughty, dreamy, droll, earnest, easy-going, ebullient, educated, efficient, eloquent, endearing, energetic, engaging, enthusiastic, erudite, faithful, feisty, flinty, forgiving, friendly, frisky, generous, genial, genteel, gentle, glad, gleeful, gregarious, hardworking, helpful, honest, honourable, humane, humble, independent, informed, innovative, inquisitive, inspirational, intrepid, intuitive, jocular, kindhearted, learned, liberal, likeable, loyal, majestic, mellow, open, patient, pawky (sly, dryly humorous), perky, pleasant, plucky, polite, reliable, respectable, sassy, self-made, sensible, sensitive, serene, shrewd, sincere, skilled, smart, sophisicated, spontaneous, stable, steely, suave, sultry, sweet, tactful, tenacious, thorough, thoughtful, tolerant, unflappable, upbeat, upright, urbane, versatile, vigilant, virile, well-groomed, well-heeled, well-mannered, wily, winsome, witty, wordly

NEGATIVE

acerbic, adulterous, aggressive, aloof, angsty, antisocial, anxious, arrogant, austere, authoritarian, batty, bellicose, belligerent, benign, berserk, bilious, bitter, bland, boorish, brittle, brusque, bumptious, callous, cantankerous, caustic, censorious, chauvinistic, churlish, clownish, closed-minded, clumsy, cocky, cold-blooded, common, condescending, conniving, contemptuous, contrary, corrupt, cowering, crabby, cranky, craven, crazy, creepy, crestfallen, culpable, cynical, daft, decrepit, deranged, destitute, devious, dim, dippy, disingenuous, dissolute, dour (glum, morose, saturnine, sullen), duplicitous, dysfunctional, dyspeptic, evil, exasperating, expedient, facetious, farouche (shy but cranky), feckless, fickle, flaky, flighty, foolish, forlorn, foul-mouthed, fractious, frail, fretful, gauche, glib, gormless, grandiose, greedy, guileful, guileless, gullible, hapless, haughty, hen-pecked, high-maintenance, histrionic, hopeless, hostile, hubristic, humourless, hypocritical, hysterical, icy, impatient, imperious, impetuous, implacable, inefficient, insecure, intolerant, irascible, irritating, listless, louche, lowbrow, lumbering, macho, malevolent, malicious, masochistic, maudlin, mean, mean-spirited, meek, melancholic, menacing, mendacious, messed-up, misanthropic, misogynistic, moody, morose, mouth-breathing, murderous, myopic, naive, narcissistic, narrow-minded, needy, neurotic, nondescript, oafish, obdurate, oblivious, obsequious, obstreperous, odious, offhand, paranoid, passive-aggressive, pathetic, peaky, peevish (querulous, complaining), petulant, philandering, phony, pompous, possessive, predatory, preening, prickly, priggish, prim, prissy, profligate, prolix, puckish, pugnacious, puritanical, restive (impatient, difficult to control), righteous, ruthless, sadistic, sanctimonious, scatterbrained, schizophrenic, self-centred, self-indulgent, self-interested, self-pitying, self-righteous, shrill, simpering, skanky, smug, snappish, snarky, snide, sniffy, snobbish, snooty, solipsistic (characteristic of extreme egotism), sour, spiteful, splenetic (irritable or spiteful), stingy, stroppy, stubborn, stupid (clueless, dumb, foolishness, idiotic, moronic), sullen, supercilious, surly, tetchy, timid, tortured, treacherous, troubled, truculent, unctuous, underemployed, unhinged, unravelling, uppity, uptight, vacuous, vain, vapid, vile, vindictive, vinegary, violent, virile, vitriolic, vituperative, whitebread (milquetoast, n), wicked, vulgar, wayward, withdrawn, work-shy

NEUTRAL OR AMBIGUOUS

acquiescent, anarchic, androgynous, bashful, bereft, besotted, biddable, blasé, blithe, bluff, bohemian, brooding, cagey, cerebral, complicated, conflicted, confused, conservative, coy, diehard, diffident, diminutive, docile, eccentric, extroverted, fey, flamboyant, flirty, frugal, furtive, gamine, garrulous, giddy, goofy, grave, highbrow, impassive, inscrutable, insouciant, introspective, introverted, itinerant, laconic, loquacious, love-struck, lugubrious, meticulous, middlebrow, mild-mannered, mischievous, naughty, nomadic, nonchalant, notorious, obsessive, ostentatious, passive, patrician, pedantic, penitent, peripatetic, pious, placid, quirky, rebellious, regal, reluctant, repentant, restless, rueful, sanguine, sceptical, shy, sly, smitten, sober, solemn, sombre, stern, stoic(al), subdued, superstitious, taciturn, talkative, teetotal, thrusting, tipsy, tongue-tied, unemployed, unrepentant, vocal, volatile, voluble, vulnerable, wary, world-weary

PHYSICAL ASPECTS

APPEARANCE

archetype, attribute, behaviour, caricature, character, characteristic, cliché, complexion, countenance, criterion, disposition, ethos, feature, figure, garb, humour, ideal, idiosyncracy, impression, lines, looks, mannerism, measure, model, morality, peculiarity, persona, personality, physiognomy, stamp, stereotype, temperament, trait, type

BODY

parts: artery, bone, bowel, brain, cartilage, flesh, gristle, gut, hair, heart, liver, lungs, muscle, sinew, skin, skull, spine, spleen, stomach, torso, trunk, vein; bodily fluid: blood, milk, menses, mucus, perspiration, phlegm, pus, saliva, semen, sperm, spittle, sweat, tears, urine, vomit

BODY HAIR

body hair: down, lanugo (fine hair on newborns and anorexics), pubic, stubble, terminal (thick and dark), vellus (fine and light); facial hair description: bare-faced, bearded, goateed, grizzled, hirsute, pogonotrophy (growing of facial hair), salt and pepper; facial hair: beard, chin puff, five o'clock shadow, Fu Manchu (a moustache that extends down beyond the jaw), goatee,

handlebar moustache, Hitler / Charlie Chaplin, imperial (a small triangular patch under the lip), mutton chops, RAF, stubble, vandyke (a goatee connected to the moustache), whiskers; famous moustaches: Albert Einstein, Magnum PI, Stalin, Village People; famous stubble: Don Johnson in *Miami Vice*, George Michael; famous beards: Charles Darwin, Ernest Hemingway, Grizzly Adams, John Lennon, Karl Marx, ZZ Top

BOTTOM

arse / ass, backside, bottom, bum, butt(ocks), callipygous / steatopygous (having well-proportioned or fat buttocks), derrière, haunches, rear, rump; famous bums: Beyonce, Jennifer Lopez, Kylie Minogue, Marilyn Monroe

CHEST

barrel, buff, gym, pigeon; breast parts: areola, mammary, nipple; alternative: amazon, buxom, cleavage, corset, décolletage, embonpoint, implant, mammary, pectoral, pneumatic, thoracic, other: corset, brassiere, lingerie

DEMEANOUR

attitude, bearing, bent, calibre, carriage, cast, character, comportment, constitution, deportment, disposition, ego, front, gravitas, gravity, guise, inclination, makeup, manner, mentality, mettle, mien, mindset, nature, outlook, personality, poise, pose, posture, presence, sensibility, spirit, stance, temperament, timbre

Persona

anima, avatar, caricature, character, cipher, effigy, emulation, entity, facade, guise, identity, imago, imitation, impersonation, imposture, incarnation, manifestation, mask, masque, mimesis, mirror, pantomime, personality, personification, portrayal, representation, self, simulacrum

FACE

parts: brows, cheeks, chin, dewlap / jowls, ears, eyes, facial hair, hairline, lashes, lips, mouth, nose, wrinkles; jaw: cleft, clenched, mandible (lower jaw), maxilla (upper jaw), orthognathous (having a non-projecting jaw), prognathous (having a projecting jaw), square; complexion: flushed, jaundiced, pale, pallor, sallow, swarthy; face shape: diamond, heart, oblong, oval, pear, rectangular, round, square, triangular

Eye

colour: amber, blue, brown, green, grey, hazel; movement: blink, dilate, flicker, flutter, saccade, wink; look: gaze, glance, glare, glimpse, peek, peer, scan, see, sight, squint, stare, watch; part: bags, cornea, crow's feet, eyebrow, eyelash, eyelid, iris, lens, pupil, retina, sclera (white), sty, tear duct

Facial expressions

blank, deadpan, frown, grimace, grin, laugh, moue (pout), pained, poker, rictus, scowl, smile

Lips

pouty, rubbery, thin; famous lips: Angelina Jolie, Fat Albert, Jocelyn Wildenstein, Mick Jagger, Mona Lisa, Scarlett Johansson, Steven Tyler

Look

angry, apathetic, arch, blank, bored, carefree, come-hither, concerned, confused, daggers, deadpan, dismissive, downward, fascinated, focused, friendly, grimacing, happy, hopeful, hopeless, insulted, inviting, laughing, longing, menacing, mocking, mystified, open, petulant, pleading, polite, quizzical, sad, scathing, searching, seductive, smiling, smouldering, smug, sorrowful, surprised, terrified, thoughtful, unconcerned, unfocused, unfriendly, unhappy, unreadable, unsurprised, vacant, withering, worried

Nose

parts: ala (wing), bridge / dorsum (ridge), nostril or naris, philtrum (ridge below nose), septum (membrane between nostrils), tip; types: aquiline / Roman (prominent bridge), bulbous, hooked ('Jewish'), 'Nubian' (wide-nostrilled), pug, retrousse, ski jump, turned-up, snub, straight; famous noses: Barry Manilow, Cleopatra (in René Goscinny and Albert Uderzo's *Asterix and Cleopatra*), Cyrano de Bergerac, Gerard Depardieu, Jean-Baptiste Grenouille, Michael Jackson, Pinocchio, Sneezy

Teeth

buck, gapped, Hollywood, vampire, whitened; type: baby, canine, fang, incisor, milk, molar, wisdom; other: braces, bridge, crown, denture, enamel, filling, tartar, veneer; famous teeth: Austin Powers, the Big Bad Wolf, Dracula, Freddie Mercury, George Washington, Janet Street-Porter,

Julia Roberts, Ken Dodd, Mike Tyson, Ricky Gervais, the Wife of Bath

FIGURE

apple, athletic, beanpole, bootylicious, courgette, curvy (built, curvaceous, junoesque, Monroe-esque, rubenesque, shapely, sonsy, stacked, voluptuous), flabby, hourglass, pear, stick; historical body theories: ectomorphic, endomorphic, mesomorphic

HAIR COLOUR

ash, auburn, black, blonde, brown, ginger, grey, red, salt and pepper, strawberry blonde, streaked, thinning, white

HANDS AND ARMS

type: artist's, bony, gnarled, hand model's, piano player's, thin; finger nail: cuticle, lunula (= crescent of white at base), quick; action: clap, gesture, gesticulate, smack, wave; arm parts: armpit, bicep, elbow, forearm, funny bone, knuckle, palm, shoulder, tricep (chicken wings), wrist

LEGS AND FEET

legs: bow-legged (knees apart), knock-kneed (knees together), pigeon-toed (toes pointing inward), splayed feet (toes pointing outward); feet: fallen arches, flat-footed, tiptoe

MOVEMENT

gait, limp; posture: academic stoop, dowager's hump, hunchback, kyphosis (outward curvature of spine), lordosis (inward curvature of spine), Quasimodo, ramrod, Sergeant Major, slacker, slouch

SKIN

marks: birthmark, eczema, freckle, mole, piercing, rash, tattoo, wart; complexion: Aryan, black, bronzed, brown, dark, etiolated, fair, freckled, melanin, Mediterranean, mocha, olive, pale, permatan, ruddy, swarthy, tanned

SMELL

aroma, body odour (BO), cologne, fragrance, musk, perfume, perspiration, olfactory, pheromone, pong / reek / stink / stench, pungency, redolence, scent, sniff, sweat

STOMACH

abdomen, beer belly, breadbasket, gastric, gut, indigestion, muffin top, paunch, pot belly, six pack, solar plexus, tummy, washboard, whisky belly

HUMAN DESCRIPTIONS: PHYSICAL

POSITIVE

burly, chiselled, comatose, comely, curvy (built, curvaceous, junoesque, Monroe-esque, Rubenesque, shapely, sonsy, stacked, voluptuous), dapper, dishy, elegant, fit (buff, toned), handsome, hunky, kittenish, limber (lissome, supple), natty, nubile, rugged, sexy, shaggy, short, silken, small (petite), studly, sturdy, svelte, tall (leggy, lofty, long-limbed, towering), tanned (bronzed, mahogany), thin (delicate, lean, slender, slight, slim)

NEGATIVE

arthritic, ashen-faced, bedridden, bleary, bulimic, cack-handed, cadaverous, clumsy, comatose, dowdy, dyslexic, emaciated, faded, frail, gawky, glowering, groggy, haggard, jittery, klutzy, mumsy, pallid, peaky, pinched, pouty, puny, queasy, runty, sallow, sclerotic, short (pint-sized, small, squat, stunted, tiny, undersized), snaggle-toothed, strutting, swaggering, tall (gangly, giant, lanky), tanned (permatan, tanorexic), thin (anorexic, beanpole, bony, bulimic, emaciated, reedy, skinny), threadbare, ugly, wan

NEUTRAL OR AMBIGUOUS

ageing (baby-boomer, elderly, older, senior, superannuated), baby-faced, bespectacled, big bosomed, décolleté (with bare neck and shoulders), deshabillé (undressed or partially dressed), donnish, epicene (androgynous, asexual, effeminate, gamine), etiolated (pale, especially due to lack of sunlight), feline, jolie laide (attractive but not conventionally beautiful), pale, paraplegic, petite, protean (changeable in form), rangy, short (diminutive, little, stocky, tiny), tetraplegic, trembling, willowy

VOICES

accent, articulation, brogue, burr, cadence, coloratura, colour, consonant, croon, delivery, dialect, diction, diphthong, drawl, embouchure, enunciation, growl, guffaw, harmonic, idiom, inflection, intonation, lilt, lisp, modulation, murmur, music, nasality, oratory, phrase, pitch, plangency, polemic, power, pronunciation, quality, range, register, resonance, reverberance, rhetoric, rhythm, rumble, shrillness, slur, sonority, sotto voce, squillo, stammer, stress, stridence, stutter, tessitura, timbre, tone, treble, trill, twang, undertone, vernacular, vibrancy, vibrato, vowel, warble, whisper

SINGING VOICE

female: soprano, mezzo-soprano, contralto (alto); male: countertenor, tenor, baritone, bass (castrato, falsetto, treble)

TONE OR QUALITY

adenoidal, bombastic, booming, breathy, bullfrog, chesty, clipped, cracked, crackling, croaky, cut-glass, droning, dulcet, flat, foghorn, fruity, gravelly, gruff, gurgling, halting, hoarse, husky, inflected, kvetching, lazy, lilting, low, mellifluous, melodic, movie trailer (Don LaFontaine, Hal Douglas), muffled, musical, nasal, plummy, radio DJ, rasping, received pronunciation (RP), reedy, rich, rotund, round(ed), rumbling, sententious, sepulchral, shrill, silky, slow, smoky, sneering, soft, sonorous, squeaky, staccato, stentorian, sultry, tinny, tremulous, undertone, urgent, ventriloquist, warm

ACCENTS, DIALECTS, LANGUAGE

US accents
African-American, Appalachian, Baltimore, Boston, Midland, New England, New Jersey, New Orleans, New York, North Central (Fargo), Philadelphia, South Carolina, Southern drawl, Texan

English regional accents
Black Country (Wolverhampton), Brummy (Birmingham), Cornish (Cornwall),

Estuary (London and surrounds),
Geordie (Newcastle upon Tyne), Mackem
(Sunderland), Mancunian (Manchester),
Pitmatic (Northumberland and Durham),
Scouse (Liverpool), Tyke (Yorkshire), West
Country (south-west England); others:
Cockney (East Midlands), East Anglia
(Norwich etc.), Grimsby (Lincolnshire,
Lancashire, Norwich, Oxford, Sheffield)

Other accents

Australian Aboriginal, Australian,
Canadian, Indian, Irish (Cork, Dublin,
Donegal, Kerry, Limerick, Londonderry,
Ulster), Jamaican, Maori, Native American,
New Zealand, Scottish (Aberdeen, Borders,
Edinburgh, Fife, Glasgow, Inverness,
Shetland Islands, West Highlands),
Singlish, South African, Welsh (Cardiff,
North Wales, South Wales)

Slang types

Cockney rhyming (English working-class
variety), Grypsera (Polish prison slang),
Mat (Russian slang, heavily sexual), Polari
(UK slang, traditionally used by gay and
theatre subcultures), Singlish (Singaporean
English creole), Verlan (French teenage
slang)

Youth language

awesome, bail, bare, bling, breh, bro, co-
dee, diss, dope, dude, epic, fiend, gay, ghey,
gnarly, grody, heinous, honed, jingus, killer,
laters, like, mega, meh, mugged, pee, peeps,
phat, piff, pinky, player, rad, seen, shizzle,
sick, so, stunting, totally, trippin', wack,
whatever, wicked

PHYSICAL APPEARANCE

HAIRSTYLES

afro, beehive, bob, bouffant, bowl cut, braids,
bun, buzz cut, Caesar cut, chignon (knot
at nape of neck), chonmage (Sumo cut),
coiffure, comb-over, cornrow, crew cut,
crop, curls, cut and blow dry, dreadlocks,
fauxhawk, French braid, fringe (bangs),
hairdo, highlights, Jheri curl (loose, greasy
curl popular in 1980s), mohawk/mohican
(shaved at sides, spiked ridge at top),
mullet (short in front, long in back), No
1, pageboy (longer bob), periwig/peruke
(17th–18th-century man's wig), perm,
pigtails, pompadour (gelled and brushed up
from forehead), ponytail, plait, quiff, rattail,
ringlets, short back and sides, skinhead,
tonsure, toupe, whiffle cut (short haircut of
US soldiers in WWII), wig

CLOTHES

anorak, Bermuda shorts, blouse, boa, bodice,
bolero (a woman's lightweight short jacket),
breeches, bustle, cagoule (a weatherproof
jacket, often knee-length), camisole, cape,
cargo pants, cassock, chaps, chemise, cloak,
codpiece, corset, cowl, cravat, culottes,
cummerbund, domino (historical jacket
with hood worn at masked balls), downie
(down jacket), duffle coat, dungarees,
fisherman's jacket, gilet (a woman's padded
waistcoat), gown, guernsey (a patterned
knitted jumper), habit, halter neck,
Hawaiian shirt, hoodie, jeans, jerkin (man's
jacket without sleeves), jersey (woollen
jumper), jodhpurs, kilt, lederhosen, mantilla
(a lace shawl worn by women in Spain
and Latin America), mantle, moleskins,

muu-muu, negligee, overalls, overcoat, overskirt, pannier (an 18th-century skirt support), parka, petticoat, plus fours, poncho, robe, sari, sarong, scarf, shawl, stockings, suit, tank top, tie, toga, trench coat, trousers, tunic, underskirt, vest, waistcoat, wimple (head covering of nuns)

Exotic clothes

abaya (an Islamic black robe), araqchin (an Islamic cloth cap), burka (a full body cloak for Muslim women), chador (women's cloak worn in Iran and Pakistan), cheongsam (a tight, one-piece Chinese dress for women), dhoti (a sarong-like Indian Hindu garment for men), djabella (an Egyptian male garb), fustanella (the white pleated skirt of Greek soldiers), jilbab (the long loose coat worn by Muslim women), keffiyeh / shemagh (Palestinian neckscarf), kimono (a long-sleeved Japanese robe), niqab (Muslim veil for face), shalwar kameez (South Asian tunic and pyjama-like trousers), soutane (cassock, often buttoned at front), thawb / dishdasha (a Middle Eastern, robe-like, ankle-length garment, often with long sleeves)

Historical clothes

doublet (a man's tight jacket), chiton (basic floor-length garment in Ancient Greece), farthingale (an Elizabethan skirt support), frock coat (a man's 19th-century, knee-length coat), himation (cloak-like garment in Ancient Greece), peplos (body-length garment in Ancient Greece), toga

HATS

Akubra, Ascot cap, baseball cap, beanie, beaver, beret, boater, bonnet, bowler, bucket hat, Cossack hat, cheesecutter, chullo, cloche, cloth cap, coolie, cowboy hat, deerstalker, derby, fedora, felt hat, fez, flat cap, homburg, hood, kepi (French military), kippah, kufi, Panama hat, pill box, pork pie, skullcap, slouch hat, sombrero, stetson, tam, taqiyah, top hat, topi, toque (chef), tricorn, trilby, turban, yarmulke, zucchetto

SHOES

Balmoral, Birkenstock, blucher, boat shoe, boot, brogue, cleat shoe, clog, court, cross trainer, derby, galoshes, gumboo, high heel, hiking boot, hi-top, jandal, loafer, moccasin, mule, Oxford, platform, rollerblade, running shoe, sandal, skate, slipper, sneaker, snow shoe, stiletto, thong, trainer, tramping boot, walking shoe, Wellington boot; historical: brodequin, espadrille, patten, poulaine, sabot

HUMAN STATES

POSITIVE

accomplishment, acumen, admiration, affection, affinity, affirmation, agreement, allure, amusement, aplomb, approval, ardour, atonement, awe, benevolence, bliss, bonhomie, bravura, brilliance, buzz, camaraderie, candour, catharsis, caution, celebration, charisma, cheerfulness, chivalry, civility, clarity, companionship, compassion, competence, composure, conscience, consolation, contrition, courage, courtesy, credence, decency, decision, decorum, dedication, derring-do, dignity, discernment, discretion, earnestness, ease, ebullience, ecstasy, endearment, enthusiasm, epiphany, erudition, euphoria, exhilaration, exuberance, fantasy, fascination, favour, fervour, fidelity, finesse, flair, forgiveness, freedom, friendship, generosity, genius, gladness, glee, gratitude, gregariousness, gumption, happiness, hilarity, honesty, honour, hope, ingenuity, innocence, insouciance, inspiration, integrity, intelligence, joy, knack, leisure, liberty, liking, love, loyalty, luck, mercy, merit, mettle, mirth, modesty, moral, mystique, panache, patience, perfection, pleasantness, pluck, politeness, prestige, proficiency, profundity, promise, propriety, prosperity, prowess, rapport, rapture, refinement, rejoicing, relief, respect, revelation, reward, righteousness, salvation, satisfaction, scruple, self-composure, serenity, skill, spirit, success, succour, tact, tolerance, triumph, truth, vigour, vim, virility, virtue, vitality, wealth, will(power), willingness, wisdom, wonder, worth, zeal, zest

NEGATIVE

abandonment, absent-mindedness, accusation, acrimony, adversity, affectation, aggravation, aggression, aggressiveness, alarm, alienation, aloofness, anathema, anger, angst, anguish, animosity, annoyance, antagonism, antipathy, anxiety, apathy, apprehension, arrogance, attack, audacity, avoidance, bafflement, bereavement, betrayal, bigotry, bile, bitterness, blame, boredom, bravado, bribery, brinkmanship, burden, capriciousness, chagrin, cheek, chutzpah, cold sweat, complicity,

condescension, confinement, confrontation, confusion, conspiracy, consternation, contempt, corruption, cowardice, credulity, crisis, curse, cynicism, death, debauchery, debt, deceit, deception, defeat, deflation, delusion, demise, denial, dependence, depravity, depression, deprivation, derision, despair, deterioration, detriment, difficulty, disappointment, disapproval, disbelief, discomfort, discourtesy, disdain, disfavour, disgust, dishonesty, dishonour, disillusionment, dislike, dismay, disobedience, disorganisation, disparagement, dispossession, disrepute, disrespect, dissatisfaction, distaste, doom, dotage, doubt, dread, drudgery, dysfunction, effrontery, embarrassment, enmity, ennui, envy, evil, exasperation, failure, fear, folly, foolishness, foreboding, fright, frustration, funk, fury, gaucherie, gloom, grief, grimace, grudge, grumpiness, guile, guilt, hardship, hatred, heartache, heartbreak, hindrance, hopelessness, horror, hostility, hubris, humiliation, hurt, hypocrisy, ignominy, ignorance, illness, immorality, impatience, imperfection, indifference, indignation, indignity, indolence, ineptitude, inferiority, ingratitude, insanity, insensitivity, insolence, intolerance, ire, jealousy, jeopardy, jingoism, lassitude, laziness, lechery, loathing, loneliness, loss, lunacy, malaise, malevolence, malice, meanness, melancholy, menace, misanthropy, misconduct, misery, mistrust, monotony, mourning, negligence, nerve, neurosis, notoriety, opprobrium, outrage, pain, panic, paranoia, peril, pessimism, petulance, pique, pomposity, poverty, prank, prejudice, privation (deprivation by others or self), punishment, qualm, rage, rancour,

recalcitrance, regret, rejection, reproach,
resentment, retaliation, retribution, revenge,
revulsion, ridicule, rivalry, ruin, sadness,
sanctimony, scorn, self-doubt, servility,
shame, shamelessness, shock, showmanship,
sin (envy, gluttony, greed, lust, pride,
sloth, wrath), slight, sorrow, spite, spleen,
stress, strife, struggle, stupidity, subjection,
suffering, sullenness, suspicion, terror,
tomfoolery, torment, torpor, torture, trauma,
treachery, trepidation, tumult, turmoil,
twinge, uncertainty, uncleanliness, unease,
unpleasantness, vacuity, vanity, vengeance,
vertigo, vexation, vice, vindictiveness,
vulgarity, weakness, wickedness, worry,
zealotry

NEUTRAL OR AMBIGUOUS

ability, abstinence, acceptance, amnesia,
apology, appetite, appreciation, artifice,
astonishment, attention, attentiveness,
authority, autonomy, awareness, belief,
bluster, celibacy, certainty, chastity,
compromise, compulsion, concealment,
concentration, concern, conviction, credit,
cunning, curiosity, defence, deference,
defiance, delay, delegation, deliberation,
deliverance, deputation, desire, detachment,
determination, disagreement, disguise,
disinterest, disposition, dissuasion, duty,
duress, eccentricity, ego, empathy, emptiness,
entitlement, equivocation, escape, excess,
exhaustion, extravagance, familiarity, fault,
flattery, foible, folly, formality, fortune,
fortitude, frenzy, fretfulness, gallantry,
gamesmanship, giddiness, glibness,
goodness, grandeur, grandiosity, gullibility,
harshness, haste, health, humility, humour,
hunch, hygiene, hysteria, idealism, illusion,

imagination, impetuousness, improvisation,
impulsiveness, inaction, inattention,
incognito, inconsistency, indecision,
independence, indulgence, infatuation,
informality, insight, intention, interest,
interference, intrigue, introspection,
intuition, irascibility, irony, isolation,
judgement, knowledge, lamentation,
languor, largesse, leniency, lethargy, levity,
libido, listlessness, longing, maturity,
memory, mischief, mood, morale, morality,
mortality, motivation, mystery, naivety,
negotiation, nonchalance, nostalgia,
obedience, obligation, observance, obstinacy,
optimism, parsimony, passion, pathos,
patriotism, penitence, perdition, permission,
perseverance, persuasion, philanthropy, pity,
plight, possession, power, predisposition,
prejudgement, preparation, presumption,
pretension, pride, principle (ethic), privilege,
professionalism, provocation, prudence,
purpose, purposelessness, pursuit, rationality,
reason, recognition, reconciliation, recovery,
redemption, redundancy, reflection,
refusal, rehabilitation, reluctance, remorse,
repentance, repute, reserve, resignation,
resistance, resolution, respectability,
restraint, reverence, reverie, ridiculousness,
ruthlessness, scepticism, scrutiny, secrecy,
security, self-assurance, self-awareness,
self-confidence, self-deprecation, self-
discipline, self-esteem, self-indulgence,
selflessness, self-pity, self-regard, self-
restraint, self-righteousness, self-sacrifice,
self-sufficiency, sensitivity, seriousness,
sincerity, singlemindedness, smitten,
sobriety, sociability, solace, stealth,
stimulation, submission, superiority,
superstition, support, surprise, surrender,

sympathy, temerity, temperance, temptation, tenaciousness, thoughtfulness, thoughtlessness, thrift, understanding, unfamiliarity, unpredictability, unsociability, vacillation, vigilance, volition, vulnerability, wariness, weariness, wherewithal, whimsy, widowhood, wilfulness, work, world-weariness, worship, worthlessness, yearning, youth

PHYSICAL

activity, addiction, age, anorexia, arousal, bulimia, cleanliness, cold, concussion, consciousness, dexterity, dirtiness, divorce, dream, drunkenness, dyslexia, fatigue, hunger, hypothermia, immortality, impotence, infertility, insomnia, marriage, monogamy, mortality, nausea, polygamy, relaxation, shock, sleep, solitude, strength, tantrum, thirst, warmth, weakness, youth

UNUSUAL

abstemiousness (moderation in eating and drinking), acedia (spiritual lethargy), acharnement (ferocity, fierce determination, with gusto), admonition (mild but serious rebuke), animus (ill will), anomie (social alienation), ataraxia (calmness of mind), braggadocio (empty bragging), cafard (hypocrisy; melancholy), brio (liveliness of spirit), calumny (a malicious attack; the act of defaming), ennui (weariness deriving from boredom), froideur (coolness of manner), hauteur (arrogant pride), improvidence (failing to provide for the future), limerence (state of romantic infatuation), lucidity (clarity of mind), penury (extreme poverty), perfidy (treachery), perspicacity (keen insight), pleonexia (excessive covetousness), politesse (courteous formality), ressentiment (generalised resentment or hostility, often chronic and without any outlet), sang-froid (composure, particularly under pressure), turpitude (inherent depravity), Weltschmerz (melancholy over state of world)

INDIVIDUALITY

aberration, abnormality, anomaly, apartness, bent, bizarreness, character, characteristic, crankiness, curiousness, dottiness, eccentricity, deviance, deviation, feature, foible, freakishness, habit, hallmark, idiosyncrasy, inclination, incongruity, independence, irregularity, mysteriousness, nonconformity, oddity, oddness, outlandishness, peccadillo, peculiarity, personality, predilection, predisposition, proclivity, propensity, quaintness, quality, quirk, quirkiness, rebellion, singularity, strangeness, streak, taint, trademark, trait, trick, unconventionality, uniqueness, warp, weirdness, whim, whimsicality, whimsy

CONVENTIONALITY

acceptance, accord, accommodation, acquiescence, adjustment, agreement, allegiance, buttoned-down, comme il faut, complaisance, compliance, concordance, conformity, congruity, convention, decorum, deference, de rigueur, docility, duty, group-think, herd-think, humility, kosher, meekness, obedience, orthodoxy, passivity, propriety, servility, submission, toeing the line, traditionalism, uniformity

OTHER STATES

absence, affluence, anarchy, austerity, bedlam, catastrophe, censorship, change, chaos, clarity, cleanliness, coincidence, combat, completeness, complexity, conformity, confusion, consequence, conservatism, continuity, cooperation, crime, danger, debate, decadence, defeat, deprivation, desecration, destruction, difficulty, disarray, disease, disorder, disrepair, disruption, dissent, disuse, diversity, entropy, equality, escape, exclusion, exile, existence, exploitation, famine, fantasy, filth, force, fraud, fury, futility, globalisation, havoc, hegemony, help, inclusion, incompleteness, injustice, intolerance, jingoism, justice, juxtaposition, liberalism, looting, mayhem, misuse, murder, mutiny, nihilism, oblivion, opposition, order, originality, permanence, plunder, poverty, power, powerlessness, precedence, presence, production, protest, purity, racism, reality, rebellion, refuge, regularity, retribution, safety, sanctity, sanctuary, scandal, security, separation, simplicity, stability, theft, torture, uniformity, union, use, vice, victory, violence, war

GROUPS OF PEOPLE

alliance, amalgamation, assemblage, assembly, association, band, battery, bloc, bunch, cabal, cabinet, cadre, caravan, cartel, caucus, circle, claque, class, clique, cluster, clutch, coalition, cohort, collection, committee, commune, company, confederacy, confederation, congregation, consortium, convoy, corps, coterie, covey, crew, crowd, deal, deputation, diaspora, duo, ensemble, faction, federation, gaggle, gang, gathering, grouping, horde, host, junta, knot, lobby, mass, menagerie, mob, multitude, muster, orchestra, outfit, pack, pact, parliament, partnership, party, phalanx, platoon, populace, posse, quartet, quorum, rally, relationship, retinue, schism, set, sort, squad, syndicate, swarm, throng, treaty, tribe, trio, troika, troupe, turnout, type, union, unit

HUMAN MOVEMENTS

blink, bow, brandish, careen, caress, cartwheel, chug, clamber, clout, copulate, crawl, cuddle, doze, exhale, faint, fiddle, fidget, flinch, flirt, flit, fondle, frisk, frown, fumble, gesture, gobble, grimace, grip, guzzle, heave, hop, huddle, hug, inhale, jostle, knee, leap, lurch, nibble, nod, nudge, parkour, pat, peek, peer, pinch, pose, pucker, pummel, queue, quiver, rinse, rummage, scowl, scurry, shimmy, shiver, shrug, shrivel, shudder, slouch, slump, smother, snooze, spring, spy, squat, squint, squirm, stamp, start, stomp, stoop, straddle, stretch, stroke, swallow, sway, swerve, teeter, tingle, tremble, tumble, tussle, twirl, twitch, vomit, waltz, wiggle, wince, wink, wobble, wrestle, wriggle, wring, writhe

WALK OR RUN

walk: amble, dawdle, gambol, hike, hobble, kneel, limp, lope, lumber, meander, mince, mosey, prance, roam, saunter, shuffle, sidle, skip, skulk, stagger, stride, stumble, strut, swagger, tiptoe, totter, traipse, trample, wander; run: barrel, bolt, bound, bustle, canter, career, dart, dash, flit, fly, gallop, hurry, jog, race, rush, scamper, scramble, scurry, scuttle, skip, sprint, trot

swaddle, swelter, swoon, tamper, taunt, thrash, thrive, thwart, tinker, tweak, urge, venerate, verify, vilify, waffle, wallow, waver, wheedle, wield, wilt, wince, woo, yearn

HUMAN ACTIONS

abandon, accost, adulate, ambush, amend, appal, assert, assuage, baffle, bask, beg, behave, besmirch, bewilder, bicker, blame, bless, blunder, brag, bribe, bristle, brood, cadge, cajole, cavort, chasten, chastise, chide, cling, coddle, coerce, collude, complain, confuse, conquer, conspire, convince, crave, cringe, crow, cuss, dally, dangle, delve, despise, devote, dither, divulge, drag, dream, drift, dwell, encourage, escape, espouse, excuse, fail, falter, ferret, feud, fight, fix, flaunt, flee, flout, flummox, forge, fossick, fret, frighten, fritter, fuss, gather, gawp, glean, gloat, glower, grapple, grieve, gripe, grizzle, grovel, gush, hanker, heckle, hinder, hoodwink, hunker, infiltrate, insinuate, inspire, interpret, juggle, kindle, labour, languish, loathe, loiter, maroon, marvel, meddle, milk, mingle, mock, mooch, mourn, muffle, mug, mull, nag, neglect, niggle, nobble, nurture, pamper, persevere, pester, philander, pillage, pillory, placate, plead, plunder, postpone, potter, praise, preen, propel, prosper, provoke, quarrel, quell, quench, quibble, quip, rage, ransack, rant, rebuke, recoil, rejoice, renege, retreat, revel, revere, reward, rig, rile, romance, ruminate, rummage, scoff, scold, seduce, segue, shirk, shop, shun, simmer, slumber, smear, smirk, smother, smudge, smuggle, snaffle, snare, sneer, snoop, snub, solicit, spout, spurn, squander, squash, stalk, stare, startle, starve, strive, struggle, succeed, sulk, surrender,

HUMAN NOISES

babble, bawl, belch, bellow, blow nose, blubber, boo, breathe, burble, burp, cackle, catcall, caterwaul, chant, chatter, cheer, chew, choke, chomp, chortle, chuckle, chunder, chunter, clap, cough, croak, cry, drool, fart, gargle, gasp, giggle, groan, growl, grumble, grunt, guffaw, gulp, gurgle, hiccup, hiss, holler, hoot, howl, jeer, kiss, laugh, maunder, moan, mule, mumble, murmur, mutter, natter, prattle, raspberry, retch, roar, scream, screech, shiver, shush, shout, shriek, sigh, slur, slurp, snarl, sneeze, snicker, sniff, snigger, snivel, snore, snort, snuffle, sob, spit, splutter, squeal, stutter, swallow, thrum, titter, twitter, vomit, wail, warble, weep, whimper, whine, whinge, whisper, whistle, whoop, wince, witter, yabber, yammer, yawn, yell, yelp, yodel

GROUP NOISE

acclamation, applause, boo, chant, chorus, clamour, greeting, hubbub, outburst, outcry, salutation, shout down, tally-ho, uproar

INTERACTIONS

appointment, assembly, collaboration, communication, conference, consultation, contact, convention, convergence, date, dealings, encounter, engagement, exchange, face time, face to face, fixture, function, gathering, get-together, introduction, interface, IRL (in real life), lecture, match, meeting, parliament, reunion, seminar, shindig, soirée, summit, tête-à-tête

INTERACTIONS: SEXUAL OVERTONES

affair, assignation, clinch, frisson, liaison, relations, rendezvous, tryst

SELECTED TYPES AND ASSOCIATIONS

ORDINARY / WORKING CLASS

blue collar, citizens, cockney, commoners, common herd, common people, cor blimey, council house, demi-monde, demos, demotic, Everyman, the French Revolution, the general public, grassroots, the great unwashed, the hoi polloi, the horde, Jane/John Doe, Joe Bloggs/Public/Schmo, labourers, the lower classes/orders, lumpen proletariat, man in the street, masses, the mob, the multitude, ochlocracy, peasantry, the people, pleb(ian), populace, proletarian, rabble, rank and file, riff-raff, a rough diamond, salt of the earth, subaltern, terrace house, toilers, tradesmen, vox pop(uli), (mobile) vulgus, workers, working class

(Arthur Dent in book, TV series and films of Douglas Adams' *The Hitchhiker's Guide to the Galaxy*, Eliza Doolittle from GB Shaw's play *Pygmalion*, Yosser Hughes from 1982 Alan Bleasdale UK TV drama *Boys from the Blackstuff*)

MIDDLE CLASS

bourgeoisie, burgher, coffee groups, commuting, conformity, curtain twitching, dormitory suburb, envy, Home Counties, middle-aged, Middle America, middle income, middle management, mortgage, petit bourgeois, respectability, silent majority, small town, social climbing, station wagon, suburbia, SUV, white collar

(George F Babbitt from Sinclair Lewis's 1922 novel *Babbitt*, Mr Charles Pooter from the 19th-century George Grossmith comic novel *Diary of a Nobody*, Hyacinth Bucket from the UK TV sitcom *Keeping Up Appearances*)

PRIVILEGED

aristocracy, beau monde, beautiful people, Beverly Hills, blue blood, boarding school, bon ton, butler, cafe society, chosen few, corduroy, cosmopolitan, country club set, cravat, cream of society, crème de la crème, elite, establishment, fashionable society, the Four Hundred, the (landed) gentry, the Gilded Age, glitterati, globetrotter, haut monde, hereditary titles, high life, high society, House of Lords, idle rich, in-crowd, Ivy League, jet set, *jeunesse dorée*, the leisured class, lords and ladies, Malibu, the moneyed class, nobility, noblesse oblige, nouveau riche, Oxbridge, parvenu, patriarchy, peers of the realm, polite society, Regency period, rich and famous, right people, ruling class, salon, Sloane Ranger, smart set, snobbery, social climber, toff, trustafarian, upper classes, upper crust, *Upstairs, Downstairs*, valley girl, *Vanity Fair*, well-born

(The Flyte family in Evelyn Waugh's novel *Brideshead Revisited*; the above-stairs characters in Robert Altman's 2001 film *Gosford Park*)

WEALTHY

banker, baron, Bermuda, blue blood, Caymans, the City, comfortable, Côte d'Azur, country club, drawing room, Easy Street, El Dorado, gentry, Golconda, golf, the Hamptons, the haves, helicopter, junk bonds, Learjet, limousine, luxury, magnate, mogul, moneyed, money markets, nabob, nouveau riche, old money, philanthropy, plutocrat, private island, privilege, propertied, rich (affluent, flush, loaded, mammon, prosperous, well-heeled, well-to-do), silver spoon, snob, solvent, stinking rich, sugar daddy, super yacht, Swiss bank, tiara, tycoon

(Jett Rink in George Stevens' film *Giant*, Croesus, King Midas; in real life: Bill Gates, Liliane Bettencourt, Rockefeller, Warren Buffett)

(luxury brands: Aspesi, Balenciaga, Breitling, Bulgari, Burberry, Cerruti, Chanel, Christian Dior, Christian Lacroix, Christian Louboutin, Dolce & Gabbana, Giorgio Armani, Gucci, Hermès, Louis Vuitton (LV, LVMH), Manolo Blahnik, Montblanc, Moschino, Prada, Rolex, TAG Heuer, Tiffany & Co., Tod's, Versace, Yves Saint Laurent (YSL))

POOR

bankrupt, begging, benefit, broke (hard up, impoverished, needy, penniless, skint), Chapter 11, charity case, council estate, deprived (disadvantaged, dispossessed), destitute, down and out, *favela*, food stamps, ghetto, hand-to-mouth, the have-nots, the needy, Old Mother Hubbard, pauper, poverty, the projects, public housing, Queer Street, reservation, shanty town, Skid Row, sleeping rough, slum, squatter, township, underprivileged, wolf at the door

OLD

aged, Alzheimer's, anorak, antediluvian, the blue rinse brigade, cardigan, Chelsea Pensioner, doddering, dotage, early riser, elderly, fogey, fuddy-duddy, granny, grey, grouch, mature, memory, nostalgia, the past, pension(er), pensioned, pipe, reactionary, rest home, retirement, Returned Services' Association (RSA), senescent, senile, senior moment, slippers, superannuitant, teacakes, twin set and pearls, veteran, Victorian, walking stick, the war, wig, wisdom, world-weary, wrinkles, Zimmer frame

(Father Time, Methuselah, Moses, Nestor, Noah)

YOUNG

adolescent, at school (preschool, kindergarten, primary, secondary, university), baby, beanie, blooming, boy(ish), boarding school, budding, callow, child, daughter, delinquent, driver's licence, formative, Generation Y, girl(ish), green, hoody, innocent, juvenile, kid, mumbling, naive, offspring, preteen, puberty, puerile, sleeping in, son, student, teen(ager), tween, under age, virgin, youthful

(Harry Potter, Hermione and Ron from JK Rowling's *Harry Potter* novels; Shakespeare's Romeo and Juliet; Vicky Pollard from the UK TV series *Little Britain*)

FAT
adipose, ample, appetite, beer belly, blubber, broad, bulky, cellulite, chubby, chunky, corpulent, dewlap, diet, double chin, dumpy, embonpoint, endomorphic, flab, fleshy, heavy, jowly, junk food, mesomorphic, obese, overweight, paunch, plump, plus-size, podgy, porky, portly, potbellied, pudgy, rotund, sizeable, squat, stocky, stout, sturdy, thickset, tubby, Weight Watchers, weighty, zaftig

(Billy and Bessie Bunter from the Charles Hamilton children's stories, Bubbles from *Little Britain*, Falstaff from Shakespeare, Fat Albert from *The Bill Cosby Show*, Gargantua from Francois Rabelais's novels, Norbit and Rasputia from the film *Norbit*, Oscar Wao from Junot Diaz's novel *The Brief Wondrous Life of Oscar Wao*, Santa Claus, the reality TV show *The Biggest Loser*)

THIN
anorexic, beanpole, bony, bulimic, cadaverous, catwalk (model), deep-eyed, diaphanous, emaciated, fine-boned, gangly, gaunt, haggard, lanky, lean, pinched, reedy, scrawny, size 0, skeletal, slender, slight, slim, spindly, supermodel, twiggy, underweight,

waif, wasted, weedy, wiry, wispy, wizened

(Olive Oyl from EC Segar's Popeye cartoons)

CONSERVATIVE
Aga, anti-abortion, bourgeois, buttoned-down, cigar, Colonel Blimp, country house, *Daily Mail*, *Daily Telegraph*, diehard, double-breasted, drawing room, fox-hunting, fusty, gated community, grandee, grandiloquent, guns, hidebound, horses, hunting, individualist, Ivy League, leather armchair, libertarian, orotund, private club, reactionary, Republican, reserve, right, sherry-drinking, stuffy, sunbelt, Tory, traditionalist, trahison des clercs, true blue, tweed, unilateral, wood-panelled

PROGRESSIVE
activist, broad-minded, Democrat, factional, green, human rights, Labour, left-liberal, left-wing, liberal, moderate, multilateral, politically correct, progressive, reformist, right-on, socialist, union, welfare, Whig

BRAINY
academic, BBC (ABC, CBC, PBS), boffin, bookish, computer programmer, eccentric, Einstein, elite, geek, glasses, highbrow, intelligentsia, ivory tower, nerd, out of touch, pocket protector, pointy-headed, professor

(contestant Charles Van Doren, played by Ralph Fiennes in Robert Redford's 1994 film *Quiz Show*; Matt Damon's janitor Will Hunting in Gus Van Sant's 1997 film *Good Will Hunting*; the idiot savant child Simon in Harold Becker's 1998 film *Mercury Rising*; the mathematician John Nash, played by Russell Crowe in Ron Howard's 2001 film *A Beautiful Mind*; physicists Niels Bohr and Werner Heisenberg in Michael Frayn's 1998 play *Copenhagen*)

SLOW OR FOOLISH
backward, birdbrain, blonde jokes, challenged, clod, dense, dim, dumb, feeble-minded, ignoramus, impaired, Jackass, (having a) learning difficulty, low IQ, not the full quid, reality TV, senior moment, Simple Simon, simpleton, slow, slow to twig, *The Weakest Link*, yokel

(dumb: Lennie in John Steinbeck's 1937 novel *Of Mice and Men*, Malvolio in Shakespeare's *Twelfth Night*, Lloyd and Harry from Peter Farrelly's 1994 film *Dumb and Dumber*; dumb blonde: Kelly Preston's air hostess Sherry from the 2003 Bruno Barreto film *View from the Top*, Gwyneth Paltrow's waitress Clementine in Paul Thomas Anderson's 1996 film *Hard Eight*, Reese Witherspoon's optimistic Elle Woods in the 2001 Robert Luketic film *Legally Blonde*)

HYPERACTIVE
ADD / ADHD, akathisia, dynamo, fidgeting, go-getter, goldfish, inattentive, insomnia, jumpiness, memory loss, overachiever, pottering, restless, Stakhanovite, St Vitus's dance, tireless, wanderlust, wild goose chase, workaholic

(Ellen DeGeneres's blue tang fish Dory character in Andrew Stanton's 2003 film

Finding Nemo, Josh Brolin's young George W Bush character in Oliver Stone's 2008 film *W*, Tom Hanks's overactive FedEx executive character in Robert Zemeckis's 2000 film *Cast Away*, Paul Bettany's Chaucer in Brian Helgeland's 2001 film *A Knight's Tale*)

EVIL
abuse, atrocity, Beelzebub, charm, cruel, curse, demoniacal, depravity, devil, diabolic, hate, Hitler, malevolence, malice, molestation, murder, Nazi death camps, paedophile, Pandora's box, pervert, plague, Satan, sin, Stalin, suicide bomber, terrorist, voodoo, wickedness

(Damian from the Omen film series, Lord Voldemort from the Harry Potter novels by JK Rowling, Michael Myers from the Halloween films, John Doe from film *Se7en*, Louis Cypher from *Angel Heart*, Jigsaw from the Saw films, Leatherface from the film *The Texas Chainsaw Massacre*, Jason from the Friday the 13th film series, Freddy Krueger from the Nightmare on Elm Street film series, Vlad the Impaler)

PAST ONE'S BEST
also-ran, bankrupt, cop-out, dud, excuse, failure, flop, has-been, loser, manqué, non-starter, past glories, washed-up, washout, weak-kneed, yesterday's man

VIRTUOUS
altruism, benevolence, blamelessness, chivalry, Christian, conscience, decency, etiquette, formal, good Samaritan, goody-goody, idealism, knight in shining armour,

law, martyr, model/upright citizen, moral, noble, obedience, paragon, philanthropy, principles, prudence, saintly, self-control, selflessness, self-righteousness, stiff upper lip, straight and narrow, straight back, temperance

HIPPIE
acid, backpack, beads, beard, beatnik, bohemian, brown rice, counterculture, crystal, dreadlocks, dream-catcher, drop out, free-living, free-loading, free love, green, Greenham Common (the Greenham Common Women's Peace Camp), gypsy, headband, kaftan, lentils, herbal tea, hummus, marijuana, muesli, multigrain, mung beans, muslin, new age, non-conformist, peacenik, pipe-smoking, poetry, protester, rebel, sandal-wearing, sexual revolution, tie-dyed, touchy-feely, tree-hugging, Vietnam protester

(characters from the 1967 musical *Hair*, Neil from TV series *The Young Ones*, the title character's sometime girlfriend Jenny from the 1994 Robert Zemeckis film *Forrest Gump*, Mark from Michaelangelo Antonioni's 1970 film *Zabriskie Point*, Wyatt and Billy from Dennis Hopper's 1969 film *Easy Rider*)

COWBOY
bandit, bandolier, black/white hat, blacksmith, boots, bounty hunter, bronco, buffalo, cattle drive, Comanche, Conestoga, cowpoke, drink, dynamite, frontier, gambling, gun belt, gunfighter, horse, Indian (feather headdress, moccasins, peace pipe, papoose, scalping, wigwam),

prostitutes, railroad, rattlesnake, rifle, robbery, rodeo, saddle, sagebrush, saloon, shoestring tie, shotgun, Sioux, six-shooter, spurs, stagecoach, stetson, teepee, telegraph, train, tumbleweed, wagon, western (cowboy movie), whip, whorehouse, wigwam, wilderness, Wyatt Earp

(famous real cowboys: Annie Oakley, Billy the Kid, Buffalo Bill, Butch Cassidy, Calamity Jane, Doc Holliday, Harry Longabough (the Sundance Kid), Jesse James, Pat Garrett, Wild Bill Hickcock, Wyatt Earp; famous Indians: Big Foot, Crazy Horse, Geronimo, Pocahontas, Sitting Bull; famous fictional cowboys: the Cisco Kid, Hopalong Cassidy, the Lone Ranger, Shane; famous fictional Indians: Tiger Lily, Tonto; famous actors and directors of westerns: Clint Eastwood, John Ford, Howard Hawks, Sam Peckinpah, John Sturges

CONFIDENT
alpha male, A-type, big swinging dick, braggadocio, brass, champ, cheek, chutzpah, cojones, entrepreneur, gall, hawk, gusto, livewire, medallist, moxie, nerve, nous, smarts, thruster, victor, winner

(Bud Fox and Gordon Gekko from Oliver Stone's film *Wall Street*)

NON-ACHIEVER
Chilled out, defeat(ist), dole-bludger, dope, dope-head, frustration, impotence, layabout, loser, marijuana, munchies, reefer, slacker, slouch, stoner, unemployed, video games

(Adam in Neil LaBute's *The Shape of Things*, Cheech and Chong from the *Cheech and Chong* movies, Dale Denton and Saul Silver from *Pineapple Express*, The Dude in *The Big Lebowski*, Ed in *Shaun of the Dead*, Gollum in JRR Tolkien's *The Lord of the Rings*, James Stevens the butler in Kazuo Ishiguro's *The Remains of the Day*, Joey from *Friends*, Pilon from John Steinbeck's *Tortilla Flat*, Prufrock in TS Eliot's 'The Love Song of J. Alfred Prufrock', Willy Loman in Arthur Miller's play *Death of a Salesman*)

NEGATIVE

anarchist, churlish, contrary, crabby, crank, cynic, denial, disparage, doubting Thomas, dove, grinch, grouch, grump, irony, misanthrope, mischievous, naysayer, nitpicker, pedant, perverse, pessimist, rejection, sarcasm, veto

(The Grinch from Dr Seuss's *How the Grinch Stole Christmas!*, Grumpy from *Snow White and the Seven Dwarfs*, HAL-9000 from *2001: A Space Odyssey*, Dr Niles Crane from *Frasier*, Oscar from *Sesame Street*, Victor Melgrew from *One Foot in the Grave*)

GAY / LESBIAN / BI / TRANS

butch, camp, closet, cottaging, cruising, dance party, drag, E, effeminate, fa'afafine, fag hag, femme, Harvey Milk, haunt, homoerotic, leather, Lesbos, limp-wristed, Mardi Gras, mincing, out, queen, queer, rainbow, rough trade, same-sex relationship, San Francisco, sapphic, Stonewall, straight-acting, takatapui, vamp, YMCA

(Connie and Carla from *Connie and Carla*, Ellen DeGeneres, Ennis Del Mar from *Brokeback Mountain*, Father Greg Pilkington from *Priest*, Felicia Jollygoodfellow in *Priscilla, Queen of the Desert*, Gay Perry from *Kiss Kiss Bang Bang*, Johnny from *My Beautiful Laundrette*, Maurice Hall from EM Forster's *Maurice*, Molina from Manuel Puig's *Kiss of the Spider Woman*, Petra von Kant from Fassbinder's *The Bitter Tears of Petra von Kant*, Roy Cohn from *Angels in America*)

DRINKER

alky, bacchanalia, bartender, bibulous, blepharitis, brew, carouser, crapulent, dipsomaniac, distillery, Eighteenth Amendment, hair of the dog, hangover, highball, hooch, kava, liquor, lush, nightcap, prohibition, proof, pub, quaffer, reveller, rosacea, saloon, soused, tavern, tippler

(drunk: beery, befuddled, bibulous, blotto, high, horizontal, inebriated, intoxicated, loaded, mellow, paralytic, pixillated, plastered, shickered, sloshed, smashed, souse, squiffy, tipsy, toasted; non-drinker: abstemious, sober, teetotal, three sheets to the wind, wowser)

(Henry Chinaski from Barbet Schroder's film *Barfly*, John Travolta's Bobby Long in Shainee Gabel's 2004 movie *A Love Song for Bobby Long*, Meg Ryan's Alice Green in Louis Mandoki's 1994 movie *When a Man Loves a Woman*, Johnny Depp's Captain Jack Sparrow in Gore Verbinski's *Pirates of the Caribbean* movies, Sebastian Flyte from Evelyn Waugh's novel *Brideshead Revisited*)

COOL

chi-chi, collected, detached, James Bond, insouciant, phlegmatic, smooth, soigné, suave, swanky

(pool player Eddie Felson from Robert Rossen's film *The Hustler*, The Fonz in TV series *Happy Days*, The Motorcycle Boy from Francis Ford Coppola's *Rumblefish*, Rick Blaine from Michael Curtiz's film *Casablanca*, Captain Jack Sparrow from the *Pirates of the Caribbean* films, James Bond, James diGriz in the Harry Harrison series of *Stainless Steel Rat* sci-fi novels, Hawkeye Pierce in the *M*A*S*H* TV series)

DERANGED

addict, alcoholic, bedlam, bonkers, crazy, delusion, dementia, derelict, doolally, glue-sniffer, loco, mad cow disease, men in white coats, mental hospital, meshuga, non compos mentis, psychiatrist, psychopath, psychosis, schizophrenia, screw loose, serial killer, sociopath, woo-woo

(Brad Pitt's Jeffrey Goines in Terry Gilliam's 1996 film *Twelve Monkeys*, Hannibal Lecter and the serial killer Buffalo Bill / James Gumb from the novels by Thomas Harris and the 1991 Jonathan Demme film, the inmate characters in *One Flew Over the Cuckoo's Nest*, Ophelia in Shakespeare's *Hamlet*, Patrick Bateman in Bret Easton Ellis's novel *American Psycho*)

CHARACTERISTICS

CHARACTER AND PRESENTATIONAL STYLES

Aristophanic – satirical with serious intent, after Ancient Greek comic poet Aristophanes

Babbit – narrow-minded, self-satisfied, materialistic person, after the character by novelist Sinclair Lewis

Beckettesque – focused on the human condition, at expense of conventional plot, characterisation, time–place unity, after playwright Samuel Beckett

Bellovian – after Saul Bellow, writer as prophet or interpreter of world; themes such as isolation, self, enlightenment, difficulty with women, anti-modernism

Boswellian – as of a companion and close observer, as in James Boswell, biographer of lexicographer Samuel Johnson; also bawdy, given Boswell's liking for alcohol, gambling and prostitutes

Brechtian – emphasising drama as vehicle for social and political use, after playwright Bertholt Brecht

Buchanesque – of a story, full of adventure and conspiracy; of a character, a resourceful action hero, after John Buchan's series of novels beginning with *The Thirty-Nine Steps*

Bunyanesque – allegorical, after John Bunyan, 17th-century writer

Canute-like / King Canute – after the Viking king: one who believes he can command everything, including nature; the representation of powerful rulers who are unable to halt or change the course of irresistible forces

Capraesque – endorsing cheery, brave buckers of authority for social good, after the movies of US filmmaker Frank Capra

Cartesian – after Descartes, especially anything mechanistic

Cassandra – forecasting doom (but not believed)

CP Scott-like – respect for truth (after UK *Guardian* newspaper editor)

Croesus-like – extremely wealthy

Dickensian – harsh working conditions, especially for children, after novels of Charles Dickens

Dorian Gray – character who makes Faustian pact so he doesn't get old in Oscar Wilde's novel *The Picture of Dorian Gray*, with themes of hedonism, double lives

Dreiserian – gritty, idiomatic, working class, rootless characters, after novels by Chicago writer Theodore Dreiser

Eeyorish – picky, negative and depressed, after the donkey in AA Milne's Winnie the Pooh stories

Faulknerian – set as a puzzle, after the novels of William Faulkner

Faustian – deal, often made with devil that involves a massive gain at a painful price later on, or character who pursues goals to drastic consequences, after the German legend and particularly Goethe's Faust

Galilean – having objective view of external world, after 16th-century Italian physicist Galileo Galilei; from or pertaining to Galilee

Grand Guignol – gruesome and amoral horror entertainment, after 20th-century Parisian theatre

Heath Robinson – complex and fancifully impractical, particularly machines, after English illustrator

Herodesque – as of Herod, especially relating to killing of children

Hitchcockian – after the style of filmmaker Alfred Hitchcock

Hobbesian – based on 17th-century philosopher Thomas Hobbes's theory of a social contract between the individual and state and the comment that life is 'solitary, poor, nasty, brutish and short': describing a strong pursuit of self-interest; absolute submission to monarch; a difficult existence

Ishmaelite – an outcast

Jeremiah – prophet of doom, particularly one not listened to, after character in the Bible

Job – long-suffering and patient individual, after character in the Bible

Joycean – after James Joyce, so complex and convoluted, or free form

Kafkaesque – involving a nightmarish, unfathomable situation for an individual; or the disruption of the everyday by the bizarre, after early 20th-century Czech author Franz Kafka

Kiplingesque – from Rudyard Kipling: empathy with common experience; a sympathetic view of English imperialism; an appreciation of the exotic

Larkinesque – as of Philip Larkin, parents messing one up

Lazarus – one who returns against great odds or from obscurity, after New Testament character raised from the dead

Lilliputian – tiny, after land of Lilliput in Jonathan Swift's *Gulliver's Travels*

Malthusian – relating to negative outlook

on population growth, after 18th-century English economist Thomas Malthus

Mephistophelean – cynical scoffer; satanic cunning and ingenuity; after Mephistopheles in the Faustus story

Methuselah – of great age, from the Genesis figure

Miss Haversham-like – scheming and poisoned by regret, from character in 19th-century English novelist Charles Dickens' *Great Expectations*

Myrmidon-like – loyally carrying out orders without question, after the mythological Greek nation known for that trait

Orwellian – totalitarian and under constant surveillance, after 20th-century English writer George Orwell's novel *Nineteen Eighty-Four*

Ozymandias – hubris, especially in the form of a monument of a powerful king, from Percy Bysshe Shelley's 1818 sonnet

Panglossian – excessively optimistic, from Voltaire's satirical and optimism-challenging 18th-century novel *Candide*

Pantagruelian – huge or of coarse humour, after Francois Rabelais's novels

Pickwickian – marked by simplicity and kindness, or not intended to be taken literally, after Samuel Pickwick in Charles Dickens' *Pickwick Papers*; also medical syndrome relating to obesity, shortness of breath and sleep problems coined after another character, Joe

Pied Piper – one who is eagerly followed, after the fairytale figure

Pollyanna(ish) – relentlessly optimistic, from character in 1913 US novel

Procrustean – enforcing arbitrary standards by force, from mythological Greek robber who made victims fit bed

Proustian – evoking nostalgia and the complexity of memory; involuntary memory connected with cues such as smells, after the early 20th-century French writer Marcel Proust and his novel *A la Récherche du Temps Perdu*

Prufrockian – timid and conforming, after character in 1915 poem by the early 20th-century Anglo-American poet TS Eliot

Puck(ish) – a mischievous and playful sprite, from William Shakespeare's *A Midsummer Night's Dream*

Quixotic – extravagantly romantic but unpractical in aiming for unrealistic ideals, after the Don Quixote character in the novel by 16th–17th-century Spanish writer Miguel de Cervantes Saavedra

Renfield – insect-eating lunatic asylum patient under influence of the vampire Dracula in Bram Stoker's 1897 novel

Rousseauistic – following idea that humans are inherently good; celebrating simpler way of life and that modern civilisation has harmful effects; after the 18th-century French philosopher Jean-Jacques Rousseau

Runyonesque – involving demi-monde characters, or referred to by colourful nicknames; a slangy vernacular style, after Prohibition-era US writer Damon Runyon

Shermanesque – in American politics (after American Civil War general William T Sherman), a clear and direct statement by a political candidate that he or she will not run for a particular post

Solomonic – wise and powerful judge, after King Solomon of the Bible

Stakhanovite – eager to please by exceeding targets, after Soviet miner Aleksei Gregorievich Stakhanov

Stendhalian – realism with psychological insight in direct style, after 19th-century French writer Stendhal (Marie-Henri Beyle)

Svengali – one who controls actions or career of another, after character in novel *Trilby* by 19th-century English writer George du Maurier

Swiftian – amusingly but caustically or grotesquely satirical, after 17th–18th-century Anglo-Irish writer Jonathan Swift

Tammany-like – an all-controlling political machine, including patronage and dubious tactics, after Tammany Hall, New York Democratic base until 1960s

Thurberesque – surreal stories and cartoons, often featuring a timid protagonist, after the style of 20th-century US writer and artist James Thurber

Thyestean – cannibalistic, after Greek mythological figure Thyestes

Torquemada-like – fanatic pursuer of heretical thought and expulsion of Jews, after 15th-century Catholic monk Tomás de Torquemada, a leader of the Spanish Inquisition

Uriah Heep – obsequious, grasping villain from Charles Dickens' 1850 novel *David Copperfield*

Vonnegut hero – a privileged individual who wants to change things; from the characters of 20th-century novelist Kurt Vonnegut

Walter Mitty(ish) – timid person with grand dreams

Whitmanesque – with strong, exuberant and democratic feeling, after 19th-century US poet Walt Whitman

Yeatsian – multiply symbolic, especially concerned with nature, after Irish poet William Butler Yeats

Zelig-like – a chameleon character who takes on aspects of those around him or who inserts himself into famous events, after Leonard Zelig, lead character in Woody Allen's 1983 film *Zelig*

Zola'esque – frank and often dark and pessimistic naturalism; action carried out by an intellectual to change public opinion; after 19th-century French writer Émile Zola and his 'J'Accuse' article, which Zola wrote in support of Alfred Dreyfus

ALLEGORICAL FIGURES AND EMBLEMS

Damocles, Sword of – constant and inescapable threat hanging over a seemingly enviable state of existence

Darby and Joan – devoted older married couple; domestic bliss

Everyman – an ordinary individual who may prove an unwilling or unwitting hero

Griselda – patience and obedience, from European folklore

Jack Frost – personification of winter or such weather (also known as Father Winter)

Jeremiah – predictor of doom, after Hebrew prophet

Jezebel – a wicked, scheming or promiscuous woman

Judas – treachery

Little Red Riding Hood – innocence; female sexuality; womanhood

Midas – greed

Morpheus – sleep, after the Greek god of
sleep and dreams

Rip Van Winkle – old age; sleep

Rumpelstiltskin – bragging

Sandman – sleep

Shylock – greed

Svengali – evil-intentioned manipulation

Tartuffe – seemingly virtuous hypocrisy,
from 17th-century French writer
Molière's play *Tartuffe, ou l'Imposteur*

FOUR HUMOURS

yellow bile (choleric): active, prone to
anger; black bile (melancholic): thoughtful,
dejected, irritable; phlegm (phlegmatic):
calm, unemotional; blood (sanguine):
confident, hopeful

MYTHOLOGICAL CREATURES

argus, banshee, basilisk, behemoth, bunyip,
centaur, Cerberus, Charybdis, chimera,
Chupacabra, Circe, Cyclops, demon, djinn,
doppelgänger, elf, fairy, genie, ghoul, giant,
goblin, gorgon, gremlin, griffin, harpy,
hobgoblin, hydra, imp, incubus, kraken,
leprechaun, leviathan, manticore, Minotaur,
naiad, Nereid, nymph, ogre, Pegasus,
phoenix, pixie, poltergeist, roc, sasquatch,
satyr, sciapod, scylla, siren, sphinx, succubus,
sylph, taniwha, tanuki, troll, unicorn,
vampire, vetala, werewolf, zombie

TERMINOLOGY

'Criticism occupies the lowest rung in the hierarchy of literature: as regards form, almost always, and as regards moral worth, incontestably. It's lower even than rhyming games and acrostics, which at least demand a modicum of invention.'— Gustave Flaubert, quoted in Julian Barnes' Flaubert's Parrot

A useful critic needs observation, judgement, powers of argument, analysis, clarity, fairness, enthusiasm, professionalism and style, to name a few attributes. Then there's knowledge of history, economics, theory and literary technique.

CRITICISM

CATEGORISATION

aesthetics – study of art, culture and nature

aetiology – study of causation, particularly in medicine

axiology – study of quality or value

ethics – study of right and wrong behaviour, including normative ethics, meta-ethics, applied ethics and descriptive ethics

epistemology – study of the origin and nature of knowledge

hermeneutics – science of understanding texts, especially religious ones

historiography – study of historical research; body of historical literature

humanism – philosophy asserting human dignity, secular morality and fulfilment through the scientific method

ideology – set of ideas, especially political, reflecting social needs and desires of individual or group

methodology – practices, procedures and principles being used

ontogeny – the development history of individuals (phylogeny = species)

ontology – study of the nature of being

phenomenology – philosophical study that regards reality as the perceptions of human consciousness

phylogeny – the development history of a tribe (similar: ontogeny)

taxonomy – classification of plants, animals

ARGUMENT

ad hominem – attacking opponent rather than their argument, from Latin for 'to the man' ('to poison the well' = pre-emptively providing information about a person or thing to adversely affect the audience's response)

appeal to authority – argument that claim is true because someone who is said to be an expert on the subject says so, when this is not the case

biased sample – fallacy that conclusions can be made on a group based on a sample of another group despite the sample being prejudiced in some form

burden of proof – obligation to shift assumed truth to one's own position; the burden of proof fallacy is where that demand for a claim to be proven is placed on the wrong side, such as an affirmative claim that UFOs exist

casuistry – specious reasoning intended to mislead; making ethical judgements based on general examples

cherry-picking – selectively choosing evidence or data that backs an argument

deduction – coming to a conclusion based on premises which, if true, would guarantee its truth (induction = coming to a conclusion based on premises which, if true, would make its truth probable)

dialectic – establishing truth by rational discussion; a debate that attempts to reconcile two opposing theories rather than disproving either

diegesis – telling as opposed to showing

doctrine – set of principles or beliefs, especially as taught ones

dogma – principle or belief presented as unquestionably true

equivocation – evasive ambiguity

(vacillation = wavering; changing opinions frequently)

fallacy – statement or argument based on mistaken or unsound reasoning

gambler's fallacy – argument that an event will occur because it 'evens out' previous events that depart from the norm, such as a toss of a head on a coin after seven tails

guilt by association – the fallacy that a claim should be rejected on the basis that objectionable people accept the claim

haute vulgarisation – the effective presentation of a difficult concept to a mainstream audience

heuristic – pertaining to a experimental or trial-and-error method of education or problem-solving

hypothesis – provisional explanation assumed to be true for the sake of argument; an idea that forms the basis for a line of reasoning or of further research

inference – reaching conclusion from facts, observation, thought (implication = that which is implied; the act of implying)

misrepresentation – false or misleading representation, often intentionally

non sequitur – statement that does not logically follow or not related to previous

Occham's razor – the proposition that the simplest explanation to any problem is likely to be the best

paradox – proposition that appears to contradict itself or be absurd, but which may be true

polemic – argument that attacks an idea; this kind of writing or speech (polemics = the art or practice of verbal debate)

post hoc (ergo proctor hoc) – the logical fallacy of assuming that because B came after A, B must have been caused by A

premise – proposition assumed to be true as basis for conclusion or further argument

quibble – petty or irrelevant distinction or objection; to argue this way

rationalisation – justification with seemingly rational reasons, especially after the event

red herring – idea introduced to divert attention away from the real issue

reductio ad absurdum – proving premise is wrong by showing that it leads to an absurd consequence

rhetoric – the art or technique of speaking or writing well to persuade others; alternatively, 'empty', language that is ostentatious and intended to impress but meaningless

rhetorical question – one that is asked for effect rather than with the expectation of an answer

sleight of hand – deceptive hand movement used in magic tricks; other deception or distraction not readily apparent to an audience

slippery slope – an argument that an event is inevitable which lacks evidence to support that inevitability

Socratic method – attempt to find truth by finding contradiction in hypothesis or casting doubt on presuppositions

sophistry – fallacious or overly subtle reasoning; the practice of reasoning speciously

special pleading – argument that exception should be made without any evidence to support that exception

straw man – a bogus claim set up solely for the sake of argument; type of argument in which opponent's position is misrepresented and then refuted

syllogism – type of logical argument, usually in the form of, e.g. 'Every A is B. Every C is A. So every C is B'

tacit – understood but not actually stated; implied (explicit = stated openly)

thesis – proposition backed by argument (antithesis = opposite of original argument in Hegelian dialectic; synthesis = combination of thesis and antithesis in Hegelian dialectic)

tu quoque – logical fallacy that deflects criticism by irrelevantly accusing someone of doing comparable acts, from Latin for 'you also'

FIGURES OF SPEECH AND LANGUAGE TERMS

acronym – a word made of the first letters of other words, e.g. NATO

acrostic – a word or message spelt out by the first letters of words in a sentence or lines in a poem, etc.

alliteration – repetition of initial consonant in phrase, e.g. 'Tommy Tucker's tiny teddy'

anacoluthon – a change of syntax within sentence for rhetorical effect (often so the grammar is incorrect), so 'My sister is a lawyer – can you see the problem?'

ananym – name formed by reversing letters, e.g. Erewhon for nowhere

antonomasia – replacement of proper name by epithet, e.g. 'The King' for Elvis Presley

aphorism – statement of a principle within a concise, pithy construction, e.g. 'Nothing succeeds like excess' (Oscar Wilde)

aporia – rhetorical device of speaker expressing doubt, real or feigned

aposiopesis – sudden breaking off by speaker or writer in middle of sentence, often to suggest that the speaker is reluctant or unable to continue

apothegm – pithy saying expressing general truth

aptronym – name especially suited to career, e.g. Mr Death the mortician

asyndeton – omission of conjunctions, as in *The Blues Brothers'* 'You, me, them, everybody' (compare: polysyndeton)

auxesis – disproportionate hyperbole, such as calling a new novel 'a classic' (compare: meiosis); a progressively amplifying list

cacography – bad spelling or handwriting

cacology – poor diction or choice of words

calque – phrase borrowed from another language in word-for-word translation, e.g. flea market for *marché aux puces*

catachresis – misuse of language

chiasmus – in modern usage, deployment of parallel clauses in which the order of one is reversed in the other to make a larger point, e.g. 'Always remember that I have taken more out of alcohol than alcohol has taken out of me': Winston Churchill

demotic – relating to the common people, especially speech

diaeresis – mark over vowel to show that it's sounded separately or is not silent, such as naïf

elegant variation – the use of two or more expressions for the same thing in a passage to avoid repeating the term, e.g. 'The queen ... the monarch ... her majesty'

ellipsis – omission of word or phrase in sentence usually understood by reader

enjambment – where phrase or sentence in poem runs over line break

epenthesis – in linguistics, the addition of a sound to a word, as in the pronunciation of 'something' as 'SUMP-thing' (excrescent = consonant; anaptyxis = vowel; prothesis = at beginning; paragoge = at end)

epistolary – of or associated with the writing of letters

epitaph – a gravestone inscription commemorating the deceased; a short verbal or written piece along these lines

epithalamion – song in honour of bride or groom

epithet – phrase that captures essence of person or thing

epizeuxis – immediate repetition of word or phrase for emphasis

eulogy – speech or writing in praise of someone, often at funeral

euphony – having a pleasing sound

faux ami – a word in a foreign language that looks similar to one in the speaker's own, but which has a quite different meaning, such as French 'demander' for 'to ask'

festschrift – a collection of academic essays published in honour of a scholar

heteronym – same spelling, different sound and meaning, e.g. lead (verb) and lead (metal)

homonym – same sound and spelling, different meaning, e.g. row ('to row a boat,' or 'a row of chairs')

hypallage – semantic transfer between two words, such as in 'hopeful day' where people have the hope rather than the day

hypocoristic – a diminution or pet name, e.g. telly for television, Bess for Elizabeth

illation – inferring from premise

in medias res – beginning in the middle of a story

in situ – in its usual or original place

lexicon – vocabulary

lexis – all the words in a language

litotes – a figure of speech in which the opposite is denied for understatement or emphasis, e.g. 'She is not ugly'

logorrhoea – the use of more words than is necessary (similar: prolixity, verbosity; compare: pleonasm, tautology)

meiosis – disproportionate understatement, e.g. 'I just gave him a tap on the head' (compare: auxesis)

metaphor – when a thing is spoken of as if it was another, e.g. 'She's a demon at pool' (compare: simile)

metathesis – altering or reordering the sounds in a word, such as 'aks' for 'ask'

metonymy – use of phrase using characteristic to suggest whole, e.g. 'Washington was agog with the charges' instead of the US government (cf synecdoche)

mnemonic – a word-device that aids recall, especially of lists

monody – a poem lamenting another's death; a lyric poem for one voice; music in which a single melodic line predominates

motif – recurring theme or pattern in literature, music or the visual arts (similar: leitmotif, especially in music)

mythologem – basic theme of cultural story, such as revenge or redemption

non sequitur – Latin for 'it does not follow', as in a conclusion that doesn't agree with its premise or a comment that has nothing to do with a previous comment

obloquy – verbal abuse, slander; shame or infamy

onomatopoeia – words that imitate the noise they describe, e.g. moo, burp, hiss

orthography – the study of spellings of words

oxymoron – union of two seemingly contradictory words, e.g. 'stupid genius'

palindrome – word or phrase that can be spelt the same forwards and backwards, such as 'madam', or 'Able was I ere I saw Elba'

palinode – poem retracting something poet said in earlier poem

paradiastole – the use of euphemism to soften the impact of negative or occasionally positive traits

paralipsis – emphasis by seemingly trying to ignore, as in 'Far be it from me to mention the member's indiscretions.'

parapraxis – a Freudian slip

paraprosdokian – an unexpected end to a sentence or phrase that forces the reappraisal of the beginning, as in 'No pain ... no painkillers needed'

parisology – the use of evasive language (similar: tergiversate)

paronomasia – a pun; punning

passim – a term in footnotes, etc. to indicate that an expression or subject appears frequently throughout the text, e.g. 'This occurs in Nabokov passim'

phatic – communication for social ease rather than information

pleonasm – use of more words than necessary, though not exact synonyms, to express something, so 'free gift' (similar: tautology; compare: logorrhoea, prolixity, verbosity)

polysemy – the capacity of a single word to carry more than one meaning, e.g. 'book'

polysyndeton – use of multiple conjunctions, as in 'Bob and Pete and Mike and John'

prolepsis – the representation of a thing as being in a later time or state before it is applicable, e.g. 'You're fish food' (equivalent to flash-forward in film)

prolixity – the use of more words than is necessary (similar: logorrhoea, verbosity; compare: pleonasm, tautology)

prosody – the study of versification

rebus – a visual pun to represent a phrase

samizdat – forbidden writing, often politically sensitive

semantics – the study of word meaning; more casually, academic quibbling over meaning

shibboleth – historically, a language term or practice that identifies group

simile – figurative language that likens something to another thing, e.g. 'He's like a fish to water' (compare: metaphor)

solecism – non-standard usage or construction

soliloquy – in drama, a speech in which a character speaks their thoughts (usually to themselves, sometimes to the audience, but never to another character), revealing true feelings or intentions to the audience

sophistry – an argument that is plausible but logically fallacious

syllepsis – in which word does more than one duty in sentence with different senses, e.g. 'Belt your buckle, not your children'

syllogism – deductive reasoning (as opposed to induction)

synecdoche – a figure of speech in which a part is used to represent the whole, e.g. 'Many hands [i.e. people] make light work' (compare: metonym)

syntax – the arrangement of words and phrases to make sentences; logic for systems, especially computer software

tautology – the use of redundant words to say the same thing twice, e.g. 'will and testament' (similar: pleonasm; compare: logorrhoea, prolixity, verbosity)

tergiversate – to use evasive language (similar: parisology)

tmesis – the splitting of words by other words, e.g. 'abso-bloody-lutely'

toponym – a place name; a reference derived from a place name, e.g. 'Waterloo' as a crushing defeat

trope – a word or phrase used figuratively; a common theme or style (the four main types are metaphor, metonymy, synecdoche and irony)

verbigeration – the repetition of meaningless phrases

verbosity – the use of more words than is necessary (similar: logorrhoea, prolixity; compare: pleonasm, tautology)

zeugma – the rhetorical yoking of several types of verb or noun to create similar phrases (sometimes without subject-verb agreement), e.g. 'Will she lose her dignity, her mind, her life?'

IRONY, ETC.

acerbic – bitter, harsh, cutting; sour (similar: vitriolic)

arcane – understood by only a few

arch – knowing, cunning, superior, sly; self-consciously playful or coy

camp – theatrical or exaggerated, especially amusingly; code for: gay

esoteric – representing and understood by a small number (similar: arcane)

facetious – intended to be humorous, especially inappropriately (similar: tongue in cheek)

farcical – broadly humorous; ludicrous

fey – whimsically unusual and vague; otherworldly; slightly crazy; camp

ironic(al) – characterised by poignant difference between expected and actual; meaning the opposite or obliquely different to what is stated; sarcastic or mocking

pejorative – uncomplimentary (similar: derogatory)

pun – a play on similar sounding words for humorous or rhetorical effect, often used in newpaper headlines

sarcastic – expressing cutting ridicule or contempt, usually delivered ironically

sardonic – mocking, scornful, sneering

satirical – holding up human folly to ridicule

wry – lightly mocking, dryly humorous, often with irony

CASUAL LANGUAGE CATEGORIES

argot (slang used by certain group), cant (ephemera or fashionable words), colloquialism (belonging to casual speech), jargon (lexical subset special to group or profession), slang (common informal words or phrases), vulgarism (vulgar word or expression)

ART & MEDIA

PRINT JOURNALISM

TERMS

advertising, advertorial, affidavit, agency, angle, assignment, attribution, backgrounder, banner ad, beat, blag, blog / post, blurb, byline, caption, Chatham House Rule, circulation, citizen journalism, clarification, clickthrough, colour, copy, correction, coverline, CPM (cost per thousand), cross-head, cuttings, dateline, deadline, death-knock, defamation, door-step, draft, DPS (double page spread), editorial, editorialise, embargo, endnote, exclusive, feature, font, freelancer, get, hack, headline, hearsay, hook, house style, illustration, innuendo, intro, journalist, journo, junket / famil(iarisation), kerning, kill fee, layout, lead, leader, leading, libel, literal, masthead, media kit, nut graf, nut par(agraph), obit(uary), off the record, on spec, orphan, package, pap(arazzi), pitch, podcast, point size, PR, print run, proof, puff piece, pull quote, readership, reporter, retraction, round, sans serif, scoop, screamer / shriek (exclamation mark), serif, shorthand, silly season, skyscraper ad, smear, spread, source, spike, splash, standfirst, subeditor, subhead, sub judice, tip, traffic, transcript, widow, wires, writ

FASHION MAGAZINE LANGUAGE

bijou(x), bling, boho, bouncy, catwalk, celebutante, chic, clash, colour, contemporary, cool, cosmetic, cosy, cuisine, culinary, cultural, cut, cutting-edge, debut, décor, delicious, designer, digs, ditzy, divine, elegant, ensemble, epicurean, ex, expression, fabulous, fierce, fine, fitted, flash, floaty, folksy, formula, frosty, glam(our), grown-up, gush, hip, hooked, hot, hurrah, icon, impeccable, inspiration, kitsch, knit, kooky, label, lively, look, luxe, nix, outlook, pamper, party, patent, pattern, pointer, pose, rehab, saggy, satchel, saucy, scary, season, sexed-up, sexy, shabby, silhouette, spicy, squeal, standout, statement, stiletto, stylish, super, sweetie, tacky, taper, tasteful, trashy, trendy, toff, update, volume, wardrobe, weird

TELEVISION

CRITICISM ELEMENTS

acting (cameo, cast, chemistry, delivery, dialogue, dramatic licence, lead, lines, performance, portrayal, projection, range, role, scene-stealing), ad break, anchor, backstory, bathos, comedy, design, direction, drama, editing, episode, format, humour (build-up, gag, punchline, payoff, set-up, straight guy), logic, method, music, opening, pathos, pilot, plausibility, plot, production, program(me), ratings, research, screenplay, script, series, structure, subtitle, synopsis, tension, theme tune, timing, title sequence, twist, wardrobe (clothes, fashion), writers

FILM

CRITICISM ELEMENTS

acting (cameo, cast, impersonation, lead, performance, portrayal, range, role, scene-stealing), action, adaptation, antagonist, argument, art direction, auteur, backstory, box office, casting, character(isation), chemistry, chronology, cinematography (frame, shot, take, visuals), coherence, cohesion, costumes, delivery, dénouement, dialogue, direction, director (early, middle-period, late-period), dramatic licence, editing, effect, episode, exchange, exposition, focus, formula, funding, genre, goal, grandeur, hero(ine), imagery, ideology, influence, intention, interlude, interplay, lighting, logic, metaphor, method, mise en scène, momentum, motif, motivation, music (song, soundtrack, theme), opening, pace / pacing, plausibility, plot (narrative, storyline, subplot, trick), post-production, premise, protagonist, psychology, reference, research, resonance, rhythm, running length, scene, score, screenplay, script, sequence, set-piece, setting, shot, sound (editing, mix), special effects, story, storytelling, structure, style, subtext, sweep, symbolism, synopsis, tempo, tension, texture, theme, tone, twist, undercurrent, vibe, vision, wardrobe (clothes, fashion)

GENRES

action, action-adventure, animation (cartoon), anime, blockbuster, chiller, conspiracy, crime, cult, disaster, documentary, drama, dramedy, dystopia, escape, fantasy, farce, film noir, genre, heist, horror, manga, mockumentary, musical, musical comedy, period, psychological thriller, romantic comedy (romcom), sci-fi, schlockbuster, steampunk, surrealist, teen, thriller, tragedy, weepie

SYNONYMS FOR 'FILM'

account, actioner, adaptation, adventure, anthology, apologia, (auto)biography, blockbuster, burlesque, chronicle, classic, composition, concoction, confection, costumer, critique, crowd-pleaser, dissertation, doco, documentary, drama, dramatisation, DVD, entertainment, entry, epic, examination, excursion, exercise, exploration, fable, fairy tale, fantasy, farce, fare, feature, follow-up, history, homage (riff), melodrama, misfire, movie, mystery, noir, number, parable, parody, picture, portrait, portrayal, prequel, project, remake / rethink / reworking, rendition, revival, rip-off, romance, romp, rumination, saga, satire, sequel, showcase, soufflé, spoof, story, study, sudser, take, tale, talkfest, tearjerker, telling, threequel, thriller, tract, transfer, treatment, treatise, valentine, vehicle, version, western, whodunnit, work, yarn

LITERATURE

CRITICISM ELEMENTS

argument, atmosphere, author, backstory, blurb, chapter, character, characterisation, chronology, continuity, cover (art), dialogue, digression, editing, foreword, format, genre, ghostwriter, ideas, incident, irony, language, length, logic, marketing, mastery, meaning, metaphor, method, narrative (storyline, subplot, trick), opening (line), pace / pacing, paragraph, passage, person, photographs, phrasing, plausibility, plot, poetry (metre, rhyme), point of view, preface, premise, proofing, prose, publisher, realism, research, rhythm, sales, sensibility, sentence, structure, style, subtext, subtlety, symbolism, tension, text, theme, thesis, thought, twist, universe, vignette, voice

GENRES

action, autobiography, Bildungsroman, biography, chick lit, chronicle, comedy, crime, documentary, drama, essay, fantasy, fiction, gay, gothic, graphic novel, historical, historical fiction, horror, kaddish (combined biography and fiction), lad lit, lesbian, magic realism, manga, memoir, modernist, non-fiction, picaresque, poetry, polemic, police procedural, postmodern, roman-à-clef, romance, saga, satire, thriller

SYNONYMS FOR 'BOOK'

adventure, anthology, autobiography, bestseller, bible, biography, blockbuster, classic, collection, composition, concoction, confection, copy, draft, epic, essay, exercise, fable, fantasy, farce, fare, hagiography, hardback / hardcover, leaflet, manuscript, memoir, morality tale, narrative, novel, pamphlet, paperback, parable, pastoral, portrait, project, read, reading, record, revival, romp, round-up, saga, sequel, story, tale, title, tome, universe, volume, work, yarn

PUBLISHING

advance, backlist, bibliography, blad (book layout and design information – a trade marketing tool), blurb, chromalin (colour-correct proof), colophon (brief note at end of book), copy, copy edit, copyright, edition, edit, endnote, endpaper, footnote, imprimatur, imprint, index, ISBN / ISSN, launch, moral rights, preface, proof, proofread, recto (right-hand page), reprint, review, royalty, soutache (the braid at the top and bottom of a book spine), structural edit, trade, typesetting, verso (left-hand page), vignette (a decorative book design, often incorporating vine leaves; also an illustration lacking a defined border)

MUSIC

CRITICISM ELEMENTS

acoustic, album, atmosphere, audience, backing, band (duo, three-piece, trio), beat, bridge, cadenza, canon, chiming, chord, chorus, covers, crescendo, crowd, delivery, dissonance, ensemble, genre, gig, guest appearance, harmony, hook(line), influences, inspiration, instruments, key, lyrics, marketing, melody, meter, music charts / sales, note, pitch, refrain, release, repertoire, resonance, reverberation, rhythm, riff, show, song (composition, single), tempo, timbre, tone, tour, track, tune, verse, virtuosity

GENRES

alt, alternative, beatbox, big band, blues, boogie woogie, breakbeat, choral, Christian, classical, country, dance, disco, drum 'n' bass, electronic, folk, funk, gamelan, garage, gospel, grunge, hardcore, heavy metal, hip-hop, honky tonk, house, jazz, jungle, Latin, metal, new age, polka, pop, punk, ragtime, R&B (rhythm and blues), rap, reggae, rock, rockabilly, salsa, ska, skiffle, soul, techno, trance, yodelling, world

CLASSICAL TERMS

a cappella – sung without musical
accompaniment

aria – self-contained solo voice piece of
larger work

arpeggio – playing selected notes of chord
in succession

atonal – music written in no set key

bar – division of beats

beat – unit of musical rhythm

cadenza – improvised or written virtuoso
passage for soloist

cantata – musical composition, often choral
and religious in nature

chord – simultaneous playing of three or
more notes

coloratura – versatile singing with large
range, particularly soprano; ornamented
vocal music

concerto – composition for orchestra
and solo instruments, often in three
movements

finale – concluding passage

fugue – composition in which three or more
voices are variants of a basic theme

gebrauchsmusik – music, simple in
technique and style, that can be played by
talented amateurs rather than virtuosos

glissando – continuous slide from one note
to another

harmony – chord structure of piece of
music; pleasing combination of notes
played simultaneously

key – music scale based on key notes

klangfarbenmelodie – technique extending
melody to more than one instrument, so
adding tone, colour and texture

libretto – text of opera or other vocal work

madrigal – historical secular multi-voice
composition

melody – rhythmical succession of related
single notes

metre – organisation of beats

modulation – changing key within a
composition

movement – section of larger work largely
self-contained

obbligato – essential accompaniment
to piece of music, especially involving
instrument and voice

operetta – short and light opera

opus – used to list composer's work

partita – collection of musical pieces

pitch – frequency (highness or lowness)
of note

pizzicato – the picking rather than bowing
of strings

recital – solo concert with or without
accompaniment

recitative/-ivo – style in opera in which
words are sung closer in rhythm to
conversational speech to little orchestral
accompaniment

ritornello – instrumental passage, often in
vocal piece

sonata – piece of instrumental music
written in three or more movements in
varying forms and keys

spiccato – where the bow is lightly bounced
on the strings

stretto – fugue part with subject and answer
close together / overlapping

symphony – orchestral composition of
several movements

tempo – speed at which piece is performed

terzetto – vocal trio

tessitura – most musically suitable range of
voice

tremolo – effect produced by rapid repetition of same pitch

vibrato – effect produced by succession of rapid changes in pitch

CLASSICAL TERMS: PLAYING INSTRUCTIONS

accelerando – accelerating

adagio – slow tempo

allegro – fast tempo

andante – moderate tempo

animato – animated

con brio – with vigour

crescendo – increasing in volume

diminuendo – diminishing in volume

espressivo – expressively

forte – loud

largo – broad and very slow

legato – smooth, opposite of staccato

mosso – with speed or animation

presto – very fast

rallentado – becoming slower

staccato – abrupt, detached, opposite of legato

titenuto – with a sudden slowing of tempo

UNUSUAL INSTRUMENTS

balalaika (Russian three-stringed), bonang (Java gamelan metal drums), didgeridoo (Aboriginal wind), djembe (hand drum), gusli (multistring plucked), guzheng (Chinese zither-like), kazoo (mouth membrane), koto (Japanese zither-like), lyre (small Greek harp), ocarina (rounded wind), oud (Middle Eastern fretless stringed), pipe and tabor (morris dancing pipe and drum), shakuhachi (Japanese bamboo flute), sitar (long necked, plucked strings), theremin (early electronic), timbrel (tambourine of biblical times), tres (Cuban, six-stringed), tsabouna (goatskin Greek wind), zither (stringed box)

THEATRE, OPERA AND DANCE

CRITICISM ELEMENTS

act, acting (cameo, cast, character, chemistry, delivery, dialogue, enunciation, lead, lines, performance, portrayal, projection, range, role, scene-stealing, understudy), adaptation, aplomb, arrangement, audience, backdrop, backstory, bathos, choreography, chorus, conductor (baton), design, direction, drama, dramatic licence, dramatist, engagement, followspot, fourth wall, interpretation, libretto, lighting, lyrics, metaphor, monologue, music / score, musical, narrative, narrator, opening, orchestra, pace / pacing, pathos, plot, principal, production (piece, play, work), range, recital, repertoire, repertory, scene, scenery, score, set, set-piece, solo(ist), sound, stage, stage directions, stagehand, staging, step, surtitle, synopsis, tension, timing, tone, voice, wardrobe (clothes, fashion)

THEATRE: GENRES

ballet, black cabaret, children's theatre, circus, comedy, commedia dell'arte, comedy, dance, Elizabethan, epic theatre, farce, Gilbert & Sullivan, Grand Guignol, historical, improv(isational), kabuki, Lehrstücke, mime, morality play, musical theatre, music hall, Noh, opera, pantomime, physical theatre, Restoration comedy, romantic comedy, tragicomedy, vaudeville

THEATRE: BUILDING

amphitheatre (an outside auditorium), apron (the part of the stage that extends beyond curtain), auditorium (the seating area of theatre), coulisse (a piece of stage scenery in the wings, where actor can enter or exit), crossover (a walkway that lets players move between wings out of sight), downstage (the part of the stage that is closest to the audience), fly system (ropes and pulleys for moving sets, etc.), loggia (an open balcony), orchestra pit, proscenium (the front part of stage or the arch that frames it), rake (the upward slope of stage), stage left / right (to performers' left / right when facing the audience), tableau curtain (one that opens up and outwards), upstage (the part of the stage that is furthest from the audience), wings (the sides of the stage that are out of sight of audience)

TYPES OF DANCE

ballet, ballroom, barn, belly, bolero, bossa nova, breakdancing, ceroc, cha-cha, country and western, flamenco, folk, foxtrot, haka, hip-hop, hula, hustle, Irish, jazz, jig, jitterbug, jive, krumping, latin, line dancing, mambo, merengue, modern, morris, paso doble, polka, quickstep, rumba, salsa, samba, Scottish, shuffle, square, swing, tango, tap, two-step, waltz, zydeco

VISUAL ARTS: PAINTING AND PRINTMAKING

STYLES

abstract, antebellum, art brut, baroque, classicism, colour-field, constructivism, cubism, Dada, expressionism, fauvism, folk, futurism, gouache, Impressionism, mannerism, modernism, naive, neo-impressionism, op art, orientalism, Orphism, pop art, pointillism, postmodernism, primitivism, realism, Renaissance, rococo, romanticism, social realism, Stuckism, surrealism, tachism

TECHNIQUES AND EFFECTS

allegory, altarpiece, bodegón, body painting, botanical, broken colour, cartoon, charcoal, composition, drybrush, drypoint (printmaking technique), dimension, easel, figure, foreshortening, frieze, genre, grisaille (monochrome painting, usually grey or brown), halo, highlights, illustration, impasto (very thick application of paint showing brushstrokes), imprimatura, industrial, intaglio (printmaking technique), landscape, Madonna, maulstick, mezzotint (printmaking technique), miniature, mural, palette, panel, perspective, pietá, plein-air (alfresco), portrait, sfumato, still life, stippling, technique, trompe l'œil, underpainting, varnish, wet-in-wet

VISUAL ARTS: ARCHITECTURE

STYLES

Ad hocism, Ancient Egyptian, Ancient Greek, Ancient Roman, Art Deco, Art Moderne, Art Nouveau, Arts and Crafts, baroque, Bauhaus, Beaux Arts, Brutalism, Futurism, Georgian, gothic, Hindu, Islamic, MADI, medieval, Minimalism, modern, neo-classical, postmodern, Renaissance, rococo, romantic, Tudor, Victorian

PARTS OF A BUILDING

architrave – the lowest part of the
entablature that sits on top of columns

balustrade – a row of posts and rail around
a balcony or staircase

bay window – a window that projects out
from room

buttress – a support structure for wall,
usually of stone or brick

capital – the crowning feature of a column

clerestory – a row of high windows that rise
above the roof from an internal wall

colonnade – a series of columns joined by
an entablature

corbel – a stone bracket that juts out from
wall to carry a weight above

cornice – the horizontal moulding at top
of wall

cupola – a dome-like structure projecting
above a roof or dome

dado – part of a pedestal between cornice
and base

dentil – one of a series of teeth-like blocks
projecting from a building, often below a
cornice

dormer – a vertical window set into a
sloping roof

eave – the edge of a roof

entablature – a structure of moulds and
bands sitting above columns and below
the roof (comprising architrave, frieze and
cornice)

entasis – a slight convexity in a column (to
counteract the illusion of concavity in a
perfectly straight one)

frieze – a horizontal strip, often decorated,
running above windows or doors or below
a cornice

gargoyle – an ornament or rain spout in the
form of a grotesque creature

geodesic dome – a dome-like structure
composed of network of polygons

loggia – a gallery or corridor in the wall of a
building that opens on one side

mansard – a type of roof with two slopes,
a steep one from the walls and a shallow
one to the summit, on each of its four
sides (a hip or hipped roof has one slope
on each of its four sides)

mitre – a type of joint, in windows, etc.,
where surfaces are cut diagonally to form
a corner

oriel – a type of bay window that extends
out from the wall without touching the
ground

parapet – a low wall that rises above the
edge of a roof or balcony

pedestal – a solid base supporting a statue
or column

pediment – a low-pitched gable on Greek-
style buildings

peristyle – a row of columns surrounding a
temple or court

pilaster – a column built into a wall

port cochère – covered entrance for vehicles

portico – a porch or walkway with a roof
supported by columns

telamon – a man-shaped pillar

PARTS OF DWELLINGS

architrave (moulding around door or
window), balustrade (railing), cornice
(cyma, ovolo, scotia), dado (lower part of
room wall if decorated differently to upper),
eave (bottom of roof extending out from
wall), fascia (flat board running along end
of rafters), gable (triangular piece of wall
formed by pitched roof), guttering, jamb

(frame for window or door), joinery, joist (floor beams), lintel (horizontal beam over door or window), pelmet (internal frame above window for curtain rails, etc.), rafters (support beams for roof), sash (piece of window frame in which pane sits), skirting board (trim on wall adjacent to floor), stud (vertical beam of house), weatherboard

HOUSE ASPECTS
architect, area, borders, temperature / climate, colour, elevation, fittings, furnishings, landscaping, location, materials, orientation, outlook, plane

FAMOUS ARCHITECTS
Alvar Aalto, Filippo Brunelleschi, Santiago Calatrava, Antoni Gaudí, Frank Gehry, Claude-Nicolas Ledoux, Le Corbusier, Sir Norman Foster, Walter Burley Griffin, Zaha Hadid, Nicholas Hawksmoor, Herzog & de Meuron, Imhotep (pyramids), Shah Jahan (Taj Mahal), Philip Johnson, Louis Kahn, Rem Koolhaas, Claude Nicolas Ledoux, Daniel Libeskind, Adolf Loos, Edwin Lutyens, Charles Rennie Mackintosh, Richard Meier, Michelangelo, Ludwig Mies van der Rohe, Glenn Murcutt, John Nash, Oscar Niemeyer, Jean Nouvel, Andrea Palladio, IM Pei, Renzo Piano, Richard Rogers, Eero Saarinen, Rudolph Schindler, Sir John Soane, Louis Sullivan, Kenzo Tange, Jørn Utzon, Sir Christopher Wren, Frank Lloyd Wright

VISUAL ARTS: SCULPTURE

CONCEPTS
alto-relievo (high relief), armature, basso-relievo (bas- or low relief), bronze, bust, casting, chisel, clay, embossing, environmental sculpture, found art (objet trouvé), foundry, installation art, kinetic sculpture, miniature, mobile, mould, patina, plaster, readymade, relief, statue, terracotta, uttorondo (sculpture free from relief), wax, welding

STYLES
ancient: Aegian, Archaic, Classical, Egyptian, Etruscan, Hellenistic, Mesopotamian, Roman; later: Byzantine, Romanesque, Gothic, Impressionism, Medieval, Post-Impressionism, Neoclassicism, Mannerism, Renaissance, Baroque, Rococo, Romanticism, Abstract, Cubism, Surrealism, Contemporary

MATERIALS
acrylic, aluminium, basalt, bronze, clay, copper, diorite, earth, fabric, fibreglass, glass, gold, granite, ice, ivory, jade, limestone, marble, plastic, sand, silver, steel, stones, terracotta, wood

FAMOUS SCULPTORS
Jean Arp, Gian Lorenzo Bernini, Louise Bourgeois, Constantin Brâncusi, Alexander Calder, Camille Claudel, Donatello, Marcel Duchamp, Alberto Giacometti, Antony Gormley, Barbara Hepworth, Len Lye, Aristide Maillol, Henri Matisse, Michelangelo, Henry Moore, Isamu Noguchi, Claes Oldenburg, Phidias, Pablo Picasso, Nicola Pisano, Polykleitos, Auguste Rodin, Shin Sang-Ho, Richard Serra, Isaac Witkin

VISUAL ARTS: PHOTOGRAPHY

TERMS

ambient light, aperture, archival, aspect ratio, background, blow-up, buffer, CCD, close-up, CMOS, CMYK, colour, CompactFlash, contrast, cropping, darkroom, depth of field, depth of focus, DPI, double exposure, downloading, enlargement, EXIF, exposure, fill-in light, film speed, filter, FireWire, f-number, focal length, focus, foreground, frame, graininess, grayscale, image resolution, JPEG/TIFF/BMP, LCD, lens, light meter, macro, memory stick, motor drive, negative, noise, overexposure, pan, panorama, parallax, Photoshop, pixels, positive, print, processing, RAW, red-eye, reflector, resolution, retouching, RGB, saturation, sharpness, shutter, shutter lag, shutter speed, slide, telephoto, thumbnail, time exposure, tone, transparency, tripod, underexposure, USB, viewfinder, wide angle lens, zoom lens

FAMOUS PHOTOGRAPHERS

Ansel Adams, Robert Adams, Nobuyoshi Araki, Diane Arbus, Richard Avedon, David Bailey, Elmer Batters, Cecil Beaton, Margaret Bourke-White, Julia Margaret Cameron, Robert Capa, Henri Cartier-Bresson, Anton Corbijn, Edward Curtis, Patrick Demarchelier, Robert Doisneau, Alfred Eisenstaedt, Anne Geddes, David Hamilton, David Hockney, Richard Kern, David LaChappelle, Dorothea Lange, Jacque-Henri Lartigue, Annie Leibovitz, Patrick Lichfield (Lord Snowdon), Robert Mapplethorpe, Helmut Newton, Terry O'Neill, Irving Penn, Richard Prince, Man Ray, Bettina Rheims, Herb Ritts, George Roger, Joe Rosenthal, David Seymour, Cindy Sherman, Jeanloup Sieff, Alfred Stieglitz, Juergen Teller, Spencer Tunick

FOOD & DRINK

CRITICISM ELEMENTS

ambience, artwork, atmosphere, authenticity, chef, clientele, coffee, consistency, courses, crockery, cutlery, décor, design, desserts, dishes, food (adventurous, variety, exterior, flavours, hand-made, plating, portion size, preparation, sourcing), ingredients, interior, lighting, music, noise, originality, owner, sauces, seating, service (attentiveness, communication, competence, friendliness, knowledge, speed), side dishes, track record, tradition, value for money, view, wine list, wine pairing

TASTES

basic tastes: bitterness, fattiness, saltiness, sourness, sweetness, umami (meaty or savoury taste in foods such as meat, cheese or soy); other tastes: acerbic, acidic, acrid, astringent, chalky, chilly, cool, creamy, curry, dry, fresh, hearty, hot, juicy, meaty, metallic, numbness, pucker, pungent, relish, savoury, smoky, spicy, succulent, tallow, tangy, zesty

SAUCES

aioli (garlic, egg yolks, olive oil), Béarnaise (butter, egg yolks, tarragon, white vinegar), béchamel (hot milk, flour and butter roux), beurre blanc (hot butter sauce with white wine/vinegar and shallots), beurre cafe de Paris (chicken livers, thyme, butter, cream, mustard), chausseur (mushrooms, shallots, white wine), chermoula (pickled lemons, lemon juice, garlic, cumin, salt, herbs), coulis (puree of fruit or vegetables), espagnole (flour and butter roux, dark stock, tomato puree), gravy (juices from cooking meat), harissa (chilli peppers, garlic, often coriander, cumin, caraway), hollandaise (butter, eggs, lemon juice), jus (sauce primarily from natural juices of cooked food), mayonnaise (cold mix of eggs and olive oil), mole (onion, garlic, ground seeds, chillis, chocolate), mornay (béchamel and cheese), pesto (basil, pine nuts, garlic, olive oil, hard cheese), ragù (tomato sauce), remoulade (mayonnaise with chilli and mixed herbs), ribollita (savoy cabbage, butter, vegetables, stock), Romesco (almonds, roasted garlic, tomato, red peppers), salsa verde (herbs, garlic, capers, anchovies), sauce vierge (olive oil, lemon juice, tomatoes, basil), tartare (mayonnaise, capers, gherkins, shallots, parsley, lemon juice), tomato (onion, garlic, tomatoes, tomato paste), velouté (flour, butter, white meat stock), vinaigrette (oil, white vinegar)

SOUPS: A SELECTION

avgolemono (Greek chicken, lemon, egg), bisque (thick shellfish), borscht (Russian beetroot), bouillabaisse (Marseille fish stew), caldo verde (Portuguese minced cabbage), chowder (thick seafood), cock-a-leekie (Scottish chicken and leek), consommé (clear, based on stock), cullen skink (Scottish smoked haddock and potato), fasolada (Greek bean), gazpacho (Spanish cold, spicy vegetables), goulash (Hungarian spicy beef and pork), gumbo (US, Caribbean thick with okra), kimchi jjigae (Korean spicy cabbage), menudo (Mexican tripe and spices), minestrone (Italian vegetable and noodles), mulligatawny (Anglo-Indian curry-flavoured), pappa pomadoro (Tuscany tomato and bread), potage (thick), pot-au-feu (French vegetables and meat), snert (Dutch split peas), tomyumgoong (Thai spicy and sour with prawns), vichyssoise (French leek and potato), white gazpacho (almonds, bread, sherry vinegar, olive oil)

SMALL DISHES

amuse-bouches, amuse-gueules, canapés, hors d'oeuvre (France), antipasto, cicchetti, stuzzichini (Italy), pintxos / tapas (Spain), dim sum (China), antojitos (Mexico)

PLACES TO EAT

bar, bistro, brasserie, buffet, buvette, cabaret, café, cafeteria, canteen, casino, coffeehouse, coffee shop, cookhouse, deli(catessen), diner, dining hall, drive-in, eatery, eating house, fast-food chain, grill, hangout, hash house, hot-dog stand, inn, joint, kitchen, lunch counter, lunchroom, mess hall, nightspot, pizzeria, pub, restaurant, ristorante, saloon, snack bar, supper club, tavern, tearoom, trattoria

AUGUSTE ESCOFFIER'S BRIGADE DE CUISINE

chef de cuisine (kitchen chief)
sous chef (deputy kitchen chief)
chef de partie (station chef)
commis (assistant cook or junior cook)
saucier (sauce cook)
rôtisseur (broiler cook)
grillardin (grill cook)
friturier (deep fry cook)
entremetier (entrée maker)
potager (soup cook)
legumier (vegetable cook)
pâtissier (pastry cook)
garde manger (pantry chef – a chef who
    prepares cold items)
boulanger (baker)
boucher (butcher)
tournant (swing cook – a chef who rotates
    through the kitchen as needed)
apprentis (apprentice chef)
plongeur (dishwasher)

DRINK

WINE: TYPES OF GRAPE

barbera, cabernet franc, cabernet sauvignon, chardonnay, chenin blanc, cinsault, colombard, gamay, gewurtztraminer, grenache (garnacha), malbec, marsanne, merlot, mourvèdre, muller-thurgau, muscat, nebbiolo, petit meunier, petit verdot, pinot gris (pinot grigio), pinot noir, pinotage, riesling, rose, sangiovese, sauvignon blanc, semillon, shiraz (syrah), tempranillo, torrontes, trebbiano, verdicchio, viognier, zinfandel

RED WINE STYLES

Akhasheni, Amarone, Barbaresco, Barolo, Beaujolais, Bordeaux, Burgundy, Chianti, Crianza, Garnacha (Grenache), Lambrusco, Marsala, Merlot, Monastrell, Moscatel, Palomino, Pinot Meunier, Pinot Noir, Pinotage, Rioja, Syrah (Shiraz), Tempranillo, Valpolicella, Zinfandel / Primitivo

WHITE WINE STYLES

Chablis, Frascati, Meursault, Moscatel, Muscat, Orvieto, Pedro Ximénez, Pouilly-Fuisse, Retsina, Silvaner, Soave, Tokaji, Torrontes, Verdelho

SPARKLING WHITE STYLES

Asti Spumante, Cava, Champagne, Prosecco, Sekt

WINE CRITICISM ELEMENTS

qualities: acidity, alcohol, aroma, balance, bouquet, body, brix, character, clarity, cleanness, colour, complexity, expressiveness, faults, finish, fruit, integration, length, mouthfeel, nose, structure, tannin, texture; origin: country, label, region, producer, terroir, vintage

WINE DESCRIPTIONS: A SELECTION

acid, almond, apple, apricot, armpit, asparagus, blackberry, blueberry, buttery, cat's pee, cedar, cherry, chocolate, currant, earth, eucalyptus, fig, flinty, floral, fruity, gooseberry, grapefruit, green pepper, herbaceous, honey, leathery, lemon, lime, liquorice, lychee, melon, mint, mown grass, mushroom, nutmeg, oak, orange, peach, pear, pencil shavings, peppery, pineapple, plum, pomegranate, raspberry, roses, smoky, spicy, strawberry, tar, toast, tobacco, vanilla, wet wool, woody

BEER STYLES

ale – top-fermenting yeasts used at warmer temperatures, giving fruity or spicy flavours

bock – a strong dark beer made for drinking in spring

India pale ale – with extra hops to allow for transportation

lager – bottom-fermenting yeasts used, at cooler temperatures, to produce a clean, crisp beer

pilsner – a clear, malty, hoppy lager

porter – a dark ale, malty and hoppy, less strong, sweeter

stout – a dark ale, strong bodied, stronger, less sweet

weissbier (wheat beer / witbier) – a fruity beer with low bitterness, brewed with wheat as well as barley

COFFEE STYLES

affogato (a shot served over ice cream), americana / long black (a shot with hot water added), breve (a shot served with light cream), cafe au lait (a shot served with the same amount of steamed milk), caffe latte (shot with more steamed milk), cappuccino (equal parts of espresso, steamed and frothed milk), corretto (with a shot of liquor), doppio (double shot of espresso; solo = single shot), espresso con panna (a shot topped with whipped cream), flat white (two-thirds steamed milk with minimal foam), lungo (espresso letting more water through coffee), macchiato (espresso with a drop of steamed milk), mocha (a latte with chocolate syrup), noisette (espresso served with a dash of cream which turns it a hazelnut colour), ristretto (espresso letting less water through coffee

GARDENING

LANDSCAPE GARDENING
TERMS

acarpous (not producing fruit), air-layering (method of propagation by cutting into bark to form roots), alcove, *allée* (formal planting of trees either side of drive or path), annual (non-woody plant that dies at the end of its growing season), arbor (a latticework for supporting climbing plants), bacciferous (berry-producing), *berceau* (vaulted trellis), bonsai (practice of creating dwarfed, shaped trees), border, bosquet (a thicket of trees, often intersected by paths), bower (a shaded, leafy recess, sometimes with a seat), budding, chitting (germinating potatoes before planting), clairvoie (gate or similar in wall to show view beyond), cloche (covering for plant against cold), cloister (courtyard with covered walk), colonnade (row of columns), conservatory, cultivar (cultivated new form of plant, which will be in quotation marks after plant name), dead-head, deciduous (type of tree that sheds its leaves in winter), dioecious / monoecious (species having male and reproductive parts on separate plants / the same plant), entomophilous / anemophilous (pollinated by insects / wind), epiphyte (plant that lives on another but is nourished solely on air and rain), espalier (to train tree against a wall, often fruit tree, usually in a symmetrical shape), evergreen, forcing (artificially encouraging plant to grow or flower), friable (description of soil that is crumbly and good to grow plants in), gazebo, grafting (combining scion shoot with rootstock to form new plant), grotto, ha-ha (sunken wall or hedge), herbaceous (description of plants that are not woody), landscaping, layering (method propagation by securing part of plant to soil to encourage new roots), loam (quality friable soil, as opposed to clay), mulch (ground covering around plants to prevent weeds and retain moisture), parterre (patterned flower or vegetable garden), perennial (non-woody plant that lives for more than three years), pergola, pleaching (interlacing trees as in a border), pollarding (cutting back to trunk to encourage dense growth), pollination, potager (vegetable garden), pruning, rhizome (horizontal underground stem that can root and form a new plant), root stock (root part of grafted plant), scion (shoot to be grafted on to rootstock), standard (shrub trained as shaped tree), taxonomy (classification of plants, which have popular names and Latin names), tendril (twisting shoots that climbing plants use for support), terrace (flat area, often supported by retaining wall), thinning, topiary (the trimming of a tree or bush into an ornamental shape), trellis (lattice for supporting climbing plants), variegated (term for leaf or flower of two tones)

SPORT

FOOTBALL

TERMS

4-4-2, A-League, attacker, away / home, Bundesliga, caution, centre, chant, clearance, coin toss, commentator, corner, cross, crossbar, defender, derby, dismissed, draw, dummy, equaliser, extra time, fan, fanzine, free kick, friendly, goal, goalpost, (goal)keeper, half-volley, handball, hat-trick, header, infringement, kit/strip, La Liga, Ligue 1, late tackle, linesman / referee's assistant, manager, match, midfielder, net, non-league, obstruction, offside, onion bag, penalty, pitch, Premiership, promotion, red card, referee, relegation, score, season, sent off, Serie A, shepherd, sideline, stoppage time, striker, sweeper, tackle, through ball, throw-in, transfer fee, wall, whistle, winger, yellow card

TOP TEAMS: GROUNDS AND COLOURS

AC Milan: San Siro, red and black vertical stripes; AFC Ajax: Amsterdam Arena, white with red vertical stripe; Arsenal: Emirates Stadium, red and white; Barcelona: Camp Nou, white; Bayern München: Allianz Arena, red and white stripes; Celtic: Celtic Park, green and white stripes; Chelsea: Stamford Bridge, royal blue; Inter Milan: San Siro, black and blue vertical stripes; Juventus: Stadio Olimpico, black and white vertical stripes; Manchester United: Old Trafford, red and white; Olympiacos: Karaiskakis Stadium, red and white vertical stripes; Olympic Lyonnais: Stade Gerland, white with vertical blue and red stripe; Paris St Germain: Parc de Princes, blue with red and white vertical stripe; Porto: Estadio do Dragao, blue and white vertical stripes; Rangers: Ibrox Stadium, green and white; Real Madrid: Santiago Bernabeu, white

RUGBY

TERMS

advantage, advantage line, ankle tap, back, backline, back row, binding, blindside, blood bin, box kick, breakdown, caution, charge down, chip, conversion, crash ball, cross-bar, dead ball line, drive, drop goal, dummy, fair catch / mark, feed, fend, five metre scrum, forward, forward pass, foul, free kick, front row, Garryowen / up and under, goal post, grubber kick, haka, high tackle, kick-off, late tackle, lineout, maul, offload, offside, on side, out on the full, pack, penalty, place kick, punt, red card, referee, restart, ruck, rucking, screw, scrum, second phase, sending off, shepherd, sin bin, spear tackle, speculator, tackle, tap kick, ten metre rule, knock-on, touch judge, touchline, try, try-line, turnover, willy-away, yellow card

POSITIONS

scrum: (blindside / open side) flanker, hooker, lock, number eight, (loosehead / tighthead) prop; backline: halfback / scrum half, first five-eighths / fly half, second five-eighths / inside centre, (outside) centre, winger, fullback

RUGBY WORLD CUP WINNERS

1987 New Zealand, 1991 Australia, 1995 South Africa, 1999 Australia, 2003 England, 2007 South Africa

CRICKET

TERMS

all-rounder, appeal, bails, batsman, bouncer, boundary, bowler, break, (leg) bumper, bye, chuck, crease, cut, dead ball, delivery, (half) century, circle, classy knock, crease, declaration, dolly, doosra, dot ball, drive, (golden) duck, extra, fast, fielder, flipper, follow-on, four, full toss, googly, hat trick, hook, follow-on, four, infield, inner ring (inside the 30m circle in ODIs – one-day internationals), innings, in-out field, knock, lbw, leg side, maiden, no-ball, ODI, off side, opener, orthodox, outfield, over, partner, pitch, playing on, pull, run, seamer, shot, single, sight screen, six, sledging, slip, slog, spell, spinner, square, stance, stumping, stumps, (reverse) sweep, swing, tail-ender test, third man, ton, twelfth man, Twenty20, umpire, walk, wicket, wide, yorker, zooter (Shane Warne's mystery ball)

POSITIONS

Clockwise from noon: wicketkeeper, leg-slip, fine leg, square leg, mid-wicket, mid-on, long-on, long-off, mid-off, extra cover, cover, cover-point, backward point, third man, gully, slip (1-4), batsman, non-striker, bowler; short positions: short square leg, short fine leg, short cover, short midwicket; silly positions: silly point, silly mid-on, silly mid-off; specialist ODI positions: boundary rider, sweeper

MAJOR TEST GROUNDS

(Ground, location, capacity)

Melbourne Cricket Ground, Melbourne, Australia, 100,000

Sydney Cricket Ground, Sydney, Australia, 46,000

The Gabba, Brisbane, Australia, 42,000

The WACA, Perth, Australia, 24,000

Adelaide Oval, Adelaide, Australia, 34,000

Lords, London, England, 29,000

Old Trafford, Manchester, England, 19,000

The Oval, London, England, 23,000

Headingley, Leeds, England, 20,000

Edgbaston, Birmingham, England, 21,000

Trent Bridge, Nottingham, England, 17,000

National Stadium, Karachi, Pakistan, 34,000

Gadaffi Stadium, Lahore, Pakistan, 62,000

Eden Gardens, Kolkata, India, 90,000

Chepauk, Chennai, India, 50,000

Wankhede Stadium, Mumbai, India, 45,000

Eden Park, Auckland, New Zealand, 42,000

Basin Reserve, Wellington, New Zealand, 11,000

Carisbrook, Dunedin, New Zealand, 29,000

AMI Stadium, Christchurch, New Zealand, 36,000

Wanderers Stadium, Johannesburg, South Africa, 34,000

Newlands, Cape Town, South Africa, 25,000

Kingsmead, Durban, South Africa, 25,000

St George's Park, Port Elizabeth, South Africa, 19,000

Kensington Oval, Bridgetown, Barbados, 15,000

Sabina Park, Kingston, Jamaica, 16,000

R Premadasa Stadium, Colombo, Sri Lanka, 35,000

Galle International Stadium, Galle, Sri Lanka, 35,000

Paikiasothy Saravanamuttu Stadium, Colombo, Sri Lanka, 15,000

Asgiriya Stadium, Kandy, Sri Lanka, 10,000

Chittagong, Chittagong, Bangladesh, 20,000

Sher-e-Bangla National Stadium, Dhaka, Bangladesh, 25,000

Harare Sports Club, Harare, Zimbabwe, 10,000

BASKETBALL

TERMS

air ball, alley-oop, assist, backscreen, basket, block, carrying, centre, charging, chucking, defence, downcourt, dribble, elbowing, endline / baseline, fake, fast break, field goal, (small / power) forward, foul, free throw, full-court press, (point / shooting) guard, hook shot, jump ball, jump shot, layup, offence, rebound, shoot, shot clock, sidelines, sixth man, slam dunk, technical foul, three-pointer, tie, time-out, tip-off, travelling, turnover

RACQUET SPORTS

TENNIS TERMS

ace, advantage, approach, backhand, baseline, break, break-point, bye, call, clay / grass court, crosscourt, Davis Cup, deuce, doubles, drop-shot, fault / double fault, first service, foot fault, forehand, game, game point, ground stroke, let, line judge, lob, love, match point, net, new balls, out, overhead, passing shot, point, rally, rubber, seed, serve, serve and volley, service line, set point, sideline, singles, slice, smash, spin, stroke, sweet spot, T, tie, tiebreak, topspin, tramlines, umpire, unforced error, volley, wildcard, winner

SQUASH TERMS

ace, appeal, attempt, backswing, board, cutline, die, down, follow through, game, game ball, half-court line, hand, length, let, match, nick, not up, out, out line, point, rail, ralley, service, service box, service line, side wall, stroke, tin

BADMINTON TERMS

alley, back alley, back court, backhand, baseline, carry, centre line, clear, court, doubles, drive, drop shot, fault, feint, flick, forecourt, forehand, flick, game, half court, kill, let, match, midcourt, net shot, passing shot, push shot, rally, serve, service court, set, shuttlecock, singles, sling, smash, throw, wood shot

GOLF

TERMS

albatross, amateur, ambrose, approach, apron, back nine, backspin, birdie, bogey, borrow, bunker (sand trap), caddie, card, carry, chip shot, clubhouse, divot, dogleg, double bogey, eagle, fade, fairway, flag, fore, fringe, front nine, gimmie, green, handicap, hole in one, hook, iron, lie, links, lip, match play, mulligan, out of bounds, par, pitch, play through, professional, pull, push, putter, range, rough, round, run, scratch golfer, slice, slope, stableford, stance, stroke play, swing, tee, tiger tees, topped shot, water hazard, wedge, wood, yips

CYCLING

TERMS

attack, bidon (water bottle), block, bonk, breakaway, bridge, cadence, caravane, chase, chicane, cleat, commissaire, criterium, danseuse, derny, domestique, draft (slipstream), echelon (paceline), etage (stage), derailleur, gear, handicap, honk, jump, keirin, madison, motorpace, musette, omnium, palmares, pannier, parcours, peloton (bunch, field, pack), poursuivant, prime, prologue, red lantern, road race, saddle, slicks, slipstream, soigneur, souplesse (suppleness), split, stage, stagiaire, time trial, velodrome, yellow jersey

BOATING

NAUTICAL TERMS

aft, aground, anchor, anchorage, ashore, bar, beacon, beam, bearing, Beaufort Scale, belay, berth, bilge, bimini, bollard, boom, bow, bridge, brigantine, bulkhead, bulwark, buoy, capsize, capstan, catamaran, clew, crow's nest, deck, draft, flotsam / jetsam, fore, forehatch, founder, gaff, galley, gangplank, genoa, gunwale, halyard, hammock, hatch, helmsman, hull, jib, keel, ketch, lanyard, lazarette, leeway, lifeboat, list, luff, mainbrace, mast, mess, moor, oars, pitch / roll / yaw, pontoon, poop deck, port, porthole, quarterdeck, rig, rigging, rowlocks, row, sail, skipper, sloop, sonar, sounding, spar, spinnaker, splice, stanchion, starboard, stay, stern, transom, trawl, trim, wake, wash, windward, yardarm

TYPES OF BOAT

barge, bark / barque, brigantine, canoe, carrack or nau (Portugal), catamaran, clipper, coracle, corvette, cutter, dhow (Arabia), dinghy, dragon boat, dugout, felucca (Egypt), freighter, frigate, galleon, galley, gondola (Venice), houseboat, hovercraft, hydrofoil, inflatable, jangada (Brazil), jet boat, jetski, junk, kayak, ketch, kolae (Thailand), laser, launch, lifeboat, longboat, longship, luzzu (Malta), paddle steamer, patrol boat, pedalo, pirogue (West Africa), pontoon, PT boat, punt, runabout, sampan (China), schooner, scow, shikara (India), skiff, skipjack, sloop, speedboat, superyacht, trawler, trireme (ancient Mediterranean), tug, waka (New Zealand), whaler, yacht

MOUNTAIN SPORTS

SKIING TERMS

après ski, base, basket, bindings, boots, bunny slope, carve, chair lift, christiana / christy turn, crud, DIN settings, downhill, dump, edge, extension, fall line, flexion, freestyle, garland, gondola, herringbone, jib, jump, mogul, piste, poles, powder, quad, rope tow, schuss, slalom, snow plough / wedge, traverse, whiteout

SNOWBOARDING TERMS

alley-oop, backside, blindside, bonk, boost, camber, cant, carve, crud, dampening, duckfoot, face plant, flex, forward lean, freeriding, frontside, goofy foot, halfpipe, handplant, hard boots, insert, job, leash, lip, mogul, nose, ollie, quarterpipe, rail, railing, soft boots, stomp pad, tail, toe edge, traverse, wall

CLIMBING

Terms

alpenstock, anchor, approach, arête, bandolier, belay, bergshrund, bivouac, bolt, buttress, cairn, chimney, cirque, clean, col, cornice, couloir, crampon, crevasse, death zone, descender, Diamox, etrier, face, fluke, free climb, glacier, glissade, Grigri, gumby, harness, headwall, hook, Jumar, karabiner, moraine, moulin, névé, nut, pass, pitch, piton, prusik, rappel / abseil, rime, rivet, roof, route, saddle, scree, serac, shoulder, snout, spur, tarn, traverse, verglas, whipper

Maladies
altitude sickness, frostbite, hypothermia, hypoxia, cerebral / pulmonary oedema

Famous peaks
Mt Everest, Nepal / Tibet, 8848 m
K2, Pakistan / China, 8611 m
Aconcagua, Argentina, 6962 m
Mt McKinley, Alaska, USA, 6194 m
Kilimanjaro, Tanzania, Africa, 5895 m
Mt Elbrus, Russia, 5642 m
Vinson Massif, Antarctica, 4897 m
Mont Blanc, Italy / France, 4808 m
Matterhorn, Italy / Switzerland, 4479 m
Mauna Kea, Hawaii, USA, 4205 m
Mt Fuji, Japan, 3776 m
Aoraki / Mt Cook, New Zealand, 3754 m
Olympus, Greece, 2919 m
Mt Kosciuszko, Australia, 2228 m

HORSE RACING

TERMS (AND DEFINITIONS)
Aboard, age (January 1 birthday for all thoroughbreds), allowance, amateur, apprentice, banker / lock, bet (accumulator / parlay, each way, exacta / forecast / perfecta, pick six, place, quinella, superfecta, trifecta, win), barrier, blinkers, bloodstock, bookmaker (bookie), breeding, cap, career, class, connections, cup, derby (stakes event for three year olds), distance, dividend, double / treble, favourite, fence, field, flat race, form, freshened, front-runner, furlong (about 200 m), gait (pacer = lateral gait, trotter = diagonal gait), gallop, going (fast, firm, good, heavy, soft), guineas, hack, hand (about 10 cm or 4 in), handicap, harness, home turn, horseflesh, hurdle, inquiry, jockey, jumps, leg, length (head, neck, nod, nose), nursery (handicap for two year olds), oaks (stakes event for three-year-old fillies), odds, owner, pacer / trotter, penalty, placing, pool, prizemoney / purse, punt(er), racecard, rail, roughie, scratching, silks, sire, stable, stablehand, stablemate, stakes, stayer, steeplechase, steward, straight, stride, stripes, sulky, thoroughbred, Totalisator, track, trainer, trials, turf, wager, weight, whip

FAMOUS RACES
(Key race, course, country, distance, month)
Canadian International Stakes, Woodbine, Toronto, Canada, 2400 m, October
Caulfield Cup, Caulfield, Melbourne, 2400 m, October
Cox Plate, Mooney Valley, Melbourne, 2000 m, October
Dubai World Cup, Nad Al Sheba, United Arab Emirates, 2000 m, March
Durban July Handicap, Greyville, Durban, South Africa, 2200 m, July
Grand National, Aintree, Liverpool, UK, 7200 m, April
Hong Kong Cup, Sha Tin, Hong Kong, China, 2000 m, December
Japan Cup, Tokyo Racecourse, Tokyo, 2400 m, November
Kentucky Derby, Churchill Downs, Kentucky, USA, 2000 m, May

Melbourne Cup, Flemington, Melbourne,
  3200 m, November
Prix de l'Arc de Triomphe, Longchamps,
  Paris, 2400 m, October
Prix Royal-Oak, Longchamps, Paris,
  3100 m, October

HORSES BY AGE/SIZE

colt – ungelded male four years or younger
filly – female four years or younger
gelding – castrated male
juvenile – two year old
maiden – horse without win; unbred female
mare – female five years or older
pony – horse under about 145 cm high
stallion – male used for breeding
yearling – horse or pony under one year

COMMON HORSE BREEDS

abyssinian, andalusian, appaloosa, arabian,
Australian brumby, clydesdale, criollo,
Dartmoor / Exmoor pony, fleuve, friesian,
miniature, morgan, mustang, palomino,
paso fino, pinto, Przewalski, quarter horse,
shire, standardbred, thoroughbred

CAR RACING

CHAMPION FORMULA ONE DRIVERS
(driver/country of origin)
RECENT: Fernando Alonso (Spain), Mika
Hakkinen (Finland), Lewis Hamilton
(UK), Damon Hill (UK), Nigel Mansell
(UK), Alain Prost (France), Kimi
Raikkonen (Finland), Michael Schumacher
(Germany), Ayrton Senna (Brazil), Jacques
Villeneuve (Canada)
PAST: Mario Andretti (USA), Jack
Brabham (Australia), Juan Manuel Fangio
(Argentina), Niki Lauda (Austria), Nelson
Piquet (Brazil), Keke Rosberg (Finland),
Jackie Stewart (UK)

FAMOUS TRACKS
Autodromo Nazionale Monza (Italy),
Brands Hatch (UK), Circuit de Spa-
Francorchamps (Belgium), Daytona
International Speedway (Florida, USA),
Goodwood (UK), Hockenheimring
(Germany), Indianapolis Motor Speedway
(Indiana, USA), Knoxville (Iowa,
USA), Laguna Seca (California, USA),
Melbourne Grand Prix Circuit (Australia),
Nürburgring (Germany), Road America
(Wisconsin, USA), Sebring International
Raceway (Florida, USA), Silverstone (UK),
Suzuka Circuit (Japan), Tsukuba Circuit
(Japan)

MISCELLANEOUS DESCRIPTION

GEOGRAPHY

PLACES

abode, address, area, arrondissement, avenue, beginning, circle, class, condition, corner, cosmos, course, digs, district, domain, domicile, dominion, dwelling, environs, field, finish, globe, habitation, home, incumbency, lair, land, latitude and longitude, level, locale, locality, location, lodgings, miasma, milestone, milieu, neighbourhood, niche, nook, outlook, pad, point of view, position, precinct, premises, province, purview, quarter, realm, refuge, region, retreat, sanctuary, scene, setting, site, situation, sphere, spot, stage, standing, standpoint, start, state, station, status, stratum (strata), suburb, tenure, terrain, territory, theatre, time, universe, vicinity, viewpoint, whereabouts, world, zone

IMAGINARY PLACES

Arcadia, Atlantis, Cockaigne (a medieval land of plenty), El Dorado, Elysium, Erewhon, Garden of Eden, Ishmaelia, Land of Nod, Neverland, Nirvana, Oz, paradise, parallel universe, Shangri-La, Utopia, Wonderland

GEOGRAPHICAL FEATURES

ait or eyot (small island in river or lake), archipelago (chain of islands), arroyo (draw, wadi, wash = dry creek bed that fills with water after rain), atoll, ayre (Orkney term for lake separated narrowly from sea), badlands, bar, basin, bay, bayou (flat, slow-moving area of water), beach, berm, bight, billabong, bluff, bog, brae, bush, butte (small mesa), cairn, canal, canyon, cape, cave, cay, channel, cirque (valley head created by glacier, also known as combe, cwm, corrie), cliff, coast, col, cordillera (series of mountain ranges), crater, creek, cuesta (a ridge formed by movement of sedimentary rock with a gentle slope on one side and a steep one on the other), delta (river mouth), desert, dune, dyke or levee (raised earth wall to protect from floods), endorheic basin (one that has no outlet), erg (area of desert covered with windswept sand), escarpment (face or edge of cuesta), estuary, fen, fjord (drowned glacier valley), floodplain, foothill, ford, foreshore, forest, fumarole (volcanic smoke hole), geyser, glacier, grassland, gulch, gulf, gully, guyot (underwater mountain), hamada (rocky desert area with little sand), harbour, headland, heath, hill, horn, inlet, inselberg (hill that rises abruptly from plain), isthmus, jungle, lagoon, lake, lea, loess (windblown deposit of silt or clay), makhtesh (type of cirque in Israel created by erosion), marsh, meadow, medanos (continental dunes in South America), mesa (flat-topped mountain), mire, mound, mountain, mud flat, oasis, ocean, outback, paddock, pampa (South America lowland), pass (col, notch, saddle), pasture, peak, peninsula, pit, plain, plateau, playa (dry or occasional lake bed), pond, prairie, quicksand, rainforest, range, ravine, reef, reg, ria (drowned river valley), ridge, river, river mouth or source or headwater, salt flat, sandhill, savannah, scree, scrubland, sea (hole, rip, swell, tide), seabed, shoal, shoulder, spit, steppe, strath (Scottish term for flat valley with stream through middle), stream, swamp, tombolo (spit of land attached to mainland), tumulus (burial mound; plural: tumuli), tundra (treeless or near-treeless plain on arctic borders), valley, veldt (large flat areas in southern Africa covered in grass or scrub), volcano, waterfall, weald, wetland, woodland, yardang (ridge in desert worn away by wind)

king, spring), tornado (twister), trough (low pressure area between two high pressure areas), typhoon (strong cyclone in China Sea), virga (streaks of precipitation that evaporate before hitting the ground), waterspout, wave (tsunami), wind (strength = breeze, gale, gust, hurricane, squall, zephyr; world = abroholos, barber, bora, chinook, foehn, haboob, haugull, jet stream, pampero, puelche, Santa Ana, simoom, williwaw; Mediterranean: gregale, mistral, levanter, libeccio, ostro, poniente, scirocco, tramontane)

WEATHER

anabatic / katabatic (weather caused by wind flowing upwards / downwards), anticyclone (area of high pressure with rotation counter to Earth's), cyclone (tropical storm), dew, drought, fog (pea soup), haar (Scottish sea fog), frost, hail, haze, hurricane, Indian summer (unusually warm, calm period in autumn), lightning, mist, monsoon (southern Asian wind and rain system), moon (blue, crescent, equinox, full, gibbous, harvest, hunter's, wane, wax), rain (cats and dogs, deluge, drizzle, flood, showers, spitting, sun shower), Scotch mist (thick mist and heavy drizzle in Scotland), serein (rain from clear sky, often at sunset), shade, shamal (sandstorm-creating wind in Iraq and Persian Gulf), sleet, smog, snow (blanket, blizzard, dusting, flurry, graupel = snow pellets, slush, snowflake, white-out), storm, sun (equinox, solstice; nadir, zenith), temperature (bake, boil, cool, freeze, heat, ice, lukewarm, melt, shiver, sweat, swelter), thunder, tide (ebb, flow; high, low; neap,

TIMES OF DAY AND YEAR

BASICS

Intervals: second, minute, hour, day, weekend, week, fortnight, month, year; seasons: summer (aestival), autumn (autumnal, harvest), winter (brumal, wintry), spring (vernal)

TIME AND SEASON: DESCRIPTIVE TERMS

afternoon, anniversary, birthday, black, breakfast-time, bright, brunch, calendar, candles, cat's eye, clocking in / out, closing time, cloudy, cock-crowing, dark, dawn, daylight, dim, dinnertime, dusk, epoch, era, eve, evening, eventide (latter part of day), festival, full moon, Groundhog Day, happy hour, hazy, headlights, high noon, holiday, ides (the middle of month in the old Roman calendar), lighting of lamps, lunar, lunchtime, midday, midnight, morning, morning glory, morning sickness, night, nightfall, nones (nine days before ides in

old Roman calender or the noonday meal),
noon, overcast, pitch-black, reflection,
ringing of bells, rush hour, sabbath, shadow,
sidereal, silhouette, solar, street lights,
sundial, sunrise, sunset, supper, today,
tomorrow, twilight (crepuscular), weekday,
workday, yesterday

DAILY PRAYERS
Christian Liturgy of the Hours in order
matins, lauds, prime, terce, sext, nones,
vespers, compline

Muslim daily prayers
fajr, zuhr, 'asr, maghrib, 'isha

DWELLINGS
apartment, barn, boarding house, bordello,
bungalow, caravan, caravanserai, castle,
cottage, compound, dacha, duplex, estate,
flat, farm, garage, hacienda, hostel, house,
hovel, hut, maisonette, manse, mansion
(pile), palace, paradore, ramada, ranch,
semi-detached, shed, station, teepee,
tenement, tent, villa, wigwam

UNUSUAL HUES
alabaster – off-white
amber – reddish yellow or orange
amethyst – purplish blue
apricot – yellowy-orange
auburn – reddish brown
aubergine – purplish blue
avocado – light green
azure – blue
beige – yellowish grey/brown
burgundy – red

cerise – clear cherry-red
cerulean – sea blue
champagne – light brownish yellow
charcoal – greyish black
chartreuse – yellowish green
cinnamon – brown
dusky – blackish, brownish grey
eau de nil – pale yellowish green
ebony – black
eggshell – off-white
filemot – colour of a dead leaf (also
    feuillemort)
fluorescent – vividly bright or glowing,
    often white, blue, red, green (similar: neon,
    phosphorescent)
fuscous – brownish grey
gentian – blue
glaucous – dull greyish green/blue
grège – greyish beige
henna – brown, from orange to coffee
jade – dark green
khaki – yellowish brown
lilac – light purple
magenta – red
mahogany – reddish brown
maroon – reddish purple
mauve – reddish purple
mustard – dark yellow
obsidian – blackish
ochre – brownish yellow
peach – pinky orange
pied – patched, multicoloured
puce – brownish purple
rose – light pink
russet – reddish brown
sable – black
salmon – reddish orange
sepia – reddish brown
sienna – reddish brown

slate – blackish grey
taupe – brownish grey
teal – greenish blue
umber – dark reddish brown
walnut – brown
wasabi – green

NOISES

Bang, beep, boing, buzz, clang, clap, click,
clink, clunk, crack, crash, creak, crunch,
ding, drill, hammer, horn, hum, knock,
pop, punch, rattle, ring, roar, rustle, scrape,
scratch, scream, screech, shot, shuffle, siren,
sizzle, skid, snap, splat, squeak, squeal,
tap, tear, thud, tick, whine, whirr, whistle,
whoosh

SECTION 4
REFERENCE

*'Knowledge is of two kinds.
We know a subject ourselves,
or we know where we can
find information upon it.'*
— Dr Samuel Johnson

The Reference section includes
lists of popes and prime ministers,
but also historical methods of
punishment and ways of divining
the future. Artworks are also listed
by period and type, and films by
subject.

GENERAL KNOWLEDGE

POPES FROM 1800

(Benedict is the 267th pope, by traditional counts)

Pius VII (1800–23)
Leo XII (1823–29)
Pius VIII (1829–30)
Gregory XVI (1831–46)
Blessed Pius IX (1846–78)
Leo XIII (1878–1903)
St Pius X (1903–14)
Benedict XV (1914–22)
Pius XI (1922–39)
Pius XII (1939–58)
John XXIII (1958–63)
Paul VI (1963–78)
John Paul I (1978)
John Paul II (1978–2005)
Benedict XVI (2005–)

UN SECRETARIES GENERAL

Gladwyn Jebb (1945–46), UK
Trygve Halvdan Lie (1946–52), Norway
Dag Hammarskjöld (1953–61), Sweden
U Thant (1961–71), Myanmar
Kurt Waldheim (1972–81), Austria
Javier Pérez de Cuéllar (1982–91), Peru
Boutros Boutros-Ghali (1992–96), Egypt
Kofi Annan (1997–2006), Ghana
Ban Ki-moon (2007–), South Korea

US PRESIDENTS

1 George Washington (1789–97)
2 John Adams (1797–1801)
3 Thomas Jefferson (1801–09)
4 James Madison (1809–17)
5 James Monroe (1817–25)
6 John Quincy Adams (1825–29)
7 Andrew Jackson (1829–37)
8 Martin Van Buren (1837–41)
9 William Henry Harrison (1841)
10 John Tyler (1841–45)
11 James Knox Polk (1845–49)
12 Zachary Taylor (1849–50)
13 Millard Fillmore (1850–53)
14 Franklin Pierce (1853–57)
15 James Buchanan (1857–61)
16 Abraham Lincoln (1861–65)
17 Andrew Johnson (1865–69)
18 Ulysses S Grant (1869–77)
19 Rutherford B Hayes (1877–81)
20 James Garfield (1881)
21 Chester Arthur (1881–85)
22 Grover Cleveland (1885–89)
23 Benjamin Harrison (1889–93)
24 Grover Cleveland (1893–97)
25 William McKinley (1897–1901)
26 Theodore Roosevelt (1901–09)
27 William Howard Taft (1909–13)
28 Woodrow Wilson (1913–21)
29 Warren Harding (1921–23)
30 Calvin Coolidge (1923–29)
31 Herbert Hoover (1929–33)
32 Franklin D Roosevelt (1933–1945)
33 Harry S Truman (1945–53)
34 Dwight D Eisenhower (1953–61)
35 John F Kennedy (1961–63)
36 Lyndon Johnson (1963–69)
37 Richard Nixon (1969–74)
38 Gerald Ford (1974–77)
39 Jimmy Carter (1977–81)
40 Ronald Reagan (1981–89)
41 George H W Bush (1989–93)
42 Bill Clinton (1993–2001)
43 George W Bush (2001–8)
44 Barack Obama (2009–)

UK PRIME MINISTERS (20TH CENTURY)

Arthur Balfour (1902–05)
Sir Henry Campbell-Bannerman
 (1905–08)
Herbert Asquith (1908–16)
David Lloyd George (1916–22)
Andrew Law (1922–23)
Stanley Baldwin (1923, 1924–29, 1935–37)
James Ramsay MacDonald (1924,
 1929–35)
Neville Chamberlain (1937–40)
Sir Winston Churchill (1940–45, 1951–55)
Clement Attlee (1945–51)
Sir Anthony Eden (1955–57)
Harold Macmillan (1957–63)
Sir Alec Douglas-Home (1963–64)
Harold Wilson (1964–70, 1974–76)
Edward Heath (1970–74)
James Callaghan (1976–79)
Margaret Thatcher (1979–90)
John Major (1990–97)
Tony Blair (1997–2007)
Gordon Brown (2007–)

ROMAN GODS AND GODDESSES (GREEK)

crops – Ceres (Demeter)
darkness – (Erebus)
death – Pluto, Dis (Hades, Pluto)
doors, gates, beginnings and endings
 – Janus
dreams – Morpheus (Morpheus)
fertility – (Priapus)
home, fire – Vesta (Hestia)
king of the gods – Jupiter (Zeus)
love – Cupid (Eros)
love, beauty – Venus (Aphrodite)
moon – Luna (Selene)
moon, hunting – Diana (Artemis)
queen of the gods, the marital sphere – Juno
 (Hera)
revenge – (Nemesis)
sea – Neptune (Poseidon)
sleep – Somnos (Hypnos)
sun – Sol (Helios)
sun, youth – Apollo (Apollo)
time, agriculture – Saturn (Kronos)
war – Mars (Ares)
wealth – Plutus (Plutus)
wine – Bacchus (Dionysus)
wisdom – Minerva (Athena)
youth – Juventas (Hebe)

TRADITIONAL GREEK TYPES OF LOVE

agape – ideal
eros – passion
philia – friendship
storge – affection
xenia – hospitality

GREEK MUSES

Calliope – epic poetry
Clio – history
Erato – lyrics/love poetry
Euterpe – music/lyric poetry
Melpomene – tragedy
Polyhymnia – sacred poetry, geometry,
 mime
Terpsichore – dancing
Thalia – comedy
Urania – astronomy, astrology

SEVEN WONDERS OF THE ANCIENT WORLD

The Colossus of Rhodes, the Hanging Garden of Babylon, the Mausoleum at Halicarnassus, the Pharos / Lighthouse of Alexandria, Phidias's statue of Zeus at Olympia, the Great Pyramid of Giza, the Temple of Artemis at Ephesus

PREDICTING THE FUTURE

Divination

anthropomancy – by human sacrifice, especially by reading human entrails

genethlialogy – by birth date (astrology)

hakata – by bones or dice (South Africa)

Ifa – by palm nuts (west Africa)

kau cim – by bamboo sticks (China)

libanomancy – by incense smoke

necromancy – by speaking to the dead

nephomancy – by clouds

numerology – by numbers

oneiromancy – by dreams

scrying – by gazing, usually using a crystal ball, mirror or water

sikidy – by seeds or lines in sand (Madagascar)

sortilege – by drawing lots (also means sorcery)

tasseography – by tea leaves, coffee grounds or sediment of wine

turifumy – by shapes in smoke

Other

astrology, casting of runes, crystal balls or gastromancy, fortune cookies, Ouija board, palm reading, Tarot cards

HISTORICAL METHODS OF PUNISHMENT AND TORTURE

bastinado – caning of the soles of feet

breaking wheel / Catherine wheel – offenders were beaten while strapped to a large wagon wheel

cangue – a heavy Chinese board yoke

cucking/ducking-stool – chairs in which offenders were paraded and sometimes immersed in water

gibbet – a gallows or hanging cage

guillotine – suspended blade that was dropped to sever the victim's head, used particularly during French Revolution

hanged, drawn and quartered – the condemned was hanged by the neck until almost dead, disembowelled and their genitals were removed, then the victim's body was cut into four pieces plus the head

jougs – an iron neck collar attached to a wall by a short chain, used in Scotland

keelhauling – sailors were dragged under the ship by rope

pillory / stocks – wooden yoke for head, hands

rack – a wooden frame that stretched offender's limbs apart by way of rollers and bars

running the gauntlet – in the army and navy, the offender runs between two lines of men who beat him

sawing – the condemned was hung upside down and sawn through from the crotch

scaphism / 'the boats' – the condemned was locked in a wooden container with their head, hands and feet protruding, and left on stagnant water or exposed to the sun for insects until dead

scourge – whip

strappado – the victim's hands were tied
  behind their back, and the victim hoisted
  up by a rope tied to their wrists

transportation – deportation to another
  country, often Australia, from Britain

Historical torture: other

beheading, burning at stake (often during
auto-da-fé by the Spanish Inquisition),
crucifixion, crushing, decapitation or
beheading, flaying or removing skin,
necklacing (putting a burning tyre over
the victim), slow slicing or lingchi, stoning,
thumbscrews

WEAPONS: A SELECTION

cosh, cudgel, shiv, tomahawk, trebuchet (a
medieval European device for launching
large stones); swords: broadsword, claymore,
cutlass, falchion, foil, hanger, katana, rapier,
sabre, scimitar, spatha, yatagan; Maori
spears: pouwhenu, taiaha, tewhatewha;
Maori clubs: kotiate, mere, patu, wahaika

FAMOUS PRISONS

ADX Florence supermax, Colorado, USA
Alcatraz – San Francisco, USA
Attica – New York, USA
Château d'If – France
Devil's Island – French Guiana
Folsom State Prison – California, USA
Justizzentrum Leoben, Austria
Kresty Prison – St Petersburg, Russia
Leavenworth – Kansas, USA
Rikers Island – New York, USA
San Pedro – La Paz, Bolivia
San Quentin – California, USA
Sing Sing – New York, USA

FIELDS OF STUDY

animal behaviour – ethology
bell ringing – campanology
butterflies and moths – lepidopterology
cats – felinology
causation – aetiology
cells – cytology
church festivals – heortology
clouds – nephology
death of humans – thanatology
dental decay – cariology
dogs – cynology
duty – deontology
end of the world – eschatology
ends or final causes – teleology
fermentation – zymology
fish – ichthyology
flags – vexillology
flow – rheology
friction – tribology
fungi – mycology
geometric properties; relationships between
  parts of incidence and transmission of
  medical conditions – epidemiology
grape varieties – ampelography
horse – hippology
human growth – auxology
insects – entomology
ligaments – desmology
living tissues – histology
meaning, words – semantics
molluscs – malacology
moon – selenology
mountains – orology
muscles – myology
network – topology
old age – gerontology
pronunciation of words – orthoepy
reptiles – herpetology

rock – lithology (classification), petrology
(composition)

Shroud of Turin – sindonology

tree ring dating – dendochronology

tumours – oncology

versification – prosody

watchmaking; timekeeping – horology

waves – kymatology

weather – meteorology

wood – xylology

word origins – etymology

COMMON PHOBIAS

air travel; flying – aerophobia

bees – apiphobia

blood – haemophobia

buried alive – taphophobia

cats – ailurophobia

change; new or novel things – misoneism

crowds – ochlophobia

dirt – rupophobia

disease – nosophobia

doctors – latrophobia

ghosts – phasmophobia

needles – enetophobia

nudity – gymnophobia

open spaces – agoraphobia

pain – algophobia

public speaking – glossophobia

red, blushing – erythrophobia

sharks – galeophobia

small spaces – claustrophobia

snakes – ophidiophobia

spiders – arachnaphobia

storms; thunder – brontophobia

thirteen – triskaidekaphobia

vehicles – amaxophobia

women – gynophobia

PERTAINING TO ANIMALS

ant – formicine

ass, donkey – asinine

badger, ferret, mink, otter, skunk, stoat,
weasel – musteline

bat – noctilionine, pteropine

bear – ursine

bee – apian

bird – avine, avian

bull, ox – taurine

cat – feline

cobra, sea snakes – elapine

cow – bovine

crab – cancrine

crocodile – crocodilian

deer, elk – cervine

dog – canine

dolphin – delphine

dragon – draconine

duck, goose, swan – anatine

eagle – aquiline

elephant – elephantine

fish – piscine

fox – vulpine

frog, toad – ranine

gerbil, hamster – cricetine

gibbon – hylobatine

goat – hircine, caprine

hare, rabbit – leporine

horse – equine

kangaroo – macropine

leech – hirudine

lemming, muskrat, vole – microtine

leopard – pardine

lion – leonine

lizard – lacertine, lacertian

lobster – homarine

mouse, rat – murine

oyster – ostracine

pig – porcine
pigeon – pullastrine
porcupine – hystricine
ram – arietine
reindeer – rangiferine
seal – phocine
serpent – serpentine
sheep – ovine
shrew – soricine
slug – limacine
snake – anguine
tortoise, turtle – testudine
turkey – meleagrine
wasp, hornet – vespine
wolf – lupine
worm – lumbricine
zebra – zebrine

ANIMAL NOISES

baa, bark, bellow, bleat, boom, bray, burp,
buzz, caw, chatter, cheep, chirp, chirrup,
click, clink, cluck, clunk, coo, creak, croak,
drone, gibber, gobble, growl, grunt, haw,
hiss, honk, howl, hum, oink, low, meow,
mewl, moo, murmur, neigh, peep, phut, purr,
roar, sing, snort, squeak, trumpet, tweet,
twitter, warble, whinny, whirr, yap

US–UK PRONUNCIATION DIFFERENCES

Word	US	UK
apricot	AP-ricot	APE-ricot
bra	braw	brah
buffet	boof-ay	buff-ay
buoy	boo-ee	boi
cement	SEE-ment	se-ment
cognac	cone-yak	con-yak
complex	com-PLEX	COM-plex

combat	com-BAT	COM-bat
compost	com-poast	com-post
condom	CON-dim	con-dom
decade	di-CADE	DE-cade
fillet	fill-lay	fill-it
herb	urb	herb
leisure	LEE-shure	leh-shih
niche	nitch	neesh
produce	PROH-doos	pro-juice
recess	RE-cess	ri-cess
recluse	RE-cluse	ri-CLUSE
remit	RE-mit	re-MIT
risotto	riz-OAT-oh	riz-O-toh
scallop	skel-op	skol-op
thorough	thur-oh	thur-uh

PERFUME DESCRIPTIONS

amaryllis, amber, ambergris, bergamot,
blackcurrant, black pepper, camomile,
cardamom, cedar, chocolate, chypre,
cinnamon, coconut, coffee, coriander,
fougere, freesia, geranium, grape, grapefruit,
green apple, iris, jasmine, lavender, leather,
lemon, lotus petal, lychee, mahogany,
mandarin, melon, musk, myrrh, neroli,
nutmeg, oak moss, narcissus, neroli, orange
blossom, orchid, passionfruit, patchouli,
peach, peony, pepper, peppermint, petit
grain, raspberry, rose, saffron, sage,
sandalwood, spice, strawberry, sweet
pea, tonka bean, vanilla, vetiver, violet,
watermelon, ylang ylang

Perfume: other

notes: top, middle, base; strength of
aromatic compounds: eau de parfum =
10-20%, eau de toilette = 5-15%, eau de
cologne = about 5%, aftershave = about 2%

GEMSTONES

agate, alexandrite, amber, amethyst, ametrine, ammonite, andalusite, aquamarine, beryl, bloodstone, chrysoberyl, citrine, cobalt, diamond, emerald, garnet, greenstone / jade, iolite, jasper, lapis lazuli, moonstone, onyx, opal, pearl, quartz, ruby, sapphire, tanzanite, topaz, tourmaline, turquoise, zircon

FABRICS

astrakhan, burlap, calico, cashmere, check, cotton, dupion, éolienne, flannel, fustian, gaberdine, gauze, habutai, lamé, linen, leather, leatherette, lisle, lurex, muslin, nylon, plaid, prunella, ruche, sateen, satin, shantung, shearling, silk, taffeta, toile, tulle, tweed, velvet, voile, wool, worsted

TYPES OF WOOD

ailanthus, anigre, ash, balsa birch, cedar, cherry, coconut, elm, eucalyptus, gum, hickory, holly, jarrah, kauri, laurel, lignum vitae (guaiacum), mahogany, maple, mulberry, myrtlewood, nutmeg, oak, pecan, persimmon, pine, poplar, rimu, rosewood, sassafras, tawa, teak, walnut, wenge, willow

ALTERNATIVE THERAPIES

acupuncture, aromatherapy, ayurveda (also siddha, Unani), balneotherapy, biofeedback, chelation, chiropracty, crystals, herbalism, homeopathy, hyperbaric oxygen, hypnotherapy, iridology, lymphatic massage, meditation, moxibustion, naturopathy, Oriental medicine, osteopathy, prayer, reiki, shiatsu, visualisation

GENES AND ASSOCIATED DISEASES

BRCA1, 2 – breast cancer
PS1, 2 – Alzheimer's disease
HPC1, MSR1 – prostate cancer
MSH2, 6, MLH1 – colon cancer
SCLC1 – lung cancer
SNCA – Parkinson's disease
EPM2A – epilepsy
CTFT – cystic fibrosis
GLC1A – glaucoma
CTFR – cystic fibrosis
DEFB4 – Crohn disease

THE BRAIN

areas involved in emotion: amygdala, anterior cingulate, Broca's area, insula, limbic system, prefrontal cortex, ventral striatum; remembering faces: amygdala, fusiform cortex; brain chemicals: dopamine, endorphin, histamine, insulin, melatonin, noradrenaline, serotonin

DEADLY VIRUSES AND BACTERIA

viruses: anthrax, bird flu, cholera, CJD, Ebola, Hanta, Hendra, Lassa, Marburg, MRSA, Nipah, SARS; food-related: campylobacter, e coli, listeria, salmonella

UNITS OF MEASUREMENT

acceleration – galileo
angle – degree
area – square kilometre
density – of volume: kilogram per cubic metre; in printing: dots per inch
electricity – charge: coulomb; current: ampere; capacitance: farad; conductance: siemens; electromotive force: volt;

resistance: ohm

energy – joule, calorie

force – newton

frequency – hertz

illuminance – lux

luminous flux – lumen

luminous intensity – candela

power – horsepower, volt-ampere, watt

pressure – pascal

radioactivity – becquerel, curie

speed – metres per second, kilometres per
hour, knots, Mach

temperature – degrees, in Celsius,
Fahrenheit or kelvin

torque – newton-metre

volume – cubic metre

weight – kilogram, pound

SCALES

Beaufort wind force scale

0 – calm

1 – light air

2 – light breeze

3 – gentle breeze

4 – moderate breeze

5 – fresh breeze

6 – strong breeze

7 – moderate gale

8 – fresh gale

9 – strong gale

10 – storm

11 – violent storm

12 – hurricane force

Hurricanes

Saffir-Simpson Scale, based on intensity

Category 1 – winds 64–82 knots
(119–153 km/h), no marked damage
to buildings

Category 2 – winds 83–95 knots
(154–177 km/h), some damage to roofs
and windows

Category 3 – winds 96–113 knots
(178–209 km/h), some structural damage
to small buildings

Category 4 – winds 114–135 knots
(210–249 km/h), extensive structural
damage to small buildings

Category 5 – winds above 135 knots
(249 km/h), complete roof failures common
and some buildings destroyed

Wood hardness

*Janka scale: measured by the amount of force
it takes to drive a 11.28 mm steel ball half its
diameter into a board*

lignum vitae = 4500 pounds-force

ebony = 3220

jarrah = 1910

teak = 1000

chestnut = 540

balsa = 100

Mineral hardness

*Mohs scale: measured in relative values, in
which each substance can scratch those softer
and only be scratched by those harder*

talc = 1	feldspar = 6
gypsum = 2	quartz = 7
calcite = 3	topaz = 8
fluorite = 4	corundum = 9
apatite = 5	diamond = 10

OCCUPATIONAL SURNAMES

Barker – tanner
Baxter – baker, especially female
Bowyer – maker or seller of archers' bows
Brazier – worker in brass
Chandler – candle maker
Chapman – merchant
Conner – inspected weights and measures
Cooper – maker of barrels
Fuller – one who thickened cloth
Lorimer – horse-bit maker
Mercer – textile dealer
Palmer – pilgrim
Smith – craftsman
Stewart – keeper of noble household
Sutler – unappointed army merchant
Wainwright – wagon builder
Webster – weaver

COMPARISONS

Distance
diameter of the moon – 3474 km
diameter of the earth (average) –
  12,742 km
from the earth to the moon (average centre-
  to-centre distance) – 384,000 km
width of the universe – 93 billion light years
furthest star in our galaxy – 70,000 light
  years
furthest star in the furthest galaxy –
  15 billion light years

Thinness metaphors
thin as air, aluminium foil, cellophane,
cigarette paper, eggshells, human hair, a
layer of paint, a pencil, a rail, a rake, razor
blade, silk, a stick, a supermodel, tissue,
paper-thin, wafer-thin

Hardness
ultrahard fullerite – theoretically harder
  than diamond
diamond – 10 on Mohs scale
talc – 1 on Mohs scale
ebony – 3220 on Janka wood scale
balsa – 100 on Janka wood scale

Number
galaxies in the universe – more than 80
  billion
atoms in the universe – estimated 10^{78}
squares on a chessboard – 64 small, 204
  total

Brightest
object within 1000 light years – Antares
object in our galaxy – Cygnus OB2
  number 12

Height
Mt Olympus Mons, Mars – 24 km
Mt Everest, Nepal / Tibet – 8850 m
Burj Dubai – 818 m (160 habitable storeys)
Empire State Building, New York, USA
  – 449 m (102 storeys)
Eiffel Tower, Paris, France – 324 m
Great Pyramid of Giza, Egypt – 139 m

Length
Great Wall of China, China – 6700 km
Berlin Wall (now demolished) – 155 km

Mass
Sun – 2×10^{30} kg (333 times the mass of
  the earth)
Earth – 6×10^{24} kg (6000 billion billion
  tonnes, estimated)

Great Pyramid of Giza, Egypt – 5.9 million tonnes (2.5m cu m, estimated)

Age

the Earth – 4.54 billion years

Sun – 4.57 billion years

the moon – 4.53 billion years

first life on earth – 3.5 billion years ago

multicellular organisms – 650 million years ago

reptiles on earth – 300 million years ago

dinosaurs – 230–65 million years ago

mammals on earth – 200 million years ago

human-like creatures – 2.5 million years ago

humans – 200,000 years ago

Temperature

absolute zero – –273.15 °C

boiling point of helium – –268.93 °C

coldest temperature recorded on earth – –89.2 °C

hottest temperature recorded on earth – 57.7 °C

normal human body temperature – 36.8 °C

boiling point of water – 100 °C

boiling point of mercury – 357 °C

boiling point of gold – 2856 °C

boiling point of tungsten – 5657 °C

temperature of the moon (day) – 107 °C

temperature of the moon (night) – –153 °C

temperature of Mars (average) – –53 °C

temperature of Mars (day) – 0 °C

temperature of Mars (night) – –82 °C

temperature of Venus (average) – 460 °C

temperature of the sun (surface) – about 6000 °C

temperature of the sun (core) – about 10,000,000 °C

SEMINAL ARTWORKS BY PERIOD OR TYPE

BOOKS BY DECADE

1950s

Atlas Shrugged (1957, Ayn Rand), *Casino Royale* (1953, Ian Fleming), *The Catcher in the Rye* (1951, JD Salinger), *The Chronicles of Narnia* (1950, CS Lewis), *Doctor Zhivago* (1957, Boris Pasternak), *The Doors of Perception* (1954, Aldous Huxley), *The End of the Affair* (1951, Graham Greene), *Fahrenheit 451* (1953, Ray Bradbury), *I, Robot* (1950, Isaac Asimov), *The Lion, the Witch and the Wardrobe* (1950, CS Lewis), *Lolita* (1955, Vladimir Nabokov), *Lord of the Flies* (1954, William Golding), *The Lord of the Rings* (1954, JRR Tolkien), *Lucky Jim* (1954, Kingsley Amis), *Naked Lunch* (1959, William Burroughs), *The Old Man and the Sea* (1952, Ernest Hemingway), *On the Beach* (1957, Nevil Shute), *On the Road* (1957, Jack Kerouac), *Our Man in Havana* (1958, Graham Greene), *The Outsider* (1956, Colin Wilson), *The Quiet American* (1955, Graham Greene), *The Tin Drum* (1959, Günter Grass)

1960s

2001: A Space Odyssey (1968, Arthur C Clarke), *The Bell Jar* (1963, Sylvia Plath), *Black Like Me* (1960, John Howard Griffin), *Catch 22* (1961, Joseph Heller), *Charlie and the Chocolate Factory* (1964, Roald Dahl), *A Clockwork Orange* (1962, Anthony Burgess), *The Godfather* (1969, Mario Puzo), *In Cold Blood* (1966, Truman Capote), *James and the Giant Peach* (1961, Roald Dahl), *One Day in the Life of Ivan Denisovich* (1962, Aleksandr Solzhenitsyn), *One Flew over the Cuckoo's Nest* (1962, Ken Kesey), *One Hundred Years of Solitude* (1967, Gabriel García Márquez), *Planet of the Apes* (1963, Pierre Boulle), *Portnoy's Complaint* (1969, Philip Roth), *The Prime of Miss Jean Brodie* (1961, Muriel Spark), *Silent Spring* (1962, Rachel Carson), *Slaughterhouse-Five* (1969, Kurt Vonnegut), *Stranger in a Strange Land* (1961, Robert A Heinlein), *To Kill a Mockingbird* (1960, Harper Lee), *V* (1963, Thomas Pynchon)

1970s

Carrie (1974, Stephen King), *The Day of the Jackal* (1971, Frederick Forsyth), *Dead Babies* (1975, Martin Amis), *The Exorcist* (1971, William Peter Blatty), *Fear of Flying* (1974, Erica Jong), *Gravity's Rainbow* (1973, Thomas Pynchon), *Jaws* (1974, Peter Benchley), *Jonathan Livingston Seagull* (1970, Richard Bach), *The Lost Honour of Katharina Blum* (1974, Heinrich Böll), *The Rachel Papers* (1973, Martin Amis), *The Right Stuff* (1979, Tom Wolfe), *Watership Down* (1972, Richard Adams), *A Woman of Substance* (1979, Barbara Taylor Bradford), *The World According to Garp* (1978, John Irving)

1980s

The Alchemist (1988, Paulo Coelho), *Beloved* (1987, Toni Morrison), *Black Dahlia* (1987, James Ellroy), *Bliss* (1981, Peter Carey), *Clan of the Cave Bear* (1980, Jean Auel), *Empire of the Sun* (1984, JG Ballard), *Flaubert's Parrot* (1984, Julian Barnes), *The Handmaid's Tale* (1985, Margaret Atwood), *The House of the Spirits* (1982, Isabel Allende), *The Joy Luck Club* (1989, Amy Tan), *Life & Times of Michael K* (1983, JM Coetzee), *London Fields* (1989, Martin Amis), *Love in the Time of Cholera* (1985, Gabriel García Márquez), *Midnight's Children* (1980, Salman Rushdie), *Money* (1984, Martin Amis), *The Name of the Rose* (1980, Umberto Eco), *Neuromancer* (1984, William Gibson), *Oranges are not the only Fruit* (1985, Jeanette Winterson), *The Satanic Verses* (1988, Salman Rushdie), *Schindler's Ark* (1982, Thomas Keneally), *The Unbearable Lightness of Being* (1984, Milan Kundera), *The Wasp Factory* (1984, Iain Banks)

1990s

About a Boy (1998, Nick Hornby), *American Pastoral* (1997, Philip Roth), *American Psycho* (1991, Bret Easton Ellis), *Angela's Ashes* (1995, Frank McCourt), *Atomised* (1999, Michel Houellebecq), *The Beach* (1996, Alex Garland), *The Celestine Prophecy* (1994, James Redfield), *Cold Mountain* (1997, Charles Frazier), *Disgrace* (1999, JM Coetzee), *Fight Club* (1996, Chuck Palahniuk), *A Fine Balance* (1996, Rohinton Mistry), *Harry Potter and the Philosopher's Stone* (1997, JK Rowling), *The Hours* (1998, Michael Cunningham), *How late it was, how late* (1994, James Kelman), *The Horse Whisperer* (1995, Nicholas Evans), *The Information* (1995, Martin Amis), *Jurassic Park* (1990, Michael Crichton), *Mason & Dixon* (1997, Thomas Pynchon), *Midnight in the Garden of Good and Evil* (1996, John Berendts), *Northern Lights* (1995, Philip Pullman), *The Perfect Storm* (1997, Sebastian Junger), *Sex and the City* (1997, Candace Bushnell), *'Tis* (1999, Frank McCourt), *Underworld* (1997, Don DeLillo)

2000s

The Curious Incident of the Dog in the Night-time (Mark Haddon, 2003), *The Da Vinci Code* (2003, Dan Brown), *Falling Man* (2007, Don DeLillo), *The Human Stain* (2000, Philip Roth), *Life of Pi* (2001, Yann Martel), *Saturday* (2005, Ian McEwan), *The Sea* (2005, John Banville), *The Time Traveler's Wife* (2003, Audrey Niffenegger), *True History of the Kelly Gang* (2000, Peter Carey), *White Teeth* (2000, Zadie Smith)

WRITERS

FICTION WRITERS BY TYPE

Crime

Lawrence Block, Raymond Chandler, Agatha Christie, Harlan Coben, Patricia Cornwell, Jeffrey Deaver, Stella Duffy, Sarah Dunant, James Ellroy, Dashiell Hammett, John Harvey, Carl Hiaasen, Elmore Leonard, Henning Mankell, Sara Paretsky, Ian Rankin, Kathy Reichs, Ruth Rendell

Thriller

Dan Brown, Lee Child, Mo Hayder, Joseph Kanon, Tess Gerritsen, James Patterson, James Twining, John Twelve Hawks

Mystery

Dan Brown, Caleb Carr, Raymond Chandler, Agatha Christie, Sir Arthur Conan Doyle, Sue Grafton, PD James, Edgar Allen Poe, Ellery Queen, Ruth Rendell, Dorothy L Sayers

Horror

Clive Barker, Poppy Z Brite, Thomas Harris, Stephen King, Dean Koontz, HP Lovecraft, Anne Rice, Peter Straub

Science fiction

Douglas Adams, Isaac Asimov, Iain M. Banks, Greg Bear, Ray Bradbury, Lois McMaster Bujold, Orson Scott Card, Arthur C. Clarke, Michael Crichton, Philip K. Dick, Harlan Ellison, Philip Jose Farmer, William Gibson, Harry Harrison, Robert Heinlein, Frank Herbert, Ursula Le Guin, Anne McCaffrey, Larry Niven, Frederik Pohl, Neal Stephenson, H. G. Wells

Chick lit

Jessica Adams, Cecilia Ahern, Sarah Ball, Melissa Bank, Candace Bushnell, Imogen Edwards-Jones, Helen Fielding, Jane Green, Marian Keyes, Sophie Kinsella, Adele Parks, Allison Pearson, Plum Sykes, Jennifer Weiner, Lauren Weisburger, Rebecca Wells

Lad lit

Mark Barrowcliffe, Colin Bateman, Ray Blackston, Mike Gayle, Nick Hornby, Scott Mebus, John O'Farrell, Chuck Palahniuk, Tony Parsons, Kyle Smith, Toby Young

Children/young persons

JM Barrie, Enid Blyton, Meg Cabot, Lewis Carroll, Roald Dahl, Kenneth Grahame, CS Lewis, Margaret Mahy, AA Milne, Beatrix Potter, Philip Pullman, JK Rowling, Antoine de Saint-Exupery, Maurice Sendak, Dr Seuss, Lemony Snicket, JRR Tolkien

Airport novel

Peter Benchley, Dan Brown, Michael Crichton, Tom Clancy, James Clavell, John Grisham, Arthur Hailey, Jesse Kellerman, Robert Ludlum, James Mitchener, James Patterson, Jodi Picoult, Harold Robbins, Wilbur Smith, Danielle Steele

NOTED NOVELISTS (KEY WORK)

Kingsley Amis (*Lucky Jim*), Martin Amis (*London Fields*, 1989), Margaret Atwood (*The Handmaid's Tale*, 1985), Jane Austen (*Pride and Prejudice*, 1813), James Baldwin (*Go Tell it on the Mountain*, 1953), John Betjeman (*Summoned by Bells*, 1960), Jorge Luis Borges (*The Garden of Forking Paths*, 1941), Charlotte Brontë (*Jane Eyre*, 1847), William Burroughs (*Naked Lunch*, 1959), Albert Camus (*The Stranger*, 1942), Miguel de Cervantes (*Don Quixote*, 1605), John Cheever (*The Wapshot Chronicle*, 1957), Joseph Conrad (*Heart of Darkness*, 1902), Daniel Defoe (*Robinson Crusoe*, 1719), Charles Dickens (*Bleak House*, 1852), Fyodor Dostoevsky (*The Brothers Karamazov*, 1880), Alexandre Dumas (*The Three Musketeers*, 1844), George Eliot (*Middlemarch*, 1871), William Faulkner (*As I Lay Dying*, 1930), Henry Fielding (*Tom Jones*, 1749), F Scott Fitzgerald (*The Great Gatsby*, 1925), Gustave Flaubert (*Madame Bovary*, 1857), EM Forster (*A Passage to India*, 1924), William Golding (*Lord of the Flies*, 1954), Günter Grass (*The Tin Drum*, 1959), Graham Greene (*The End of the Affair*, 1951), Joseph Heller (*Catch-22*, 1961), Ernest Hemingway (*The Sun Also Rises*, 1926), Herman Hesse (*Steppenwolf*, 1927), Thomas Hardy (*Tess of the D'Urbervilles*, 1891), Ernest Hemingway (*A Farewell to Arms*, 1929), Victor Hugo (*Les Misérables*, 1862), Henry James (*The Ambassadors*, 1903), James Joyce (*Ulysses*, 1922), Samuel Johnson (*Rasselas*, 1759), Franz Kafka (*Metamorphosis*, 1915), Jack Kerouac (*On the Road*, 1957), Doris Lessing (*The Golden Notebook*, 1962), CS Lewis (*The Chronicles of Narnia*, 1950–1956), Cormac McCarthy (*The Road*, 2006), Norman Mailer (*The Naked and the Dead*, 1950), Thomas Mann (*The Magic Mountain*, 1924), Gabriel García Márquez (*One Hundred Years of Solitude*, 1967), Herman Melville (*Moby Dick*, 1851), Henry Miller (*Tropic of Cancer*, 1934), Vladimir Nabokov (*Lolita*, 1955), Joyce Carol Oates (*Black Water*, 1992), George Orwell (*Nineteen Eighty-Four*, 1949), Sylvia Plath (*The Bell Jar*, 1963), Marcel Proust (*In Search of Lost Time*, 1913–1927), Thomas Pynchon (*Gravity's Rainbow*, 1973), Philip Roth (*Portnoy's Complaint*, 1969), Salman Rushdie (*Midnight's Children*, 1981), JD

Salinger (*The Catcher in the Rye*, 1951), Mary Shelley (*Frankenstein*, 1818), John Steinbeck (*The Grapes of Wrath*, 1939), Stendhal (*The Red and the Black*, 1830), Lawrence Sterne (*Tristram Shandy*, 1759), Bram Stoker (*Dracula*, 1897), Leo Tolstoy (*War and Peace*, 1869), Mark Twain (*Adventures of Huckleberry Finn*, 1884), Voltaire (*Candide*, 1759), Kurt Vonnegut (*Slaughterhouse-Five*, 1969), Evelyn Waugh (*Brideshead Revisited*, 1945), Virginia Woolf (*To the Lighthouse*, 1927), Emile Zola (*Germinal*, 1855)

NOTED POETS

Anna Akhmatova, Maya Angelou, Guillaume Apollinaire, Matthew Arnold, WH Auden, Amiri Baraka, Charles Pierre Baudelaire, Elizabeth Bishop, Elizabeth Barrett Browning, James K Baxter, Beowulf, John Betjeman, William Blake, Joseph Brodsky, Emily Brontë, Robert Browning, Charles Bukowski, Robert Burns, Lord Byron, Luis Vaz de Camoes, Lewis Carroll, Miguel de Cervantes, Geoffrey Chaucer, Samuel Taylor Coleridge, Billy Collins, EE Cummings, Allen Curnow, Dante, Cecil Day-Lewis, Emily Dickinson, John Donne, John Dryden, TS Eliot, Ralph Waldo Emerson, Janet Frame, Robert Frost, Allen Ginsberg, Goethe, Seamus Heaney, Heinrich Heine, Robert Herrick, Ted Hughes, Ben Jonson, John Keats, Rudyard Kipling, Philip Larkin, DH Lawrence, Mikhail Lermontov, Henry Longfellow, Federico Garcia Lorca, Louis MacNeice, Christopher Marlowe, Andrew Marvell, Roger McGough, Czeslaw Milosz, John Milton, Gabriela Mistral, Marianne Moore, Paul Muldoon, Les Murray, Pablo Neruda, Octavio Paz, Sylvia Plath, Edgar Allan Poe, Alexander Pope, Ezra Pound, Aleksandr Pushkin, Adrienne Rich, Rainer Maria Rilke, Arthur Rimbaud, Christina Rossetti, Dante Gabriel Rossetti, Siegfried Sassoon, Friedrich Schiller, Anne Sexton, William Shakespeare, Edmund Spenser, Wallace Stevens, Alfred Tennyson, Dylan Thomas, Henry Thoreau, JRR Tolkien, Paul Valéry, Derek Walcott, Walt Whitman, Oscar Wilde, William Carlos Williams, William Wordsworth, Xu Zhi Mo, WB Yeats

CLASSICAL POETS

Aeschylus, Aristophanes, Li Bai, Catullus, Du Fu, Herodotus, Homer, Horace, Omar Khayam, Ovid, Sappho, Sophocles, Virgil, Wang Wei

NOTED DRAMATISTS

Edward Albee, Jean Anouilh, John Arden, Alan Ayckbourn, Honoré de Balzac, JM Barrie, Samuel Beckett, Alan Bennett, Steven Berkoff, Bertolt Brecht, Anton Chekhov, Agatha Christie, Caryl Churchill, Jean Cocteau, Noel Coward, Jean Genet, WS Gilbert, David Hare, Vaclav Havel, Victor Hugo, Henrik Ibsen, Eugene Ionesco, David Ives, Tony Kushner, Neil LaBute, David Mamet, Somerset Maugham, Martin McDonagh, Arthur Miller, Eugene O'Neill, Joe Orton, John Osborne, Harold Pinter, Luigi Pirandello, Dennis Potter, Aleksandr Pushkin, David Rabe, Terence Rattigan, Will Russell, William Saroyan, Arthur Schnitzler, Peter

Shaffer, George Bernard Shaw, Neil Simon, Tom Stoppard, August Strindberg, Oscar Wilde, Tennessee Williams

PRE–19TH-CENTURY PLAYWRIGHTS

Aeschylus, Aristophanes, Aphra Behn, Pierre Corneille, John Dryden, Euripides, Goethe, Ben Jonson, Niccolo Machiavelli, Christopher Marlowe, Molière, Plautus, Jean Racine, William Shakespeare, Sophocles, Terence, Voltaire

CLASSIC FILMS (BY SUBJECT)

Generally only the first of sequels and the latest version of remakes are noted.

Unconventional romance
Personal redemption
Revenge
Homecoming
Pygmalion-type
Teachers
Actors
Journalists
Prostitutes
Religion
Mathematics
Car racing
Trains
Boats
Aeroplanes
Plane crashes
Police
Heists / Bank robbers
Mafia / Gangsters
Politics

Terrorism
Prison
War
Classic westerns
Spaghetti westerns
Historical/Epics
Dancing
Letters
Environmentalism
Narrators
Memory
Interlopers
Death / afterlife
Deceased narrators
Reincarnation
Time travel
Dystopias
Computers
Chance encounters
Love triangles
Deception
Swapped / assumed identities
Mistaken identities
Twist in the tail
Fish out of water
Innocent abroad
Gay
Transvestite / transexual
Mental illness / challenge
Alcohol
Drugs
Bigotry
Boxing
Bowling
Sport
Being buried alive
Christmas, New Year's, Thanksgiving
Unlikely couples
Mismatched partners

Pregnancy, adoption, abortion
Documentaries
Mockumentaries
About making films
Apocalyptic
Paranormal
Aliens
Alien invasion
Vampires / Werewolves
Robots
Underwater
Quest
Plucky young heroes
Gambling
Cloning
Animated

UNCONVENTIONAL ROMANCE

American Beauty (1999)
Casablanca (1942)
Roman Holiday (1953)
Secretary (2002)
sex, lies, and videotape (1989)
Wall-E (2008)
White Palace (1990)

PERSONAL REDEMPTION

About a Boy (2002)
Green Mile, The (1999)
Hurricane, The (1999)
It's a Wonderful Life (1946)
Jerry Maguire (1996)
Kid, The (2000)
Leon the Professional (1994)
Princess Bride, The (1987)
Pulp Fiction (1994)
Scent of a Woman (1992)
Scrooge (1951)
Shawshank Redemption, The (1994)

Splendor in the Grass (1961)
Verdict, The (1982)

REVENGE

Carrie (1976)
Count of Monte Cristo, The (1934)
Death Rides a Horse (1967)
Death Wish (1974)
Get Carter (1971)
Gladiator (2000)
Godfather, The (1972)
Irreversible (2003)
Mad Max (1979)
Man on Fire (2004)
Mystic River (2003)
Oldboy (2003)
Outlaw Josey Wales, The (1976)
Payback (1999)
Point Blank (1967)
Punisher, The (2004)
Ran (1985)
Straw Dogs (1971)
V For Vendetta (2006)

HOMECOMING

Best Years of our Lives, The (1946)
Coming Home (1978)
Deer Hunter, The (1978)
Invitation to a Gunfighter (1964)
Quiet Man, The (1952)
Le Retour de Martin Guerre (1982)

PYGMALION-TYPE

Born Yesterday (1950)
Hoi Polloi (1935)
Miss Congeniality (2000)
My Fair Lady (1964)
Princess Diaries, The (2001)
Pretty Woman (1990)

Pygmalion (1938)
Sabrina (1995)
Trading Places (1983)

TEACHERS

Breakfast Club, The (1985)
Les Choristes (2004)
Dangerous Minds (1995)
Dead Poets Society (1989)
Election (1999)
Etre et avoir (2004)
Ferris Bueller's Day Off (1986)
Finding Forrester (2000)
Freedom Writers (2007)
Good Will Hunting (1997)
Man Without a Face, The (1993)
Mona Lisa Smile (2003)
Mr Holland's Opus (1995)
Paper Chase, The (1973)
Prime of Miss Jean Brodie, The (1969)
Substitute, The (1996)
Teacher, The (1974)
To Sir, With Love (1967)

ACTORS

8½ (1963)
Being John Malkovich (1999)
Golden Coach, The (1952)
Les Enfants du Paradis (1945)
Lost in Translation (2003)
La Nuit Americaine (1973)
Rosemary's Baby (1968)
Venus (2006)
Mephisto (1981)
My Favourite Year (1982)
Shakespeare in Love (1998)
Sideways (2004)
Withnail and I (1987)

JOURNALISTS

All the President's Men (1976)
Citizen Kane (1941)
Control Room (2004)
Defence of the Realm (1985)
La Dolce Vita (1960)
Fear and Loathing in Los Vegas (1998)
Front Page, The (1974)
Goodnight, and Good Luck (2005)
His Girl Friday (1940)
Hurricane, The (1999)
Insider, The (1999)
It Happened One Night (1934)
Naked Truth, The (1957)
Network (1976)
Paper, The (1994)
Pelican Brief, The (1993)
Quiet American, The (2002)
Reds (1981)
Salvador (1986)
Shattered Glass (2003)
Shipping News, The (2001)
Spider-Man (2002)
Superman (1978)
Sweet Smell of Success (1957)
Veronica Guerin (2003)
Year of Living Dangerously, The (1982)

PROSTITUTES

American Gigolo (1980)
Belle de jour (1967)
From Hell (2001)
Leaving Las Vegas (1995)
McCabe and Mrs Miller (1971)
Mona Lisa (1986)
Monster (2003)
Notti di Cabiria, Le (1957)
Paint Your Wagon (1969)
Pretty Woman (1990)

Risky Business (1983)
Taxi Driver (1976)

RELIGION
Black Robe (1991)
Da Vinci Code, The (2006)
Keeping the Faith (2000)
Mission, The (1986)
Name of the Rose, The (1986)
Passion of the Christ, The (2004)
Priest (1994)
Rapture, The (1991)
Saved! (2004)
Sister Act (1992)
Ten Commandments, The (1956)

MATHEMATICS
Beautiful Mind, A (2001)
Good Will Hunting (1997)
Infinity (1996)
It's My Turn (1980)
Mercury Rising (1998)
Mirror Has Two Faces, The (1996)
Pi (1998)
Proof (2005)
Sneakers (1992)
Stand and Deliver (1987)
Straw Dogs (1971)

CAR RACING
Bullitt (1968)
Cannonball Run, The (1991)
Days of Thunder (1990)
Death Race 2000 (1975)
Fast and the Furious, The (2001)
Gone in Sixty Seconds (1974)
Great Race, The (1965)
Gumball Rally, The (1976)

Love Bug, The (1968)
Talladega Nights (2006)

TRAINS
Bridge on the River Kwai, The (1957)
Brief Encounter (1945)
Closely Observed Trains (1966)
Derailed (2002)
L'Homme du Train (2002)
Railway Children, The (1970)
Shanghai Express (1932)
Station Agent, The (2003)
Strangers on a Train (1951)
Throw Momma From the Train (1987)
Titfield Thunderbolt, The (1953)
Murder on the Orient Express (1974)
North by Northwest (1959)

BOATS
African Queen, The (1951)
L'avventura (1960)
Apocalypse Now (1979)
Big Blue, The (1988)
Breaking the Waves (1996)
Deliverance (1972)
In Which We Serve (1942)
Jaws (1975)
King Kong (2005)
Night to Remember, A (1958)
Perfect Storm, The (1997)
Poseidon Adventure, The (1972)
River Wild, The (1994)
Speed 2 (1997)
Titanic (1997)

AEROPLANES
Airport (1970)
Air Force One (1997)
Catch Me If You Can (2002)

English Patient, The (1996)
Final Destination (2000)
Flight of the Phoenix (2004)
Flightplan (2005)
Pushing Tin (1999)
Redeye (2005)
Snakes on a Plane (2006)
United 93 (2006)

PLANE CRASHES

Accidental Hero (1992)
Aliens (1986)
Alive! (1993)
Aviator, The (2004)
Bounce (2000)
Cast Away (2000)
Donnie Darko (2001)
English Patient, The (1996)
Fearless (1993)
Final Destination (2000)
Flight of the Phoenix (1965)
Foreign Correspondent (1940)
Jurassic Park III (2001)
Lost Horizon (1937)
Matter of Life and Death, A (1946)
Planet of the Apes (1968)
Random Hearts (1999)
Sahara (2005)

POLICE

Basic Instinct (1992)
Cruising (1980)
Fallen (1998)
Fargo (1996)
French Connection, The (1971)
In the Heat of the Night (1967)
LA Confidential (1997)
Mississippi Burning (1988)
Serpico (1973)

Shaft (1971)
Silence of the Lambs, The (1991)
Untouchables, The (1987)
Witness (1985)

HEISTS / BANK ROBBERY

Asphalt Jungle, The (1950)
Assassination of Jesse James, The (2007)
Bandits (2001)
Before the Devil Knows You're Dead (2007)
Bonny and Clyde (1967)
Butch Cassidy and the Sundance Kid (1969)
Dog Day Afternoon (1975)
Fistful of Dynamite, A (1971)
Home Alone (1990)
Italian Job, The (1969)
Ladykillers, The (1955)
Lavender Hill Mob, The (1951)
Night of the Hunter, The (1955)
Ocean's Eleven (1960)
Panic Room (2002)
Point Break (2001)
Raising Arizona (1987)
Run Lola Run (1998)
3:10 to Yuma (2008)
Wild Bunch, The (1969)

MAFIA / GANGSTERS

American Gangster (2007)
Analyze This (1999)
Carlito's Way (1993)
Departed, The (2006)
Dillinger (1973)
Dirty Dozen, The (1967)
Donnie Brasco (1997)
Gangs of New York (2002)
Godfather, The (1972)
Goodfellas (1990)
Mean Streets (1973)

Midnight Run (1988)
Once Upon a Time in America (1984)
Reservoir Dogs (1992)
Scarface (1983)
Untouchables, The (1993)

POLITICS

All the President's Men (1976)
Art of War, The (2000)
Bob Roberts (1992)
Bulworth (1998)
Candidate, The (1972)
Dr Strangelove (1963)
Fahrenheit 9/11 (2004)
Gandhi (1982)
Good Night, and Good Luck (2005)
Interpreter, The (2005)
Last Hurrah, The (1958)
Manchurian Candidate, The (1962)
Nixon (1995)
Primary Colors (1998)
Reds (1981)
Syriana (2005)
Wag the Dog (1998)

TERRORISM

Black Sunday (1977)
Brazil (1985)
Children of Men (2006)
Crying Game, The (1992)
Die Hard (1988)
Fight Club (1999)
In the Name of the Father (1993)
Munich (2005)
Peacemaker, The (1997)
Team America: World Police (2004)
United 93 (2006)
World Trade Center (2006)

PRISON

Alien 3 (1992)
Attica (1991)
Birdman of Alcatraz (1962)
Cape Fear (1962)
Colditz Story, The (1957)
Great Escape, The (1963)
Monster's Ball (2001)
Shawshank Redemption, The (1994)

WAR

Apocalypse Now (1979)
Black Hawk Down (2001)
Born on the Fourth of July (1989)
Casablanca (1942)
Dam Busters, The (1955)
Deer Hunter, The (1978)
Full Metal Jacket (1987)
Good Morning, Vietnam (1987)
La Grande Illusion (1937)
Jarhead (2005)
Killing Fields, The (1984)
M*A*S*H (1970)
Nuit et brouillard (1955)
Platoon (1986)
Saving Private Ryan (1998)
Thin Red Line, The (1998)
Three Kings (1999)

WESTERNS

Assassination of Jesse James, The (2007)
Blazing Saddles (1974)
Brokeback Mountain (2005)
Broken Lance (1954)
Butch Cassidy and the Sundance Kid (1969)
Dances with Wolves (1990)
Good, the Bad and the Ugly, The (1966)
Hidalgo (2004)
High Noon (1952)

Lone Star (1996)
Magnificent Seven, The (1960)
My Darling Clementine (1946)
No Country for Old Men (2007)
Once Upon a Time in the West (1968)
Proposition, The (2005)
Rio Bravo (1959)
Searchers, The (1956)
Shane (1953)
These Thousand Hills (1959)
Treasure of Sierra Madre, The (1948)
Wild Bunch, The (1969)
Yellow Sky (1948)

HISTORICAL / EPICS

2001: A Space Odyssey (1968)
300 (2006)
All Quiet on the Western Front (1930)
Battleship Potemkin (1925)
Ben-Hur (1959)
Cleopatra (1963)
Doctor Zhivago (1965)
Gandhi (1982)
Giant (1956)
Gone With the Wind (1939)
Greatest Story Ever Told, The (1965)
Judgment at Nuremburg (1961)
Last Emperor, The (1987)
Lawrence of Arabia (1962)
Lord of the Rings, The (2001)
Quo Vadis (1951)
Solaris (1972)
Spartacus (1960)
Troy (2004)
Wild Bunch, The (1969)

DANCING

Dirty Dancing (1987)
Fame (1980)
Flashdance (1983)
Footloose (1984)
Grease (1978)
Pulp Fiction (1994)
Saturday Night Fever (1977)
Scent of a Woman (1992)
Singin' in the Rain (1952)
Top Hat (1935)

LETTERS / EMAILS

About Schmidt (2002)
Atonement (2007)
Broken Flowers (2005)
Cast Away (2000)
84 Charing Cross Rd (1987)
Jarhead (2005)
Lake House, The (2006)
Love Letters (1945)
Notebook, The (2004)
Shop Around the Corner, The (1940)
You've Got Mail (1998)

ENVIRONMENTALISM

Doctor Doolittle 2 (2001)
Happening, The (2008)
Inconvenient Truth, An (2006)
Silent Running (1972)
Soylent Green (1973)
Star Trek IV: The Voyage Home (1986)
Sunshine (2007)
Wall·E (2008)

NARRATORS

Amélie (2001)
Apocalypse Now (1979)
Bladerunner (1982)
Cock and Bull Story, A (2005)
Dead Men Don't Wear Plaid (1982)
Draftsman's Contract, The (1982)
Goodfellas (1990)
Lord of War (2005)
Notes on a Scandal (2006)
Pursuit of Happyness, The (2006)
Third Man, The (1949)

MEMORY

Angel Heart (1987)
Away from Her (2006)
Bladerunner (1982)
Butterfly Effect, The (2004)
Eternal Sunshine of the Spotless Mind (2004)
Fountain, The (2006)
Lo Smemorato di Collegno (1962)
Memento (2000)
Notebook, The (2004)
Science of Sleep, The (2006)
Spider (2002)
Suddenly, Last Summer (1959)
The 39 Steps (1935)

DEATH / AFTERLIFE

City of Angels (1998)
Flatliners (1990)
Ghost (1990)
Heaven Can Wait (1978)
Here Comes Mr Jordan (1941)
Just Like Heaven (2005)
Others, The (2001)
Poltergeist (1982)
Sixth Sense, The (1999)
Truly Madly Deeply (1990)

What Dreams May Come (1998)
Wings of Desire (1987)

DECEASED NARRATORS

American Beauty (1999)
Human Comedy, The (1943)
Jacob's Ladder (1990)
Lovely Bones, The (2009)
Sin City (2005)
Sunset Boulevard (1960)
Vanilla Sky (2001)

REINCARNATION

Audrey Rose (1977)
Birth (2004)
Chances Are (1989)
Dead Again (1991)
Down to Earth (2001)
Fountain, The (2006)
Heaven Can Wait (1978)
Omen, The (1976)
Orlando (1992)

TIME TRAVEL

Austin Powers (1997)
Back to the Future (1985)
Blast from the Past (1999)
Butterfly Effect, The (2004)
Donnie Darko (2001)
La Jetée (1962)
Kate and Leopold (2001)
Navigator, The (1988)
Pleasantville (1998)
Terminator, The (1984)
Time Machine, The (2002)
Time Bandits (1981)
Timecop (1994)
Twelve Monkeys (1995)

DYSTOPIAS

AI: Artificial Intelligence (2001)
Alphaville (1965)
Bladerunner (1982)
Boy and His Dog, A (1975)
Brazil (1985)
Children of Men (2006)
City of Lost Children, The (1995)
Clockwork Orange, A (1971)
Death Race 2000 (1975)
Delicatessen (1991)
Fahrenheit 451 (1966)
Gattaca (1997)
Handmaid's Tale, The (1990)
Idiocracy (2006)
I, Robot (2004)
Island, The (2005)
Logan's Run (1976)
Mad Max (1979)
Matrix, The (1999)
Metropolis (1927)
Minority Report (2001)
Nineteen Eighty-Four (1984)
Planet of the Apes (1968)
Rollerball (1975)
Scanner Darkly, A (2006)
Silent Running (1972)
Soylent Green (1973)
Starship Troopers (1997)
Strange Days (1995)
Terminator, The (1984)
Total Recall (1990)
Twelve Monkeys (1995)
TX1138 (1971)

COMPUTERS

Hackers (1995)
Independence Day (1996)
Matrix, The (1999)
Net, The (1995)
Sneakers (1992)
Stealth (2005)
Swordfish (2001)
Tron (1982)
2001: A Space Odyssey (1968)
Wall•E (2008)
War Games (1983)

CHANCE ENCOUNTERS

L'air du Temps (2004)
Brève Traversée (2001)
Brief Encounter (1945)
Lost in Translation (2003)
Love Affair (1939)
Red (1994)
Shadowlands (1993)
Sliding Doors (1998)

LOVE TRIANGLES

Being John Malkovich (1999)
Casablanca (1942)
Fatal Instinct (1993)
French Lieutenant's Woman, The (1981)
Gone With the Wind (1937)
Heaven's Gate (1980)
Intersection (1994)
Jules et Jim (1962)
Keeping the Faith (2000)
Legends of the Fall (1994)
Shopgirl (2005)
Story of a Love Story (1973)
Sweet Home Alabama (2002)
Titanic (1997)

SWAPPED / ASSUMED IDENTITIES

All of Me (1984)
Big (1988)
Body Heat (1981)
Double Indemnity (1944)
Duck Soup (1933)
Face/Off (1997)
Freaky Friday (2003)
Gattaca (1997)
Gentlemen Prefer Blondes (1953)
Hot Chick, The (2002)
I Was Monty's Double (1958)
Majestic, The (2001)
My Man Godfrey (1936)
Retour de Martin Guerre, Le (1982)
Shakespeare in Love (1998)
Sommersby (1993)
Taking Lives (2004)
Talented Mr Ripley, The (1999)
13 Going on 30 (2004)
Waking Ned (1998)
While You Were Sleeping (1995)

MISTAKEN IDENTITY

Big Lebowski, The (1998)
Le Bonheur est dans le pres (1995)
Brazil (1985)
Galaxy Quest (1999)
Life of Brian (1979)
North by Northwest (1959)
Man Who Knew Too Much, The (1956)
Third Man, The (1949)
Wrong Man, The (1956)
Vertigo (1958)

TWIST IN THE TAIL

Atonement (2007)
Brazil (1985)
Chinatown (1974)
Fight Club (1999)
Identity (2003)
Memento (2000)
Planet of the Apes (1968)
Psycho (1960)
Rear Window (1954)
Shawshank Redemption, The (1994)
Sixth Sense (1999)
Thing, The (1982)
Usual Suspects, The (1995)
Wizard of Oz, The (1939)

FISH OUT OF WATER

Cars (2006)
Devil Wears Prada, The (2006)
Doc Hollywood (1991)
Edward Scissorhands (1990)
Groundhog Day (1993)
Hot Fuzz (2007)
Kindergarten Cop (1990)
Legally Blonde (2001)
Man of the House (2005)
Meet Dave (2008)
Pretty Woman (1990)
Some like it Hot (1959)
Splash (1984)
Terminator 2: Judgment Day (1991)
Trading Places (1983)
Witness (1985)

INNOCENT ABROAD

Borat (2006)
Crocodile Dundee (1986)
Dances with Wolves (1990)
Last King of Scotland, The (2006)

Lost in Translation (2003)
Red Heat (1988)
Sleeper (1973)
Sleepy Hollow (1999)
Species (1995)
Story of a Three Day Pass, The (1968)

GAY / LESBIAN

Adventures of Priscilla, Queen of the Desert, The (1994)
Beautiful Thing (1996)
Bound (1996)
La cage aux folles (1978)
Fucking Amal (1998)
I Heard the Mermaids Singing (1987)
In and Out (1997)
Kissing Jessica Stein (2001)
Kiss of the Spider Woman (1985)
Milk (2008)
My Beautiful Laundrette (1985)
When Night is Falling (1995)

TRANSVESTITE / TRANSGENDER

Boys Don't Cry (1999)
Ed Wood (1994)
Hedwig and the Angry Inch (2001)
Hot Chick, The (2002)
Ma Vie en Rose (1997)
Tootsie (1982)
Transamerica (2006)
White Chicks (2004)

MENTAL ILLNESS / CHALLENGE

Angel at my Table, An (1990)
Beautiful Mind, A (2001)
Being There (1979)
Benny and Joon (1993)
Birdy (1984)

Butcher Boy, The (1997)
Clockwork Orange, A (1971)
Fisher King, The (1991)
Forrest Gump (1994)
I Am Sam (2001)
K-Pax (2001)
Little Voice (1998)
Memento (2001)
One Flew over the Cuckoo's Nest (1975)
Rain Man (1988)
Sling Blade (1996)
Twelve Monkeys (1995)
What's Eating Gilbert Grape? (1993)

ALCOHOL

Arthur (1981)
Barfly (1987)
Casablanca (1942)
Days of Wine and Roses (1962)
Factotum (2006)
Last Orders (2001)
Leaving Las Vegas (1995)
Lost Weekend, The (1945)
Mean Streets (1973)
My Name is Joe (1998)
National Lampoon's Animal House (1978)
Paint Your Wagon (1969)
Risky Business (1983)
Sideways (2005)
Swingers (1996)
Upside of Anger, The (2005)
Who's Afraid of Virginia Woolf? (1966)

DRUGS

Altered States (1980)
Big Lebowski, The (1998)
Bird (1988)
Drugstore Cowboy (1989)
Fear and Loathing in Las Vegas (1998)

Lock, Stock and Two Smoking Barrels (1998)
Maria Full of Grace (2004)
Midnight Express (1978)
Naked Lunch (1991)
Requiem for a Dream (2000)
Spun (2002)
Traffic (2000)
Trainspotting (1996)
Up in Smoke (1978)

BIGOTRY

American History X (1998)
Crash (2004)
East is East (1999)
Falling Down (1993)
Green Mile, The (1999)
Guess Who's Coming to Dinner? (1967)
La Haine (1995)
In the Heat of the Night (1967)
Intolerance (1916)
Lone Star (1996)
Malcolm X (1992)
Mississippi Burning (1988)
Monster's Ball (2001)
Passage to India, A (1984)
Rabbit Proof Fence (2002)
Romper Stomper (1992)
Snow Falling on Cedars (1999)
To Kill a Mockingbird (1962)
Touch of Evil (1958)
West Side Story (1961)

BOXING

Ali (2001)
Body and Soul (1947)
Girlfight (2000)
Golden Boy (1939)
Great White Hope, The (1970)
Hurricane, The (1999)

Joe Louis Story, The (1953)
Million Dollar Baby (2004)
Raging Bull (1980)
Rocky (1976)
Somebody Up There Likes Me (1956)
Unforgiveable Blackness (2005)

BOWLING

Big Lebowski, The (1998)
Bowling for Columbine (2002)
Crackerjack (2002)
Deer Hunter, The (1978)
Fatal Attraction (1987)
Five Easy Pieces (1970)
Kingpin (1996)
Lars and the Real Girl (2007)
Matchstick Men (2003)
Ordinary People (1980)
Pin Gods (1996)
Scarface (1932)
Streetcar Called Desire, A (1951)
There Will Be Blood (2007)

SPORT

Bend it Like Beckham (2002)
Fever Pitch (1997)
Field of Dreams (1989)
Hoop Dreams (1994)
Hurricane, The (1999)
Invincible (2006)
Jerry Maguire (1996)
Legend of Bagger Vance, The (2000)
Replacements, The (2000)
Shaolin Soccer (2001)

BURIED ALIVE

Blood Simple (1984)
Casino (1995)
Dirty Harry (1971)

Don't Say a Word (2001)
Double Jeopardy (1999)
Kill Bill: Vol 2 (2003)
Oxygen (1999)
Prestige, The (2006)
Raiders of the Lost Ark (1981)
Vanishing, The (1988)

XMAS, NEW YEAR'S, THANKSGIVING

Angel Heart (1987)
Bad Santa (2003)
End of Days (1999)
Family Stone, The (2005)
Home for the Holidays (1995)
Ice Storm, The (1997)
Last Day (1999)
Miracle on 34th Street (1947)
Ocean's Eleven (1960)
Peter's Friends (1993)
Sleepless in Seattle (1993)
Strange Days (1995)
Sunset Boulevard
When Harry Met Sally (1989)

UNLIKELY COUPLES

Benny and Joon (1993)
Crazy/Beautiful (2001)
Crying Game, The (1992)
Desert Hearts (1985)
Guess Who's Coming to Dinner? (1967)
Harold and Maude (1971)
It Happened One Night (1934)
Jungle Fever (1991)
King Kong (2005)
Mississippi Masala (1991)
Pretty Woman (1990)
Pygmalion (1938)
Some Like it Hot (1959)

Strada, La (1954)
White Palace (1990)

MISMATCHED PARTNERS

Alien Nation (1988)
Beverly Hills Cop (1984)
Bone Collector, The (1999)
48 Hrs (1982)
Lethal Weapon (1987)
Midnight Run (1988)
Miss Congeniality 2 (2005)
Renegades (1989)
Robocop (1987)
Rush Hour (1998)
Shanghai Noon (2000)
Showtime (2002)
Training Day (2001)
Turner & Hooch (1989)

PREGNANCY, ADOPTION, ABORTION

Ann Vickers (1933)
Cider House Rules, The (1999)
4 Months, 3 Weeks and 2 Days (2008)
High Fidelity (2000)
Juno (2007)
Knocked Up (2007)
Magdalene Sisters, The (2002)
Riding in Cars with Boys (2001)
Road to Ruin, The (1928)
Saved (2004)
Vera Drake (2004)

MUSIC

Almost Famous (2000)
Fame (1980)
High Fidelity (2000)
Last Waltz, The (1978)
Metallica: Some Kind of Monster (2004)

Monterey Pop (1968)
School of Rock (2003)
Sgt Pepper's Lonely Hearts Club Band (1978)
Stop Making Sense (1984)
This is Spinal Tap (1984)

MUSICALS

Absolute Beginners (1986)
Blues Brothers, The (1980)
Brigadoon (1954)
Calamity Jane (1953)
Chicago (2002)
Chitty Chitty Bang Bang (1968)
Dreamgirls (2006)
Duck Soup (1933)
Grease (1978)
High Society (1956)
Lion King, The (1994)
Mamma Mia! (2008)
Mary Poppins (1964)
Night at the Opera, A (1935)
Oliver! (1968)
Paint Your Wagon (1969)
Singin' in the Rain (1952)
Sound of Music, The (1965)
Sweeney Todd (2007)
Wizard of Oz, The (1939)

DOCUMENTARIES

Bowling for Columbine (2002)
Capturing the Friedmans (2003)
Fahrenheit 9/11 (2004)
Fog of War (2003)
Inconvenient Truth, An (2006)
March of the Penguins (2005)
Night and Fog (1955)
Outfoxed (2004)
Promises (2001)
Seven Up! (TV – 1964)

Sorrow and the Pity, The (1969)
Supersize Me (2004)
Touching the Void (2003)
War Game, The (1965)

MOCKUMENTARIES

Best in Show (2001)
Bob Roberts (1992)
Borat (2006)
Drop Dead Gorgeous (1999)
Falls, The (1980)
For Your Consideration (2006)
Man Bites Dog (1992)
Mighty Wind, A (2003)
Real Life (1979)
Smile (1975)
Surf's Up (2007)
This is Spinal Tap (1984)
Waiting for Guffman (1997)
Zelig (1983)

ABOUT MAKING FILMS

Adaptation (2002)
Be Kind Rewind (2008)
Bowfinger (1999)
Cock and Bull Story, A (2005)
Crimes and Misdemeanours (1989)
Ed Wood (1994)
8½ (1963)
Kid Stays in the Picture, The (2002)
Lost in La Mancha (2002)
Mulholland Drive (2001)
La Nuit Americaine (Day for Night) (1973)
Player, The (1996)
Star is Born, A (1937)
Sunset Boulevard (1950)
Tropic Thunder (2008)
Way We Were, The (1973)

APOCALYPTIC

After the Apocalypse (2004)
Armageddon (1998)
Children of Men (2006)
Deep Impact (1998)
Delicatessen (1991)
Logan's Run (1976)
Mad Max (1979)
Omega Man (1971)
Planet of the Apes (1968)
Quiet Earth, The (1985)
Silent Running (1971)
Terminator, The (1984)
Twelve Monkeys (1995)
28 Days Later (2002)

PARANORMAL

Amityville Horror, The (1979)
Audrey Rose (1977)
Blair Witch Project, The (1999)
Butterfly Effect, The (2004)
Carrie (1976)
Constantine (2005)
Exorcist, The (1973)
Frequency (2000)
Ghost Busters (1984)
Illusionist, The (2006)
Messengers, The (2007)
Ninth Gate, The (1999)
Omen, The (1976)
Poltergeist (1982)
Rosemary's Baby (1968)
Shining, The (1980)
Sixth Sense, The (1999)
Skeleton Key, The (2005)
X Files, The (1998)

ALIENS

Alien (1979)
Astronaut's Wife, The (1999)
Close Encounters of the Third Kind (1977)
Contact (1997)
Day the Earth Stood Still, The (1951)
ET (1982)
K-Pax (2001)
Meet Dave (2008)
Men in Black (1997)
Pitch Black (2000)
Predator (1987)
Thing, The (1982)
Virus (1999)
X-Files (1998)

ALIEN INVASION

Alien Nation (1989)
Arrival, The (1996)
Blob, The (1958)
Cloverfield (2008)
Dark City (1988)
Day the Earth Stood Still, The (1951)
Gojira (1954)
Hitchhiker's Guide to the Galaxy, The (2005)
Independence Day (1996)
Invasion of the Body Snatchers (1956)
It Came From Outer Space (1953)
Mars Attacks! (1996)
Men in Black (1997)
Signs (2002)
Species (1995)
Thing, The (1982)
Village of the Damned (1960)
War of the Worlds (2005)
When Worlds Collide (2008)
X Files, The (1998)

VAMPIRES / WEREWOLVES

American Werewolf in London, An (1981)
Black Sunday (1960)
Blacula (1972)
Blade (1998)
Chronos (1993)
Day Watch (2006)
Dog Soldiers (2002)
Dracula (1979)
Fright Night (1985)
From Dusk Till Dawn (1996)
Horror of Dracula (1958)
Howling, The (1981)
Hunger, The (1983)
Interview with the Vampire (1994)
Near Dark (1987)
Night Stalker, The (1972)
Nosferatu (1922)
Perfect Creature (2006)
Teen Wolf (1985)
30 Days of Night (2007)
Twilight (2008)
Underworld (2003)
Vampyros Lesbos (1970)
Van Helsing (2004)
Wild Boys (1987)
Wolf (1994)
Wolf Man, The (1941)

ROBOTS / HUMANOIDS

AI: Artificial Intelligence (2001)
Bicentennial Man (1999)
Bladerunner (1982)
Cherry 2000 (1988)
Cyborg (1989)
Day the Earth Stood Still, The (1951)
Forbidden Planet (1956)
I, Robot (2004)
Robocop (1987)

Stepford Wives, The (1975)
Terminator, The (1984)
Westworld (1973)

UNDERWATER

Above Us the Waves (1956)
Abyss, The (1989)
Big Blue, The (1988)
Cocoon (1985)
Deep, The (1977)
Deep Blue Sea (1999)
Jaws (1975)
Men of Honor (2000)
Orca (1977)
Silent Enemy (1958)
Sphere (1998)
SpongeBob SquarePants (1999)
Titanic (1997)
20,000 Leagues Under the Sea (1954)
Waterworld (1995)

QUEST

Adventures of Baron Munchhausen, The (1988)
Fisher King, The (1991)
Lord of the Rings, The (2001)
Matrix, The (1999)
Moby Dick (1930)
Monty Python and the Holy Grail (1979)
Navigator: A Mediaeval Odyssey, The (1988)
Princess Bride, The (1987)
Watership Down (1978)
Willow (1988)
Wizard of Oz, The (1939)

YOUNG HEROES

Billy Elliot (2000)
Cinema Paradiso (1988)
Cocoon (1985)
Free Willy (1993)
Client, The (1994)
Kes (1969)
Karate Kid, The (1984)
Kolya (1996)
Millions (2004)
My Life as a Dog (1985)
Neverending Story, The (1984)
Oliver Twist (1948)
Sixth Sense, The (1999)
There's only one Jimmy Grimble (2000)
This Girl's Life (2003)

GAMBLING

Amores Perros (2000)
Barry Lyndon (1975)
Deer Hunter, The (1978)
Casablanca (1942)
Gambler, The (1974)
Good Thief, The (2003)
Lock, Stock and Two Smoking Barrels (1998)
Oceans Eleven (1960)
Owning Mahowny (2003)
Snake Eyes (1998)
Snatch (2000)
Stranger Than Paradise (1984)

CLONING

Alien Resurrection (1997)
Austin Powers: The Spy Who Shagged Me (1999)
Boys From Brazil, The (1978)
Fifth Element, The (1997)
Godsend (2004)
Island, The (2005)

Jurassic Park (1993)
Multiplicity (1996)
6th Day, The (2000)
Starman (1984)
Twins (1988)

ANIMATED

Animal Farm (1952)
Barefoot Gen (1983)
Bug's Life, A (1998)
Fantasia (1940)
Grave of the Fireflies (1989)
Incredibles, The (2004)
Laputa: Castle in the Sky (1986)
Iron Giant, The (1999)
Madagascar (2005)
Persepolis (2007)
Pinocchio (1940)
Ratatouille (2007)
Toy Story (1995)
Triplettes de Belleville, Les (2003)
Shrek (2001)
Spirited Away (2001)
Simpsons Movie, The (2007)
Wall·E (2008)
Wind in the Willows, The (1983)
Wrong Trousers, The (1993)

CLASSIC FILMS (BY DECADE, 1920s–2000s)

1920s

The Cabinet of Dr Caligari, The Freshman, The General, The Gold Rush, The Kid, Metropolis, Napoleon, Sunrise, The Wedding March

1930s

Alexander Nevsky, All Quiet on the Western Front, Un Carnet de Bal, La Chienne, City Lights, Un Coeur en Hiver, Death Takes a Holiday, Destry Rides Again, Duck Soup, Follow the Fleet, 42nd Street, Gone With the Wind, The Grand Illusion, It Happened One Night, The Lady Vanishes, The Life of Emile Zola, The Lost Patrol, M, Modern Times, Olympia, Rules of the Game, They Won't Forget , The Wizard of Oz

1940s

Adam's Rib, All the King's Men, Bambi, Beauty and the Beast, Bicycle Thieves, The Big Sleep, Black Narcissus, Brief Encounter, Casablanca, Children of Paradise, Citizen Kane, The Grapes of Wrath, The Great Dictator, In Which We Serve, It's a Wonderful Life, Kind Hearts and Coronets, The Life and Death of Colonel Blimp, The Lost Weekend, The Maltese Falcon, The Miracle of Morgan's Creek, Ossessione, The Ox-Bow Incident, Passport to Pimlico, Pinocchio, Rebecca, Red River, Stray Dog, They Were Expendable, The Third Man, A Tree Grows in Brooklyn

1950s

The African Queen, All About Eve, Ben Hur, The Bridge on the River Kwai, The Devils, Diabolique, The Four Hundred Blows, High Noon, The Ladykillers, The Lavender Hill Mob, Lili, The Night My Number Came Up, Night of the Hunter, North by Northwest, On the Waterfront, Paths of Glory, Rashomon, Rear Window, Rebel Without a Cause, Roman Holiday, Sawdust and Tinsel, The Searchers, Seven Brides for Seven Brothers, Seven Days to Noon, Seven Samurai, The

Seventh Seal, Some Like it Hot, La Strada, Strangers on a Train, A Streetcar Named Desire, Sunset Blvd, 3:10 to Yuma, Touch of Evil, 12 Angry Men, Vertigo, The Wages of Fear, Wild Strawberries

1960s

Alfie, L'avventura, The Battle of Algiers, Belle de Jour, The Birds, Bonny and Clyde, Breathless, Butch Cassidy and the Sundance Kid, Doctor Zhivago, La Dolce Vita, Dr Strangelove, Easy Rider, Fist in his Pocket, The Good, the Bad and the Ugly, Goldfinger, The Graduate, Hiroshima Mon Amour, Knife in the Water, Lawrence of Arabia, Lolita, Mary Poppins, Midnight Cowboy, Once Upon a Time in the West, Othello, The Pawnbroker, Psycho, Ship of Fools, The Sound of Music, Spartacus, The Train, Tunes of Glory, 2001: A Space Odyssey

1970s

Aguirre: The Wrath of God, Alice Doesn't Live Here Anymore, Alien, All the President's Men, Apocalypse Now, Being There, Chinatown, A Clockwork Orange, The Conversation, Day for Night, Dog Day Afternoon, The Exorcist, The French Connection, The Godfather, The Last Picture Show, Manhattan, Marathon Man, M*A*S*H, Mean Streets, Monty Python's Life of Brian, Network, O Lucky Man!, One Flew over the Cuckoo's Nest, Paper Moon, Patton, Seven Beauties, Small Change, The Sting, Straw Dogs, Taxi Driver, The Tree of Wooden Clogs, An Unmarried Woman, Vincent, Francois, Paul and the Others

1980s

American Gigolo, Blade Runner, Body Heat, Brazil, Danton, Drugstore Cowboy, ET: The Extra-Terrestrial, Fanny and Alexander, The Fly, Full Metal Jacket, Glory, Hannah and Her Sisters, Marianne and Juliane, My Left Food, Once Upon a Time in America, Platoon, The Princess Bride, Raging Bull, Ran, Sex, Lies and Videotape, The Shining, Summer, The Terminator, The Thin Blue Line, The Tin Drum, The Untouchables, The Vanishing, When Harry Met Sally

1990s

After Life, All About My Mother, Boogie Nights, The Crying Game, Election, The English Patient, Fight Club, Gattaca, Goodfellas, Good Will Hunting, Groundhog Day, Kolya, Magnolia, The Matrix, Memento, Moonlighting, Pulp Fiction, Raise the Red Lantern, Reservoir Dogs, Se7en, The Silence of the Lambs, Smash Palace, The Vanishing

2000s

2046, Amelie, Amores Perros, The Assassination of Jessie James, Bad Santa, Boogie Nights, The Death of Mr Lazarescu, The Diving Bell and the Butterfly, Donnie Darko, Eternal Sunshine of the Spotless Mind, Lost in Translation, March of the Penguins, Maria Full of Grace, No Country for Old Men, Pan's Labyrinth, Requiem for a Dream, Sideways, The Son's Room, There Will Be Blood, Volver, Wall•E

PROMINENT FILM DIRECTORS

Robert Aldrich, Woody Allen, Pedro Almodovar, Robert Altman, Paul Thomas Anderson, Wes Anderson, Michaelangelo Antonioni, Michael Apted, Gillian Armstrong, Darren Aronofsky, Hal Ashby, Ingmar Bergman, Bernardo Bertolucci, Peter Bogdanovich, John Boorman, Robert Bresson, Luis Bunuel, Tim Burton, James Cameron, Jane Campion, Frank Capra, John Carpenter, John Cassavetes, Claude Chabrol, Charlie Chaplin, Ethan and Joel Coen, Francis Ford Coppola, David Cronenberg, Cameron Crowe, Alfonso Cuarón, George Cukor, Michael Curtiz, Terence Davies, Cecil B DeMille, Jonathan Demme, Brian De Palma, Carl Dreyer, Clint Eastwood, Blake Edwards, Sergei Eisenstein, Rainer Werner Fassbinder, Federico Fellini, David Fincher, John Ford, Milos Forman, John Frankenheimer, Stephen Frears, Terry Gilliam, Jean-Luc Godard, Peter Greenaway, DW Griffith, Christopher Guest, Curtis Hanson, Michael Haneke, Howard Hawks, Todd Haynes, Werner Herzog, Alfred Hitchcock, Ron Howard, John Huston, Alejandro González Iñárritu, James Ivory, Peter Jackson, Jim Jarmusch, Jean-Pierre Jeunet, Norman Jewison, Spike Jonze, Wong Kar-Wai, Lawrence Kasdan, Elia Kazan, Mathieu Kassovitz, Aki Kaurismaki, Krzysztof Kieslowski, Stanley Kubrick, Akira Kurosawa, Fritz Lang, David Lean, Patrice Leconte, Ang Lee, Spike Lee, Mike Leigh, Sergio Leone, Barry Levinson, Richard Linklater, Ken Loach, Joseph

Losey, Ernst Lubitsch, George Lucas, Sidney Lumet, David Lynch, Terrence Malick, Louis Malle, Joseph Mankiewicz, Michael Mann, Paul Mazursky, Deepa Mehta, Jean-Pierre Melville, Anthony Minghella, Vincente Minnelli, Lukas Moodysson, Michael Moore, Nanni Moretti, Mike Nichols, Manoel de Oliveira, Yosujiro Ozu, Alan J Pakula, Alan Parker, Alexander Payne, Sam Peckinpah, Arthur Penn, Wolfgang Petersen, Roman Polanski, Sydney Pollack, Michael Powell, Otto Preminger, Cristi Puiu, Sam Raimi, Nicholas Ray, Rob Reiner, Jean Renoir, Alain Resnais, Jacques Rivette, Nicholas Roeg, Eric Rohmer, George A Romero, Roberto Rossellini, Ken Russell, Walter Salles, John Sayles, John Schlesinger, Volker Schlondorff, Paul Schrader, Martin Scorsese, Ridley Scott, Tony Scott, M Night Shyamalan, Don Siegel, Bryan Singer, Douglas Sirk, Jerzy Skolimowski, Steven Soderberg, Todd Solondz, Steven Spielberg, Oliver Stone, Preston Sturges, Quentin Tarantino, Jacques Tati, Bertrand Tavernier, Guillermo del Toro, Francois Truffaut, Gus Van Sant, Luchino Visconti, Lars von Trier, Margarethe von Trotta, John Waters, Orson Welles, James Whale, Billy Wilder, Robert Wise, John Woo, William Wyler, Zhang Yimou

APPENDIX

WORD ASSOCIATIONS

20TH-CENTURY DECADES

1950s

Alfred Kinsey, Beatniks, *Ben-Hur*, Bettie Page, Betty Boop, Brigitte Bardot, *Cat on a Hot Tin Roof*, Charlie Parker, Cold War, comic book, Eamon de Valera, Elvis Presley, Federico Fellini, Franco, frisbee, full skirts, Glenn Ford, *Grease*, hula hoop, Ingmar Bergman, Jack Kerouac, James Dean, Jerry Lee Lewis, Korean War, the Lone Ranger, *Lord of the Flies*, *The Lord of the Rings*, Lucille Ball, Mao Zedong, Marilyn Monroe, *Peanuts*, Perry Como, pop art, quiz shows, rock and roll, social conservatism, Sophia Loren, *A Streetcar Named Desire*, Suez Crisis, tail fins on cars, television, Tony Curtis, Tony Hancock, *War of the Worlds*, Warsaw Pact, westerns, *West Side Story*, Winston Churchill, *The Wizard of Oz*

1960s

1968, *2001: A Space Odyssey*, acid, Bay of Pigs, The Beatles, The Beach Boys, Bob Dylan, Bob Marley, Bonnie and Clyde, Charles de Gaulle, civil rights, conceptual art, counter-culture, Cuban Missile Crisis, Deep Purple, The Doors, draft dodger, *Easy Rider*, *The Feminine Mystique*, flower child, folk music, free love, *The Graduate*, hippies, Janis Joplin, Jefferson Airplane, JFK, Jimi Hendrix, Johnny Cash, Led Zeppelin, Lee Harvey Oswald, long skirts, LSD, Mamas and Papas, marijuana, Martin Luther King, mods and rockers, moon landing, Motown, Neil Armstrong, Pink Floyd, *Planet of the Apes*, Prague Spring, psychedelia, *Psycho*, Richard Nixon, The Rolling Stones, Second Vatican Council, Six Day War, *The Sound of Music*, space race, Stonewall riots, Swinging Sixties, The Velvet Underground, Vietnam, Woodstock

1970s

acid rock, *All in the Family*, anti-apartheid, *Apocalypse Now*, Arab-Israeli War, Augusto Pinochet, The Bee Gees, bellbottoms, Betty Friedan, *Black September in Munich*, Brezhnev, Bruce Lee, Charlie's Angels, *Close Encounters of the Third Kind*, computing, *The Deer Hunter*, disaster movies, disco, environmentalism, *The Exorcist*, feminism, Gloria Steinem, *The Godfather*, hippie, hot pants, Hoxha, Idi Amin, Indira Gandhi, Iranian Revolution, *Jaws*, kaftan, kitsch, kung fu movies, leisure suit, Mark Spitz, Mary Tyler Moore, *M*A*S*H*, miniskirt, oil crisis, *One Flew over the Cuckoo's Nest*, the Osmonds, paisley, peace symbol, pet rocks, the Pill, platform heels, Pol Pot, polyester, Pope John Paul I/II, President Ferdinand Marcos and Imelda Marcos, Richard Nixon, Rocky, roller skates, *Saturday Night Fever*, Sean Connery as James Bond, stagflation, *Star Wars*, Stephen King, Steve Biko, *Taxi Driver*, Tito, vinyl records, Voyager, Watergate

1980s

AIDS, *Aliens*, anti-apartheid, Ayatollah Khomeini, B52s' 'Rock Lobster', *Back to the Future*, the Berlin Wall, Bhopal disaster, big hair, Cabbage Patch Dolls, Carl Lewis, Challenger disaster, Chernobyl, democracy movements, drum machine, Duran Duran, economic liberalisation, *ET*, Exxon Valdez, Falklands War, Fiji coups, Filofax, gay rights, glasnost, Haiti, heavy metal, hip-hop, Intifada, Iran-Contra, Iran-Iraq War, *The Karate Kid*, keyboard, lace gloves, Lebanon War, leopard prints, Libya bombing, Live Aid, Margaret Thatcher, materialism, Madonna, Manuel Noriega / Oliver North, *Miami Vice*, Michael Jackson, Mikhail Gorbachev, Mt Saint Helens, *MTV*, multinational, My Little Pony, neoliberalism, neon colours, New Romantic, New Wave, *An Officer and a Gentleman*, parachute pants, patriotism, perestroika, power suits, *Raiders of the Lost Ark*, the *Rainbow Warrior* sinking, Ray-Ban Wayfarers, recycling, Richard Gere, ripped jeans, Ronald Reagan, Sandinista, shoulder pads, Solidarity, Soviet troops in Afghanistan, Space Invaders, stonewashed jeans, synthesiser, *The Terminator*, Tiananmen Square, Velvet Revolution, War on Drugs

1990s

anti-fashion, anti-globalisation protests, apartheid ends, Asian financial crisis, Balkan Wars, Bill Clinton, *The Blair Witch Project*, Boris Yeltsin, Burma junta, Channel Tunnel, Chechnya, Chinese economic growth, climate change, CNN, Cold War ends, *Dances With Wolves*, democracy goes global, Dolly the sheep, Ethiopia peace, euro launch, *Friends*, Generation X, the Good Friday Agreement, goths, GPS goes live, grunge, Gulf War, Hale-Bopp, Hubble telescope, Human Genome Project, the internet, Kosovo, Kyoto Protocol, Mars Rover, Monica Lewinsky, NAFTA, Nelson Mandela, OJ Simpson, Oklahoma City bombing, Oslo Accords, personal computers, piercings, Prozac, raves, reality TV, retro, Rodney King, Rwandan genocide, Sarajevo, *Seinfeld*, *Sex and the City*, *The Silence of the Lambs*, *The Simpsons*, Soviet Union break-up, the Spice Girls, Taliban, tattoos, techno music, Y2K, Yugoslavia separation, Waco siege, the Wonderbra, *X-Files*

2000s

9/11, *American Idol*, animated films, Barack Obama, Beijing Olympics, *Big Brother*, biofuels, boho, Britney Spears, broadband, Chinese economic boom, camouflage patterns, chav, credit crunch, Crocs, dance music, *The Da Vinci Code*, digital cameras, dot-com crash, DVD, Eminem, emo, Enron, gay marriage, George W Bush, global warming, Google, green, Harry Potter, hip-hop, housing market crash, hybrid vehicles, indie, internet commerce, iPod, Jackass, Kanye West, Large Hadron Collider, London bombings (7/7), *The Lord of the Rings*, lowrise jeans, mobile phones, music downloading, neo-atheism, Nintendo Wii, oil crisis, pop punk, social networking, stock market boom and crash, Sydney Olympics, telecommunications, YouTube

SUBJECTS

RELIGION AND DEATH

RELIGION

adherence, agnostic, altar, apostasy, apostle/
disciple, atheist, belief, the Bible, blasphemy,
bless, bodhi tree, burial, caliphate, chapel,
church, clergy, cleric, cloister, committed,
conservative, creed, credo, cremation,
cross, crusade, cult, deity, desecration, devil
/ diabolical, devotion, devout, diocese,
divine, doctrine, dogma, dome, eulogy,
excommunication, faith, gentile, godly,
gospel, hajj, halal / haram, heathen, heaven,
hell, heresy, holy, infidel, koan, kosher
/ shechita / treif, Inquisition, jihad, lay,
liberal, liturgy, martyr, mass, menorah,
messiah, minaret, monastery, morality,
mortal, mosque, mysticism, netherworld,
ordination, orthodox, pagan, pagoda,
pantheon, parish, penitence, perdition,
persecution, pew, piety, pogrom, practising,
prayer, profane, proselytise, prostrate,
pulpit, puritan, rapture, requiem, reverent,
righteous, rite, rosary, sabbath, sacrament,
sacred, sacrilege, sacrosanct, saint, salvation,
sanctity, saviour, schism, scripture, sectarian,
secular, shrine, shroud, sin, soul, spiritual,
steeple, supererogation, synagogue, synod,
tabernacle, taboo, temple, temptation,
testament, theological, venial, vestments,
vow, worship, zealot

RELIGIOUS TITLES

archbishop, ayatollah, bishop, brother,
cantor, cardinal, deacon, elder, father, friar,
gothi, *granthi*, imam, *kohen*, minister, monk,
mufti, mullah, nun, pastor, pope, priest,
rabbi, reverend, sangha, shaman

DEATH

auto da fé, autopsy, burial, capital
punishment, cemetery, coffin, coma, corpse,
cremation, crossbones, cryogenics, crypt,
danse macabre, death knell, demise, dodo,
embalming, eschatology, euthanasia, fate
(destiny, karma, kismet, moksha, nirvana,
samsara), funeral, grief, guillotine, hangman,
hearse, immortal, inquest, last rites, Lazarus,
lethal, martyr, mausoleum, mortal, mortuary,
mourning, mummy, necrophilia, necropsy,
noose, ossuary, posthumous, postmortem,
pyre, rigor mortis, sarcophagus, seppuku,
shiva, shroud, suicide, tomb, wake

FIGURES OF DEATH

Azrael (Muslim), Ceres (Greek female
violent-death spirits), Father Time, Fourth
Horseman of the Apocalypse, Grim Reaper,
Izanami (Japanese), Michael (Roman
Catholicism), Samael (Christianity /
Judaism), Satan, Thanatos (Greek), Yama
(Hindu)

AFTERLIFE

Aaru – heavenly paradise of ancient Egypt

Dis – city of the dead in Dante's *Divine Comedy*

Elysium – Greek place for blessed and heroic

Gehenna – Jewish hell

Hades – Greek lower world

Heaven – place of God and righteous in Christianity and other religions

Hell – place of endless punishment in Christianity and other religions

Jannah – Islamic heaven

Jahannam – Islamic hell

Limbo – Place for dead without original sin in Roman Catholic thought

Naraka – Buddhist / Hindu lowest realm

Purgatory – Roman Catholic place of temporary punishment

Sheol – Hebrew word for afterlife

Styx – river around Hades (Stygian = gloomy)

Tir nan Og – Celtic land of eternal youth

Valhalla – Norse place of heroic souls

Xibalba – Mayan underworld

Yggdrasil – tree joining heaven, earth and hell in Norse myth

Yomi – Japanese underworld

ORDERS OF TRADITIONAL MEDIEVAL ANGELS

seraphim, cherubim, thrones, dominations, virtues, powers, principalities, virtues, powers, archangels, angels

SEX

adultery, arouse, bondage, carnal, coitus, copulation, cottaging, crotch, erection, flirt, fornicate, frottage, gay, genital, gigolo, groin, how's your father, in flagrante delicto, intercourse, kinky, orgasm, pederast, perverse, pimp, pornography, promiscuous, prostitute, pubic, pudenda, sadomasochism, scrotum, sodomy, straight, swinger, trick, tryst, virgin, voyeur

POLITICS AND SOCIETY

administration, agitprop, anarchy, apparatchik, aristocracy, authoritarian, autocracy, ballot, budget, cabinet, campaigning, capital, capitalism, centrist, church-state, civic, civil liberty, colonialism, commission, commonwealth, communism, congress, conservative, constituency, contract, corruption, coup d'état (putsch), customs, democracy, democrat, department, détente (relaxing of previously hostile relations between nations), diplomacy, dirigisme (economy strongly directed by government), division, dove, economy, egalitarianism, election, embassy, entente cordiale (UK–France post-colonial agreement), environment, equality, executive, fascism, federal, federation, filibuster, foreign aid, foreign relations, globalisation, gulag, hawk, hegemony, human rights, ideology, immigration, independent, infrastructure, judiciary, junta, justice, labour, laissez-faire, law and order, lawmaking, leader, left-right, legislation, legislature, legitimacy, liberal, libertarianism, lobbyist, lower house, Machiavellian, mandarin, mandate, manifesto, market,

Marxism, military, monarchy, nationalism, neocon (servative), oligarchy (rule by elites), parliament, patriotism, patronage, pinko, platform, plebiscite, policy, politburo, politician, politico, poll, polling, pollster, poverty, PR, press, progressive, propaganda, property, protest, public, public works, radicalism, reactionary, realpolitik, rebellion, reform, refugees, regime, regulation, renegade, republican, revenue, review, secretary, secularism, sedition, shuttle diplomacy, slogan, social contract, social democracy, socialism, sovereignty, speaker, spin, state, tariff, taxation, terrorism, Tory, totalitarianism, trade, treason, treasury, tyranny, upper house, utilitarianism, utility, veto, vote, welfare, whig, whip

POLITICAL THINKERS

Aristotle, Edmund Burke, Cicero, Confucius, Friedrich Engels, Antonio Gramsci, Friedrich Hayek, Thomas Hobbes, David Hume, John Maynard Keynes, John Locke, Karl Marx, John Stuart Mill, Montesquieu, Plato, Karl Popper, Ayn Rand, John Rawls, Jean-Jacques Rousseau, Adam Smith, Voltaire

TYPES OF RULING SOCIETY

anarchy – without government
aristocracy – by privileged order
autocracy – by single individual
communism – by one-party; a Marxist-Leninist state where all property is publicly owned
democracy – by the people
fascism – nationalistic authoritarianism
feudalism – warrior nobility and vassals
kakistocracy – by society's worst
meritocracy – by persons selected by merit
monarchy – by sole hereditary head of state
ochlocracy – mob rule
oligarchy – by the few
plutocracy – by the wealthy
republic – non-monarchy based on rule of law; by elected representatives
thalassocracy – primarily maritime
thearchy/theocracy – by gods or through a priestly order
timocracy – a style of government in which only land owners can vote

USEFUL WEBSITES

WORDS

thefreedictionary.com – dictionaries

freethesaurus.net - thesaurus

rhymezone.com – rhymes, synonyms, related words and more

onelook.com – meta-dictionary search

dictionary.cambridge.org – UK dictionaries

merriam-webster.com – US dictionaries

wiktionary.org – community-created dictionary

dictionary.die.net – dictionary

bartleby.com – word-related reference

wordspy.com – new words and phrases

tiscali.co.uk/reference/dictionaries/difficultwords – difficult words

buzzwhack.com – buzzwords

medterms.com – medical dictionary

innerbody.com – human anatomy

biology-online.org – biology

biotech.icmb.utexas.edu – life sciences resources

businessdictionary.com – business dictionary

investorwords.com – glossary of financial terms

infovisual.info – visual dictionary

creativeproverbs.com – international proverbs

quotationspage.com – quotes

whatquote.com – quotes

brainyquote.com – quotes

www.peevish.co.uk/slang – slang dictionary links

urbandictionary.com – community-created slang dictionary

USEFUL

imdb.com – movie information

wikipedia.org – community-created encyclopedia

onlineconversion.com – conversion of measures

xe.com/ucc – currency conversion

chemical-ecology.net/java/lat-long.htm – distance between world cities

nationmaster.com – statistical comparison of nations

thepeerage.com – idiosyncratic British and European aristocracy site

bl.uk – the British Library
icom.museum/vlmp – online museum directory
europeana.eu - virtual European gallery and museum
wga.hu/index1.html – gallery of European art
artcyclopedia.com – visual art links
artnet.com – galleries and auctions
freetranslation.com – multi-language translation
babelfish.yahoo.com – multi-language translation
translate.google.com – multi-language translation
sparknotes.com – study guides
cliffsnotes.com – study guides
loc.gov/nls/other/sayhow.html – US name-pronunciation guide
dotolearn.com/games/facialexpressions/face.htm – facial expressions
acwl.org/links.htm – crime writing resources